DATE DUE

Marxism and the Reality of Power 1919-1980

Olga A. Narkiewicz

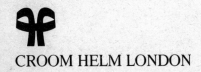

CROOM HELM LONDON

© 1981 Olga A. Narkiewicz
Croom Helm Ltd, 2-10 St John's Road, London SW11

British Library Cataloguing in Publication Data

Narkiewicz, Olga A.
   Marxism and the reality of power 1919–1980.
   1. Communist parties — History
   324.2'09'04   HX40

ISBN 0-85664-806-X

Printed and bound in Great Britain
by Billing and Sons Limited
Guildford, London, Oxford, Worcester

Contents

Preface

When Marxist theories were outlined in the nineteenth century they assumed that a new proletarian culture would eliminate nationalist sentiments and that an international system would grow, which would allow the working classes to abolish both the capitalist system and the system of national states.

The test of these theories came in 1914 and was found wanting. The Social-Democratic parties in most European countries supported their national governments in a war effort and neglected the international bonds. This brought about an ideological split, which deepened further when the Russian Revolution broke out in 1917. The Bolshevik government signed a separate peace treaty with Imperialist Germany, instead of fostering European revolutions in early 1918. The failure of communist revolutions in Europe in the following years, and the break-up of Social-Democratic parties into Communist and Socialist parties added a new dimension to the split.

The development of the theory of 'socialism in one country' in the USSR further inhibited the growth of internationalism. This was perceived immediately by the left wing of the Bolshevik Party. Trotsky, in his essay *Against National Communism*, warned that the 'truly Russian' theory of 'socialism in one country' would inevitably lead to the development of nationalistic tendencies in all sections of the Comintern. However, as the USSR became more powerful the theory of 'socialism in one country' seemed to be justified in practice, and after the Second World War the setting up of communist governments in several European countries made the theory of internationalism even more difficult to implement.

Stalin's death and the ensuing Sino–Soviet split produced the polycentric theory, which owed much more to power politics and local conditions than to the early internationalist beliefs. 'Socialism in one country' became the rule, rather than the exception.

Preface

This book outlines the way in which the early ideology had been phased out, first by the CPSU[1] and later by other communist parties, at the expense of the politics of reality. The author has acknowledged the leading role of the CPSU in the development of other communist parties, but has concentrated mainly on those parties, both ruling and non-ruling, which have played an important role in the shaping of policy since the setting up of the Communist International. Their changes of policy and the reasons for which they were carried out are analysed and a direct line is drawn between the initial theory of 'communism in one country' and the emergence of 'national' communist parties, both in Europe and in other continents. Special attention has been devoted to the implementation of communist theories in Eastern and South-eastern Europe, as well as to the phenomenon of Eurocommunism. There are also sections on communist parties in the Far East, with its specific problems and on the Latin American 'hispanic' brand of Marxism. African Marxism is also examined in order to compare how its implementation varied in different local conditions. Some space is given to the 'New Left' and its theories to analyse the reasons for the disillusionment with orthodox communism among the radicals.

The book owes a debt to my students, their work and their interest. Many people have given generous help. I must single out Lady Bowden, the President of the Lucy Cavendish College, at the University of Cambridge, who offered me College hospitality and placed the resources of the University at my disposal during my study leave; Professor Leonard Schapiro, who discussed the book with me and suggested many ideas, as well as enabling me to use the facilities of the London School of Economics in the final stages of research; and Barry Hills, who read the manuscript with his usual thoroughness, made valuable suggestions on the sources used and helped with the editing of the final version. Needless to say, the opinions expressed in the book are my own.

The select bibliography reflects some of the materials used in preparing the work. As it was impossible to include all the sources drawn upon over a long period of time, I have selected as many current works as was possible in order to facilitate the readers' acquaintance with the latest literature. The spelling of foreign names and place-names was kept in the original wherever possible, with the exception of forms generally accepted in English.

O.A.N.

Note

1. For the sake of simplicity the term CPSU (Communist Party of the Soviet Union) has been used throughout the book although the party had different names during the period examined.

Part one:

Marxist Internationalism and Nationalism

1

How the Bolshevik Party Came to Power and Retained It

The revolution of 1917 . . . was a 'national'
revolution . . . (Pokrovsky, *Izbrannye Proizvedeniya*,
Vol. 4, p. 66).

The Bolsheviks and the National Revolution

When Pokrovsky wrote the words quoted above he was unaware
that he was setting a pattern for the revolutions of the twentieth
century. He applied his statement to the unique experience (as it
then was) of the Russian revolution in 1917. With the benefit of
hindsight, it can be seen that he was correct. What appeared to be
a socialist revolution in Russia was bound, for reasons which will
be outlined below, to become a national revolution.

A brief look at the conditions in Russia at the beginning of the
twentieth century will show that it was a country ideally suited to
such a revolution. The developments in the eighteenth and
nineteenth centuries have created two nations: the middle and
upper classes were brought up on Western European models and
conformed to Western rules of behaviour, dress and culture. The
lower-middle classes and the peasantry stayed Russian in every
respect. This dichotomy was, if anything, strengthened by the
development of various political parties, which attempted to
model themselves on Western European patterns. It is, perhaps,
symptomatic that the only party which had a wide following in the
countryside was the one which followed a completely Russian
'national' pattern: the Social Revolutionaries.

The Tsarist governments contributed to the development of a
national ideal through their chauvinistic policy in the last quarter

of the nineteenth century. Through the ideology of 'autocracy, nationality and orthodoxy' the Russians were made aware, perhaps for the first time since Peter the Great, that they were separate and possibly superior to other nationalities: certainly superior to the nationalities within the Empire. While this ideology was rejected by the educated liberal classes, it did appeal to the Slavophile element as much as to the masses, who were told that they were being exploited by foreign interests, not by the Russians themselves. As a noted Russian historian put it:

> 87 per cent of the population (according to the census of 1897) lived in rural areas and were as untouched by any cultural influence as though they dwelt on another planet. The gulf between the educated classes and the masses was the basic and fatal weakness of Russia's social structure. In appearance, customs, standards, and way of life the *barin* ... and the muzhik had nothing in common and both, literally and figuratively, spoke a different language... The persecution of national and religious minorities — Finns, Poles, Jews, Ukranians, and others — bred disaffection and separatist tendencies. Finally, the failure to produce a decent standard of living for the peasants and industrial workers weakened among those groups the stimulus to fight for the country against the external enemy and prepared fertile ground for subversive propoganga. In 1914–1917, as in 1905, the strain and stress of the war brought to the fore the disruptive forces that had long been at work behind the imposing facade of the empire.[1]

The modern Russian political parties, like the Social-Democrats, were so taken up with improving the social and economic conditions of the people (and rightly so) that they did not see the essential problems of nationality, at least, as regarded by the Russians themselves. Even the Bolshevik programme on nationalities, which took account of all the national minorities in the Empire, neglected the Great Russians. Yet it was the Great Russians, or the lower classes among them, who felt that they were being oppressed by the alien upper classes, and even more by foreign bureaucracy and industrialists.

It was against this background of national grievances and feelings that one has to observe the Bolshevik Revolution. It is notable that this revolution was made on a pattern designed by foreign theoreticians, and was carried out by Russians whose experience was much more connected with foreign countries than with Russia itself. Moreover, it was well known that the theoreticians of the revolution, Marx and Engels, did not expect that a socialist revolution would break out in an underdeveloped country, and had in mind advanced, industrial countries, with a well-emphasised national consciousness.

The analysis of the practical makers of the revolution reveals that the main ones — Lenin, Trotsky, Bukharin, Kamenev, Zinoviev and Radek — had either spent many years in exile and were imbued with foreign ideology or were, in Stalin's later phraseology, 'cosmopolitan' elements. Some of them, like Radek, were better known in the Polish Social-Democratic Party and the German Social-Democratic Party than in the Russian party. The very city where the revolution was made, Petrograd, was generally known to be 'un-Russian' in contrast to Moscow, the genuinely Russian capital.

If this was the case of the leaders and of the locality, what about those who made the revolution possible in practice? They were, in the first instance, sailors from the Imperial Navy; second, the Petrograd workers; third — in the countryside — the peasants. Of these three elements only the peasants could be said to be untouched by foreign influences; in the long run it was only because of their grievances that the revolution was a successful one. Nobody would claim that the Russian peasants had any international experience or links. On the other hand, nobody would claim that the peasant revolution was a socialist one. The peasant revolution of 1917 had exactly the same pattern that all peasant revolutions had taken; it was an economic one, designed to seize land and other wealth from the landlords. Its ideology owed much more to the populist ideology of social revolutionaries than of the Bolsheviks. This fact was constantly stressed by Lenin in his post-revolutionary speeches and writings. The 'petty bourgeois' peasant element was in fact the social revolutionary element, and it was for this reason that the only coalition the Bolsheviks ever established, even for a short time, was with the left wing of the Social Revolutionary Party. The reason was plain: if the Bolsheviks were to claim any legitimacy in the countryside it could only be through a party which had a programme of land distribution for the peasants. It was this coalition which brought about the neutrality, or sometimes active help, from the Russian countryside, and probably saved the Bolshevik government at its very inception.

If the Revolution itself was foreign in concept it was Russian in its passage, i.e. it tended to be spontaneous. Had it not been for the efforts of Lenin and Trotsky in first producing a small and coherent communist organisation and then in establishing a disciplined army and labour force (by recalling White officers and NCOs to the first and by militarisation of labour in the second), the Revolution would have been lost in the first period, particularly after the German collapse on the Western front. This collapse deprived the Russians of material aid from Germany and released the Entente forces for intervention in Russia. Fortunately for the Bolsheviks by then the Red Army was organised, the railways were running on the most important lines and some armaments were being produced. Hence the Bolsheviks stayed in power, though very precariously, as the various national movements and the Polish war provided at least as much danger as the White Russian forces.

Lenin was particularly aware of the danger: his early speeches always stressed the idea that a separate revolution in Russia was unthinkable; that the revolution was an international one, which merely *started* in Russia; and that it was but a matter of time (the less the better) before a European revolution was successful and world revolution would follow. While this was a sound ideological premise, well in line with Marxist theory, it was also based on the practical worry about the Russians being able to sustain a revolutionary order for long, and being even less able to construct a socialist system.

Hence the whole system was geared to international developments. The citizenship of the Russian Socialist Republic was offered to all foreigners who would profess loyalty to the Bolshevik government (to prisoners of war in particular, which is significant in itself), and the Constitution of the RSFSR conferred rights of citizenship without any formalities on all foreigners working within the territory of the Russian Republic, provided that they had appropriate class status. Similarly, the Red Army was to be an international army, not a Russian army, and in early 1918 an appeal was made to form an international detachment, whose language would be English. This in itself was rather interesting in view of the fact that Germany was the most communised country in Europe, and most Russians' second language was French, not English. But if the revolution was to spread outside Europe, to

Britain and to the United States, then English was the appropriate language of the new communist forces.

In line with this idea Radek announced his views of world citizenship, saying that the Bolsheviks were no longer 'Muscovites', or citizens of 'Sovdepia', but the advance guard of world revolution, and Trotsky contemptuously dismissed the need for keeping up diplomatic relations with other countries. A few revolutionary proclamations to the nations of the world and the need for diplomacy would cease — there would be a worldwide revolution. The funds of the new Commissariat for Foreign Affairs were almost solely devoted to subsidising foreign revolutions, and Radek himself was put in charge of revolutionary propoganda abroad, particularly among the 'German brothers'. The failure of other nations to respond fully to such propaganda was one of the major disappointments for the Bolsheviks, but this was deemed to be but a temporary setback, one which would be rectified as soon as possible, either by internal decay or by an external stimulus.

In the meantime the setback was most dangerous in its effects for the Russians themselves: the expectation of a world revolution was so strong, and lack of experience of government was so marked among the new leaders, that orderly government did not have much chance. If there were a world revolution and the state would wither away, there was little need to set up new state institutions. In their place *ad hoc* committees and coercion, where persuasion was insufficient, would have to be enough.

The Revolutionary Forces

In recent years more attention has been paid to the fact that the Bolsheviks carried out a *coup d'état* which, in conjunction with a peasant revolution in the countryside, had been called a socialist revolution. Latest Soviet research appears to lay the emphasis much more on the armed services' role in the revolution than on the role of the political leaders. This approach conforms with what we already know: the Bolshevik government did not stand a chance of survival unless it could produce a disciplined armed force; and indeed, it only began to consolidate its position after Trotsky built up the Red Army and militarised the labour force. But many sources in the Soviet Union point to a much more active part of the armed services in the process of revolution-making itself.

When the cruiser *Aurora* was sent to Petrograd for refitting in the autumn of 1916 contacts were established between the workers and the sailors. Those workers are named as T.E. Lyachin, N. Kozyrev, P. Voytek, A.A. Danovskaya-Spivak, I.Ya. Krutov and others in memoirs of the *Aurora*[2] — the real makers of the Revolution, yet completely forgotten at a later stage. More links were set up between the many sailors who worked in the naval establishments in Petrograd, which also employed civilian workers. These shipyards employed some 100,000 workers in June 1917. The political leaders were well aware of the fact that the army and fleet were the most revolutionised parts of the population, mostly because of the bad conduct of the war.

The March Revolution began in the *Aurora* when a group of political agitators were put in cells on the cruiser on 27 February 1917. The sailors demanded their immediate release, and when the authorities attempted to send the prisoners ashore to local prisons they announced a revolt, invited on board a group of armed workers and together took over the cruiser.[3] Large numbers of sailors from the *Aurora* and other ships disarmed the police and gendarmerie, took over railway stations and arrested the Tsarist government. The sailors stormed military prisons and fortresses, allowing more dissenting soldiers to join the revolution. The Viborg and Kronstadt Soviets were set up in these areas for the very reason that here there were large numbers of disaffected sailors. The sailors kept close links with the Petrograd Committee of the Bolshevik Party. In Kronstadt itself a Bolshevik sailors' committee was established at the beginning of March and a Bolshevik paper, *Golos Pravdy*, began to appear there on 15 March.[4]

The reason for the emphasis on Kronstadt was not only the large fleet stationed there but also the fact that most naval specialist schools were sited in the area. The nearness to Petrograd, the revolutionary stance of the sailors and their military skills and discipline were all of importance to the Bolsheviks.

Throughout the summer of 1917 a struggle went on between the Bolsheviks and the Provisional Government for the allegiance of the sailors. On 28 August Boris Savinkov, then the military governor of Petrograd, sent back 2000 sailors who had come to the city from Kronstadt on their own. The sailors' revolutionary newspapers were sent round the whole Petrograd region in September 1917 as an example for others to follow. On 10 October a member of the

Petrograd Soviet described the sailors as the 'flesh and blood' of the revolutionary proletariat.[5] At the beginning of October a large number of guns and ammunition was taken from Petrograd to Helsinki. On 24 October 1917 detachments of sailors left Helsinki for Petrograd in order to take part in the Bolshevik Revolution. Ensign Dybenko was already a member of the Military Revolutionary Committee in Petrograd from 12 October; simultaneously, sailors took a leading part in political meetings in major factories in Petrograd. They were organised into groups of two to three people by Sverdlov, and carried out pro-Bolshevik agitation among the workers. By 25 October there were eleven warships and over ten thousand sailors in Petrograd, all at the disposal of the Military Revolutionary Committee.[6] The value of such a large force in the October coup cannot be underestimated, neither can the firepower of so many warships in close proximity to the seat of the Provisional Government.

Indeed, the role the Baltic Fleet sailors played in the October Revolution is well attested, though Soviet historians have preferred to give the priority to the army detachments and Red Guard detachments. To take one example, the *History of the CPSU* describes the sailors' role in these words: 'The workers' Red Guard detachments formed the principal fighting force of the insurrection, the sailors of the Baltic Fleet sharing the glory of victory with them,' and later: 'From the Neva, the cruiser Aurora fired a shot, giving the signal for attack.'[7] But contemporary revolutionary forces were aware of the importance of the sailors' input into the insurrection. The Petrograd Soviet sent a special message of thanks to the Baltic Fleet, ending it with the words: 'Glory to the sailors who are selflessly spilling their precious blood for the happiness of the people and for socialism!'[8] Had the sailors not later taken up weapons yet again these eulogies may have continued. But in the long run, the sailors from the Baltic Fleet proved to be too independent and less willing to follow the Party's calls for discipline.

In the meantime, other parts of the Russian fleet were giving reason for disquiet. One incident can be quoted: under the provisions of the Brest-Litovsk Treaty, the Black Sea fleet was to return to Sevastopol from Novorossiysk. Some of the crews refused to follow this order, given by Lenin, and enforced by Yoffe: in the event, part of the fleet had to be scuttled. The fleet which remained in Sevastopol and some ships which returned (one

battleship and six minelayers) were later seized by the interventionist forces and taken to Bizerta.[9] The sailors refused to follow Lenin's personal orders in this respect and the sailors of lower ranks were not the only ones to be disciplined. Ensign Dybenko became suspect early in 1919: in October 1919 Lenin sent a special despatch in cypher to Smilga, asking him 'whether you can use Dybenko as a Divisional Commander or on other work. I advise you to give him a trial, while keeping him under strict control'.[10] Dybenko had already been accused of undisciplined behaviour in the Ukraine: he was given the command of the 37th Division in Siberia on Lenin's advice.

As the position of the Red Army improved the interventionist and White Forces were being routed, and the Bolsheviks switched their attention to war on land (as in the Polish-Bolshevik War) and the sailors' role began to be of less importance. Had it not been for the Kronstadt Revolt in 1921 the sailors might have been forgotten. The Bolsheviks, in the meantime, had built up the army, rather than the fleet, for traditional reasons and it was the army which ran the country for several years, longer in the outlying districts such as the Far East of Russia or the Caucasus.

The writer has already discussed the role of the Military Revolutionary Committees in a previous work[11] and has shown that they acted as local government authorities in most areas. The Eighth Party Congress in 1919 turned its attention to the liquidation of 'guerrilla activities' in the army, and the safeguarding of strict submission of the army to the Party.[12] The political role of the army was stressed through the creation of the Political Department in the Revolutionary Military Council of the Republic (known as PUR), which became responsible for the work of political commissars and departments throughout the armed forces.

A series of political conferences were arranged after the Eighth Party Congress on all fronts and in all large cities. They took place in April and May 1919 and were designed to impress upon the political leadership of the army the necessity, on the one hand of following the party line and, on the other, of not interfering with the military commanders in the running of the campaigns. Nevertheless, the situation in the Red Army remained sufficiently ambiguous for further measures to be taken. These were also necessitated by the continuing civil and interventionist wars. The government had few trustworthy military commanders; the belief that political commissars could run the war on several fronts simultaneously did not stand up to the test; other measures had to be taken. 'Single command', i.e. the abolition of the powers of political commissars (though not of the institution itself), came to be adopted much more widely. By January 1920 Lenin announced that some fifty per cent of commands were in single hands.[13] Later on in the spring discussions began on whether the abolition of the political commissars would help the military commanders to win the war more efficiently. It was considered that there were insufficient grounds for the abolition of the office of political commissar; instead, even greater efforts were made to communise the Red Army, both by increasing political work among the recruits and by assigning newly recruited communists to army units as soldiers and officers. Many conferences of political workers in the armed services were held throughout 1920, and in December it was decided that greater control had to be exercised over all political work in the Red Army. To control the work better, C.I. Gusev was appointed the head of the PUR in January 1921.

It was agreed that political work had to be subordinated to the more important task of winning the war and that often ideology had been the cause of serious losses or errors in battles. Political workers were directed towards other tasks; for instance, they were to liquidate illiteracy among the troops, and were asked to run propaganda sessions among the local civilian population in order to produce a sympathetic approach towards the Red Army. In liberated territories political workers were incorporated in the local soviets, and often ran the executive committees of those soviets. Other work carried out by the political commissars included mobilisation of new army recruits, supply of food to the army and the maintenance of revolutionary order.

There was a basic change in attitudes during the Civil and Polish wars: this was that wars were too important to be left to political commissars. In time of danger wars had to be left to the military; the political workers could be entrusted with important, but lesser tasks of propaganda, food supply or recruitment, and kept away from the front, where they could do less harm.

Since the years 1917 to 1921 are generally accepted as the formative years of the Soviet Union it is perhaps not surprising that cooling off towards political workers (which began in this period) provided a model for later history. The military became the leaders in times of stress; political workers were allowed to support them in less important areas of government. The party and the military did not clash; they fused (as is well demonstrated in the person of Trotsky) both on a personal and on a government level, and inevitably the pacifists, the utopians and the opponents of violence in general lost out in the process. For this reason the early proposals to abolish a standing army, regular police forces and military discipline in all military and paramilitary bodies never really took root. Because of the fusion of functions between the military and the party, the 'utopian' elements had no chance of putting their ideas into practice.

The Victory of National Forces

As the Bolshevik government took over power in more and more areas it began to face the problems of opposition, both from the non-Russian groups within the former Empire and, even more cogently, from the Russian groups and mostly from the peasants. The reasons for this were clear: the peasants distrusted the Bolsheviks, even though they were happy to receive land from their hands. The Bolsheviks were alien; they were townspeople; they were often not ethnically Russian; they were violently anti-clerical. Even if all these reasons were overlooked (and they were not), the peasants were sufficiently parochial to feel that anyone who came from outside the area was a foreigner.

Hence the Bolshevik emissaries were seldom welcomed with joy in the villages, even though the very same people would have been loath to give away the gains which came with the Revolution: the land. When the period of forced requisitions arrived the Bolshevik detachments were often attacked and killed by the peasants. The alliance between the Bolsheviks and the peasants, which was the essence of Lenin's strategy, was at risk. It was for this reason that Lenin gave in to the demands from the countryside in 1921 and introduced the New Economic Policy.

The new course, called a return to a 'mixed economy', was in fact a climbdown before the national forces: the Russian peasant. It remained for Stalin to develop the second part of the strategy: first to evolve a new theory, owing little to Marxism and still less to the forces of internationalism, and call it 'socialism in one country'; and second, to begin a new policy of national integration, which culminated in the chauvinistic excesses of the 1930s, and which served him in good stead during the Second World War.

While developing a national policy for the Russians the Soviet government was intent on following the Tsarist policy of retaining the outlying parts of the Empire. Much has been said about the brutality of the Soviet conquests of Georgia, Soviet Central Asia and the Far East. The Soviet historians have always maintained that these areas have become voluntary members of the Union. But even if this were not so, one has to look at the possibility of Tashkent reverting once again to a theocratic regime, of Outer Mongolia in Japanese or Nationalist Chinese hands, or of Georgia, whose whole economy depended on Russia, to realise that these outlying territories had a better rationale within the Union than outside it.

Moreover, thanks to the ideology of international communism it was possible to demonstrate that this was a true union of the working classes of various nations. And the Soviet nationalities policy, when contrasted with the Tsarist policy of extermination of national differences, has been a very liberal one. Nevertheless, it cannot be disguised that the policy was one of national interest and that it has remained such.

Hence, what had begun as a communist, internationalist revolution soon gave way to a government devoted to its national interests. The internationalist wing of the party had to go, and in its place were put particularist, Russian, interests. What had taken shape was not what Marx had envisaged and Lenin had hoped for. But what had taken place was much more viable than the dreams of international solidarity of the workers and the uprooting of the capitalists. The revolution was successful, the outcome different, but in its way highly successful. It will be attempted to demonstrate below that the revolutions made in the name of Marxism tend to become national ones.

Notes

1. M.T. Florinsky, *Russia: A History and an Interpretation*, vol. 2, pp. 1256-7.
2. S.S. Khesin, 'Revolyutsionnye Svyazi Petrogradskogo Proletaryata s Baltiiskimi Moryakami v 1917 g', in D.A. Baevskii *et al.* (eds), *Ot Oktyabryia k stroitelstvu kommunizma*, p. 7, quoting an article in *Voenno-Istoricheskii Zhurnal*, No. 11, p. 72, 1960.
3. Ibid., p. 9.
4. Ibid., p. 12.
5. Ibid., p. 31.
6. Ibid., pp. 32-6, quoting various sources.

7. B.N. Ponomaryov (ed.), *History of the CPSU*, p. 255.
8. Khesin, 'Revolyutsionnye Sviyazi', p. 36.
9. J.M. Meijer, *The Trotsky Papers*, vol. 1, p. 57. n. 7.
10. Ibid., pp. 683-5.
11. O.A. Narkiewicz, *The Making of the Soviet State Apparatus*.
12. N.M. Vyunova *et al.* (eds), *Partiyno-Politicheskaya Rabota v Krasnoy Armii*, Documents, 1964, p. 4.
13. Ibid., pp. 11-12.

2

The Comintern and International Socialism

The Founding of the Comintern

What of internationalism, then, since the Russians had captured revolutionary Marxism and adopted it for their own? 'Russia... has long been standing on the threshold of an upheaval; all the elements of it are prepared.... This time the revolution begins in the East, hitherto the unbroken bulwark and reserve army of counter-revolution.'[1] In 1917 the revolution began in the East as Marx had, rather surprisingly, surmised in 1877; but the East — and that applies not only to Russia in 1917 but to China in 1949 — had always been the bulwark of counterrevolution. How could one impose a popular democratic system on a society which had only experienced autocracy? And how could one spread such a new system to make it into a global one? These were the questions to which the leaders may have addressed themselves soon after the revolution. But for very good reasons, they were forced to ignore them. As one author opines:-

Before tsarist rule was toppled civil society had not advanced enough to gain a genuine constituency .... Until the very end of tsarist rule Russian civil society remained uncomfortably squeezed between the hammer of the autocratic tsarist bureaucracy and the anvil of inert and illiterate masses.

As a result of this lack of political development

The problem which confronted the Soviet power was unique in requiring the legitimation of the rule of an elite committed to modernity in a country which had never before generated a modern legitimation of power.[2]

25

Moreover, this was only the beginning of the leadership's troubles. Even ignoring the fact that Marxist theory had to be manipulated to accommodate the revolution in an agrarian country to the theory of a socialist revolution in an advanced industrial country, and the fact that the failure of other European revolutions forced the Soviet leaders to produce the theory of 'socialism in one country', one could not ignore the undeniable truth that the European workers, while not averse to profiting from the Bolshevik Revolution by claiming more rights from their capitalist bosses, were as far from making socialist revolutions in 1921 as they had been in 1913. The onset of a world revolution or even of a European revolution seemed to be as far away as ever. The problem of rousing the proletariat to a revolution — unless it is in the last stages of despair — is fully acknowledged nowadays. As one author states:

> The first socialist revolution occurred in Russia, which was both a semi-imperialist and a semi-colonial country. Marx had anticipated that one or more of the advanced countries of Western Europe would lead the way in abolishing capitalism. The Yugoslav, Chinese and Cuban revolutions have since shown that the Russian experience was not unique. Was Marx all wrong? Why have the more backward countries been the first to have a socialist revolution? Will the rest of the colonial world also take the road to socialism?[3]

But this suspicion had already crossed the minds of the more analytical revolutionaries earlier. Writing after the failure of the 1905 revolution in Russia, Trotsky suggested that:

> It is of course true that the growth of political consciousness depends upon the growth of the numbers of the proletariat, and proletarian dictatorship presupposes that the numbers of the proletariat will be sufficiently large to overcome the resistance of the bourgeois counterrevolution. But this does not at all mean that the 'overwhelming majority' of the population must be proletarians and the 'overwhelming majority' of the proletariat conscious socialists. It is clear . . . that the conscious revolutionary army of the proletariat must be stronger than the counter-revolutionary army of capital, while the *intermediate, doubtful or indifferent strata* of the population must be in such a position

that the regime of proletarian dictatorship will attract them to the side of the revolution and not repel them to the side of its enemies.[4]

The problems, as Trotsky saw them in 1905–6, were not limited to class ones. They were geographical as well. A revolution in Europe could only happen if there was a geographical connection between Western Europe and Russia. This posed problems: 'Let us take the example of Poland as a link between the revolutionary East and the revolutionary West, although we take this as an illustration of our idea rather than as an actual prediction. The triumph of the revolution in Russia will mean the inevitable victory of the revolution in Poland.' The German and Austro–Hungarian governments would send troops to quell the Polish revolution, which would spread from the Russian-occupied provinces to those under German and Austrian domination. 'A war between feudal-bourgeois Germany and revolutionary Russia would inevitably lead to a proletarian revolution in Germany.'[5] The key to the revolutionary situation then, as Trotsky foresaw, lay in turning an agricultural country into a socialist one — not an easy task, despite the success of the 1905 Revolution in Russian-occupied Poland. Without revolutionising Poland, any Russian revolution might be stopped before it reached the heart of Europe.

The creation of the Comintern was partly an answer to this dilemma, though it had other roots as well. One author notes that:

The difference of content between the socialist revolution in the broad sense and the socialist revolution in the narrow sense includes . . . a difference of space and time. In the first case, the space is world-wide and the time covers an entire epoch of history; in the second, the space is national (or, more precisely, countrywide) and the time is reduced to a brief period of history. When Marx and Engels speak of the possibility of a victory of the socialist revolution in some particular country . . . they are employing the concept in its narrow sense. They do not contemplate the hypothesis that this victory may remain isolated, within a nationally confined space, for a long period. This problem was thrown up by practice itself, when the proletarian revolution was crushed everywhere except in Russia, in the years following the war of 1914–18, while Soviet power became consolidated. The failure of Marxists, from Marx to Lenin, to consider the eventuality was due to the fact that their theoretical conception of the socialist revolution as necessarily a world revolution caused them to rule out any such possibility.[6]

Like Trotsky, Lenin had considered the Russian revolution as one of the links in a chain of revolutions — those in advanced capitalist countries, those in intermediate countries like Russia and those in completely underdeveloped countries like China, where the absence of a proletariat would produce a bourgeois parliamentary regime till objective conditions were fulfilled for a socialist revolution. In each case, the leader would be the consciously socialist part of the working classes, and, most importantly, the proletariat in Western and Central Europe well skilled in the doctrine of socialism. It was not till the spring and summer of 1917, when Lenin realised that in Russia a socialist revolution was possible and that proletarian power (in the soviets) already in operation during the March Revolution worked, that he changed his mind about Russia being behind the rest of Europe. But this did not solve the problem of what to do when the other European revolutions (such as in Germany and Hungary) failed, and others — even more crucial to the spread of the revolution, as in Poland — did not even take off. Some means of pressing the sluggish European proletariat into a revolution had to be found, for Lenin (unlike Stalin at a later stage) never believed that a true socialist system could be maintained in one country alone.

The means was at hand. Before the Bolshevik Revolution, the Social-Democratic Party had developed as a single international party of various nationalities in the Russian Empire. During the war and immediately after the end of the war, links were extended to the German socialists, mainly through the good offices of 'cosmopolitan' revolutionaries such as Karl Radek and Rosa Luxemburg.

The work continued in the interventionist period, when large numbers of French troops in Russia had to be withdrawn hastily because they had become communised. This seemed to prove that, exposed to a combination of socialist progaganda and internationalist ethos, almost anybody, even the Western European proletariat, would opt for a revolution. It was on the basis of such experience that Lenin proposed to set up the Comintern. This came into being, as the first article of its Statutes declares, 'in order to organise joint action by the proletariat of the various countries, with the aim of establishing a World Federal Soviet Republic ... with this not a distant aim, but the practical task of the moment'.[7] Just as the Bolshevik Party had included every nationality of the Empire so the Comintern was to become a single world party of all revolutionaries.

Despite Lenin's enthusiasm for the Comintern there was opposition to it from the very circles where he might have expected support: the German Spartakists. Rosa Luxemburg, whose wartime activity had encouraged Lenin to believe that the German left-wing socialists would support the Russians, had already disagreed with Lenin's interpretation of the mechanics of a socialist revolution. Eberlein, who represented the German Spartakists at the conference during the founding of the Comintern, said that: 'The need for a Communist International is absolutely obvious, but founding it now would be premature. The Communist International should be definitely established only when, in the course of the revolutionary mass movement gripping nearly all the countries of Europe, Communist parties have sprung up'.[8] It was only because Lenin insisted on its creation and because of his personal prestige as the maker of the first revolution in Europe that the Comintern was established, despite the misgivings of the Germans.

In January 1919 delegates of eight Marxist parties met in Moscow: — Russian, Polish, Hungarian, German, Austrian, Latvian, Finnish, the Balkan Revolutionary Socialist Federation and one unofficial delegate from the American Federation of Labor (which had already declined to go to a meeting of the Second Socialist International in Switzerland). The delegates sent out an invitation to thirty-nine parties of the left and labour organisations in the world to attend a world congress which would establish the Third or Communist International. The programme of the new organisation was drawn up by the Russian Bolshevik Party after consultation with the German Spartakist Union. There were fifteen articles, which called for revolutionary seizure of power, the disarming of the bourgeoisie and the arming of the proletariat; suppression of private property and means of production and their transfer to a proletarian state; and rejection of centre and right-wing labour parties and the establishment of a new world organisation, to be called the Communist International.[9]

There are various interpretations about the reasons for founding the Comintern. They differ from opinions that it was 'a propaganda gesture', to others that 'the Russian revolution had shown in a detailed and precise way ... the inner mechanism of the revolutionary process', and still others that it was the first Bolshevik move to organise the left-wing forces in the world under Russian domination.[10]

Whatever the reasons, the First Congress of the Third International, which took place in Moscow between 2 and 6 March 1919, was impressive. Nineteen parties and groupings were represented, and though it was called 'unrepresentative in fact, if not on paper'[11] several governments thought it sufficiently important to arrest some delegations *en route* to the Congress. The delegations which arrived came mostly from Eastern Europe — Armenia, Austria, Estonia, Finland, Germany, Hungary, Latvia, Lithuania, Poland, Russia, the Ukraine, Norway, Sweden, the Balkans, German colonies in Russia, Oriental Nationalities in Russia and Left Zimmerwaldians — and belonged to the left wings of Social-Democratic parties in those countries. There were also observers from Holland, Yugoslavia, Korea, Persia, Switzerland, Turkestan, Turkey, USA, Azerbaijan, Bulgaria, China, Czechoslovakia, France, Georgia and Great Britain.

Lenin opened the Congress and asked the delegates to honour the memory of Karl Liebknecht and Rosa Luxemburg, both recently murdered in Germany and both, incidentally, in disagreement with Lenin's theories on the dictatorship of the proletariat. Then he referred to the spread of the revolution in Europe. The Spartakist movement in Germany was mentioned but he also made much of the Birmingham Soviet of Workers Deputies in Britain, which had just been formed. The most developed country in Europe, Germany, and the oldest capitalist country in the world, Britain, were heading for a revolution, and Lenin professed to have high hopes of it spreading. The Congress adopted the programme which the earlier conference had set out, calling for dictatorship of the proletariat and the creation of a classless communist commonwealth. Lenin insisted that the Russian Communist Party should take the lead in the Comintern, because, though backward, Russia was the only country which had experienced a real and successful proletarian revolution in Europe. While the work of writing a constitution of the organisation was postponed till the next Congress, the First Congress elected an Executive Committee consisting of one member from each of the following parties: Russia, Germany, Austria, Switzerland, Sweden and the Balkan Federation, which elected its Bureau. The Bureau membership was heavily dominated by the Russians, consisting of Rakovsky, Lenin, Zinoviev, Trotsky and Platten. Zinoviev was elected as President and Angelica Balabanoff became the secretary. In his closing address Lenin said that: 'The comrades present in this hall saw the founding of the first Soviet Republic, now they see the founding of the Third International, and they will all see the founding of the World Federative Republic of the Soviets.'[12]

As usual, opinions differ on the first steps of the new organisation. Some authors maintain that the appeal of the First Congress to workers everywhere to support the young Soviet state acted as a stimulus for widespread industrial unrest. They also state that: 'For the time being, the Soviet leaders, fighting for their survival . . . showed a marked tolerance to the ideological diversities of the nascent communist movements in Europe.'[13] Other authors maintain that: 'The Comintern adopted draconian measures from the outset to ensure the purity of the new parties. This was the aim of the "21 Conditions", a model of sectarianism and bureaucratic method in the history of the working-class movement.' The purpose of the Conditions was that only true communists could be admitted to the Comintern. The criterion of being a true communist was the complete and unconditional acceptance of the Conditions. These emphasised that the members of the organisation should ensure that all posts in the media, trade unions, parliamentary groups and other bodies were taken by convinced communists, and put members on guard against centrist and right-wing tendencies. 'Reformism' was also outlawed, and the trade-union International (which at that time had nearly 20 million members in the West) was condemned as a 'yellow' organisation for showing reformist tendencies.[14]

Perhaps enough time has passed now to be able to formulate an objective assessment of the early (as opposed to the later) phase of the Comintern. Against the background of a collapsing political order not only in Russia but all over Europe the setting up of new institutions and systems would be difficult. But the Russian Bolshevik Party was faced with dilemmas hitherto unknown in Europe. It believed that it was the vanguard of a new order — but a new order had emerged in the world in any case. The European economy was in ruins; the USA was swiftly taking over world leadership hitherto held by European powers; colonialism appeared to be on the wane (though it did not finally collapse till the middle of the twentieth century); and the swift development of new technology (due mostly to the war) had changed the face of Europe and the attitudes of the people just as much as the phasing out of the empires.

Yet all the equipment the Russians had to deal with the new situation was nineteenth-century theories and some practical experience from the 1905 Revolution. All over Europe there were new trade union organisations and left-wing parties (released from pre-war controls and constraints) with a strong wish to lead their membership into the modern age. Hence the exercise had all the elements of a tight-rope act. It was hoped that left-wing organisations in Europe and in the world would follow the Russians, and that with the coming of a world revolution the others would soon cease to count. The act failed for all kinds of reasons, not all connected with right-wing reaction.

Probably the most cogent reason is encapsulated in the same philosophy which engendered the growth of Eurocommunism: left-wing parties in non-Russian territories were not willing to surrender their freedom of action, and were not over-impressed by the tactics of the Bolsheviks. And as Claudin states:

> A large number of socialists and trade-unionists who wanted to join the Comintern because they were in sympathy with the Russian revolution and shared, generally speaking, the revolutionary objectives of the new International nevertheless disagreed with it on certain points, especially where structure and methods of work were concerned. Above all they regarded the policy of splitting the labour movement as wrong, particularly in the trade-union field.

As a result, the Russians proposed

> to create chemically pure Bolshevik parties overnight, and to do this on the basis of a working-class which had for decades been trained in the reformist spirit, in parliamentary and trade-union activity — a working class which ... had supported the 'traitor' leaders in entering into *union sacrée* with their respective bourgeoisie.[15]

It was an attitude which the Russians could not readily understand, both for temperamental and traditional reasons. The publication of Lenin's essay on non-conformism in June 1920 was an attempt to eradicate dissent from the Comintern and to lay down the rules for future conduct of foreign parties.[16] Yet, despite laying down the law and stating that the Russian revolution had international significance which could not be rejected, Lenin was on the defensive:

> It would of course, be grossly erroneous to exaggerate this truth and to extend it beyond certain fundamental features of our revolution. It would also be erroneous to lose sight of the fact that, soon after the victory of the proletarian revolution in at least one of the advanced countries, a sharp change will probably come about: Russia will cease to be the model and will once again become a backward country (in the 'Soviet' and the socialist sense).[17]

Lenin had clearly changed his tactics, for under the cloak of castigating the German, Italian, Dutch and British left-wing socialists and communists, he was, in fact, calling on them to unite with other parties or factions (sometimes called 'independent') and to work through parliamentary and official trade-union channels for the ultimate establishment of a socialist system. In other words, having emphatically stated that Russia could only have achieved socialism by rejecting parliamentarism he was now conceding that in the West tactics would have to be different. Communist deputies would have to join the existing parliaments in European countries, and not refuse to acknowledge them. German communists, even a German Soviet Republic, if it was created, would have to acknowledge the reality of the Treaty of Versailles. Existing institutions would have to be not only tolerated but respected and treated as working models. Why was the recipe so different in 1920 from the recipe of 1917? Was it a mere geographical problem?

Lenin explained it himself. The difficulties of retaining true communist beliefs in a bourgeois society were great, but they 'are mere child's play compared with the *same sort* of problems which ... the proletariat will have ... to solve in order to achieve victory. ... Compared with *these* truly gigantic problems of re-educating, under the proletarian dictatorship, millions of peasants and small proprietors, hundreds of thousands of office employees, officials and bourgeois intellectuals, of subordinating them all to the proletarian state and to proletarian leadership ... compared with these gigantic problems it is childishly easy to create, under the rule of the bourgeoisie, and in a bourgeois parliament, a really communist group of a real proletarian party.' The problem was simple, and the 'left infantilists' must be put right: 'Whilst you lack the strength to do away with bourgeois parliaments and every other type of reactionary institution, you *must* work within them because *it is there* that you will still find workers who are duped by the priests and stultified in the conditions of rural life; otherwise you risk turning into nothing but windbags.'[18] A refusal to join existing parliamentary institutions would weaken the Communists without adding anything to the revolutionary zeal of the masses.

Was this a short-term stratagem in order to gain a foothold in Western European institutions? Or an attack on the left wing of the Bolshevik Party in Russia, already about to protest at Lenin's apparent return to non-Communist policies? After all, less than a year divided the Second Congress of the Comintern from the fateful Tenth Congress of the Bolshevik Party, at which semi-capitalist measures would be introduced from above. It seems that each factor may have played a small part in Lenin's reasoning; it could hardly have failed to do so. But perhaps the more important reasons have never been analysed. They were the experience of the Spartakist League in Germany in 1919 and the experience of the Soviet army in Poland.

In Germany the Luxemburg–Liebknecht attempt at a communist uprising had shown the utter isolation of the extreme left wing from the people. If it was the German government and German armed forces which quelled the uprising, it was the lack of a following among the people, the millions of peasants and workers, which condemned the communist revolution to death. Similarly in Poland, the Bolsheviks aroused little enthusiasm. Even as Lenin was writing his essay on Leftism, Polish forces entered the Ukraine and occupied Kiev in May 1920. While they were forced to abandon Kiev in June and the Red Army began its pursuit into territory which Poland claimed as her own (though it was beyond the Curzon Line awarded her by the Western Entente), a 'Polish Provisional Revolutionary Government' consisting of Feliks Dzierzynski, Feliks Kohn, Julian Marchlewski and Unschlicht (unable to participate directly because of hospitalisation) moved with the Red Army, organising Soviet government. But it would appear that their only success was at Bialystok. Here they were able to set up a government authority, a local newspaper and issue innumerable proclamations. But they met with no success between Bialystok and Warsaw, the next big city. Some time later this lack of success was being attributed to faulty tactics:

> Thus Kohn explained the failure of the Polish working class to seize the opportunity offered it by the presence of the Red Army. On the other hand, the confiscation of grain by the Bolshevik divisions who had been separated from their base in the rapid advance antagonised the peasant population. The Bolsheviks lost the support of the villages without gaining the support of the towns.

This claim is made by Louis Fischer, who states that he had been able to discuss the position with Kohn himself.[19] But Fischer commits the usual error of foreign communists or sympathisers. He maintains that all was well, despite the lack of support:

> An invincible Red Army marching to the heart of Poland. Russia united behind it, with even the petty bourgeoisie supporting the Soviets. The German proletariat still tingling from its victory over the reactionary Kapp–Ludendorff putschists by means of a lightning general strike. The British trade unions threatening to call a general strike; staid English Labor leaders using revolutionary phrases. Europe not stabilized . . . . Under the circumstances, Bolsheviks would not be Bolsheviks if they did not wish and try to exploit the situation for revolutionary expansion.

However, all was not well, and the realist in Lenin understood it better than the enthusiastic American.

'The Red Army's threat to Warsaw united the Polish bourgeoisie . . . . the moment national territory felt the tramp of foreign troops, parties buried their swords, petty differences were forgotten and a strong government emerged . . . thousands rushed to the defense of Warsaw, especially the Polish student youth.' The Red Army did not retreat from Warsaw till the second half of August, after the Second Congress had closed. But the lesson of how difficult it would be for a communist revolution to make headway, not only in an advanced Germany but in a backward, agricultural Poland, was not lost on Lenin. In the winter of 1920 he complained to Clara Zetkin:

> Yes, what happened in Poland had to happen ... our unbelievably brave, victorious advanced guard could receive no reinforcements from the infantry, could receive no munitions, not even stale bread and other prime necessities from the Polish peasantry and petty bourgeoisie. These ... saw in the Red Army soldiers not brother-liberators but foes.... The Polish revolution on which we reckoned failed. The peasants and workers, stultified by the partisans of Pilsudski and Dashinsky, defended their class enemies, permitted our brave Red Army soldiers to die of starvation, and ambushed and killed them. ... Incidentally, ... Radek foretold how everything would happen. He warned us. I was terribly angry with him, and called him a defeatist — but in the main he has proved to be right. He knows the situation in the West better than we do and he is talented. He is very helpful to us....[20]

There is an analogy between the wording of some sentences in the anti-Left essay and Lenin's admission to Clara Zetkin. It was not the fault of the revolutionaries that the Poles were stultified and refused to help them. But it was not an unexpected defeat, since Radek had foreseen it earlier. Could it not have been Radek who had advised Lenin to soft-pedal the extremist programme at the Second Congress of the Comintern, and to pursue a parliamentary road to socialism — at least for the time being? Was it all a tactical exercise, or was the essay the result of one bitter experience and an anticipation of another defeat?

Viewed in these terms, the whole tone of the Second Congress would take on a new meaning. The disciplinary measures were adopted *not* to promote world revolution but to stop the more extreme communists from promoting it. Lenin may have hoped that the capitalist governments would be pacified till such time as a real revolution could be promoted, or may have believed that, with the development of parliamentary communism, the people would acknowledge the superiority of the system — not in backward Russia but in advanced countries — and would adopt it by consent. The question is difficult to answer; it could be that it was a mixture of both hopes which motivated Lenin. But it is not an outdated problem, because it arose once again with the growth of a phenomenon called 'Eurocommunism'.

Second Congress of the Comintern and After

The opening of the Second Congress was marked by the imposition of the 21 Conditions on all communist parties, which would become sections of a single global party, and by warnings about strict discipline within the national parties, on the model of the Russian Bolshevik Party. But this was merely the start of the proceedings. Of much more interest was the new emphasis on liberating colonial nations. Lenin presented his theses on colonialism: these postulated that communist parties were in future to bring about a close alliance of all nationalist and colonial liberation movements, including bourgeois–democratic movements, so long as such support would strengthen the Soviet state and weaken capitalist states. In his speech Lenin spoke at great length of the exploited masses of Asians and Africans and of the need to overthrow imperialism. But capitalism was given a respite — it would be overthrown eventually. In the meantime the most important task was to purge the European Communist Parties. Lenin's demand at the Congress that the PCI should exclude 'revisionists' broke up the Italian party into three wings.[21]

The Bolsheviks' new stress on colonialism, to the exclusion of thoughts about a European revolution, gave rise to a bizarre meeting soon after the Second Congress. In September 1920, in Baku, Zinoviev, as President and Radek, as Secretary of the Comintern and Bela Kun, who came specially from Moscow, convened a 'Congress of the Peoples of the East'. 'It was an odd gathering, a museum of Oriental costumes, a Babel of tongues, a confusion of ideas and aims. Lenin once upon a time took pencil in hand and figured out that the United States, Britain, France and Japan with a population of about one-quarter billion were ruling countries and colonies with a population of two and a half billion. This is the lesson Lenin's disciples brought to the Baku congress.' On 1 September Zinoviev made a dramatic appeal: 'The Communist International ... turns today to the peoples of the East and says to them: "Brothers, we summon you to a Holy War first of all against British Imperialism".' The delegates shouted 'Jehad, Jehad' and brandished daggers, Damascan swords and revolvers. The nations which took part in the meeting were Turkey, Persia, Afghanistan and India. But the meeting was the only one, 'Comintern psychology receded ... and more and more, revolutionary possibilities were sacrificed to the Soviets' desire for treaty contacts with non-revolutionary states.'[22]

In this way, the European revolution receded to give way to a colonial revolution, which receded in its turn. What was left? Problems of running the Soviet state interfered with almost everything the Comintern might have undertaken. By the time the Third Congress took place in June and July 1921 the Russians had experienced the introduction of the New Economic Policy, the Kronstadt Revolt and the imposition of even more discipline in the CPSU at the 10th Congress. At the Third Congress the Russian delegation led by Lenin firmly announced that the fomenting of world revolutions was not one of the immediate needs of the Soviet state. Protesters (mainly German Communists) were soon expelled from the Comintern.

The result of the explusions was twofold: first, the retreat from revolutionary tactics produced a crisis of faith among more radical Communists; second, the Fourth Congress which met in November 1922 was a much more obedient body. It was at this congress that Lenin made his last appearance and seemed to retreat from the disciplinary clauses which had been written into the Comintern's constitution. But his speech was blurred after his severe stroke: few understood what he said, and the clauses remained.

Notes

1. K. Marx in 1877, in a letter to Sorge. *Marx and Engels: Selected Correspondence*, p. 374; see Claudin, *The Communist Movement*, n. 6, p. 651. For background, see F.W. Deakin and G.R. Storry, *The Case of Richard Sorge*, p. 35.

2. Z. Bauman, *Socialism, the Active Utopia*, pp. 81 and 82.

3. P. Camejo, in the Introduction of L. Trotsky, *The Permanent Revolution*, p. 7.

4. L. Trotsky, *Results and Prospects*, originally published in 1906, republished in *The Permanent Revolution*, p. 88. (Emphasis mine.)

5. Ibid., pp. 108-9.

6. F. Claudin, *The Communist Movement*, pp. 47-8.

7. Ibid., p. 106.

8. Quoted by Claudin, ibid., p. 104, from B. Lazitch and M. Drachkovitch, *Lenin and the Comintern*, vol. I, p. 61.

9. The literature on the history of the Comintern is not very satisfactory. The basic information from an American communist's point of view will be found in W.Z. Foster, *A History of the Three Internationals*, and there is a selection of documents in J. Degras (ed.), *The Communist International (1919-1943)*. F. Borkenau's *World Communism. A History of the Communist International* is very much out of date.

10. L. Schapiro, *The Communist Party of the Soviet Union*, p. 196; Claudin, *Communist Movement*, p. 104.

11. Schapiro, *Communist Party*, p. 196.

12. Claudin, *Communist Movement*, pp. 55-6.
13. Schapiro, *Communist Party*, p. 196.
14. Claudin, *Communist Movement*, p. 107.
15. Ibid., pp. 108-9.
16. *Left-wing Communism — an infantile disorder* was written in April 1920 to coincide with the opening of the Second Congress of the Communist International; the book was published on 12 June 1920 and in French and English in July. Foreign editions in French, English, German and Italian were published in the second half of 1920. See V.I. Lenin, *Selected Works*, note 252, p. 748.
17. Ibid., p. 516.
18. Ibid., p. 589 and 546 (emphasis in text).
19. L. Fischer, *The Soviets in World Affairs*, p. 192.
20. Ibid., pp. 193-4, also quoting C. Zetkin's *Remininiscences of Lenin*.
21. V.I. Lenin, *Selected Works*, pp. 602-6.
22. Fischer, *The Soviets*, pp. 205-6.

3

The Post-Leninist Comintern

The Period of 'Russification'

The course of policy which the Comintern followed from the Fourth Congress onwards till the mid 1930s was not always clear; it had been classed variously as 'left-wing communism', 'centralism' and a period of 'Russification'. It seems to have been an outcome of several events coinciding simultaneously: the death of Lenin; the subsequent power struggle within the Soviet Communist Party; the need of the Soviet state for a period of co-existence with the capitalist world; and with Stalin gradually emerging as the new leader of Soviet Russia, a phasing out of the theory of 'continuous revolution' and a wager on 'socialism in one country'.

These events were in themselves sufficient to cause a weakening of a commitment to revolutionary tactics. But perhaps the most important factor lay in Stalin's attitude towards the Comintern. Deutscher, whose testimony on personal attitudes is probably as good as anyone's, tells us that: 'Trotsky relates how contemptuously Stalin dismissed the potentialities of foreign communism. The Comintern, he allegedly held, would carry out no revolution for many decades. Lominadze, one of Stalin's close associates in the twenties, later attributed to Stalin the saying that "the Comintern represents nothing. It exists only because of our support".' Deutscher supports this statement, saying that he himself heard European leaders of the Comintern in the early 1920s, and Trotsky's opponents, attributing to Stalin 'remarks in substance identical with those quoted by Lominadze and Trotsky'.[1] Stalin's disregard of the Comintern is easily understandable, as he had had little influence in it; he had never been concerned with foreign policy and he had a deep suspicion of the 'cosmopolitan' elements in the Comintern. As long as the leaders of the Comintern retained their influence Stalin's position would be weaker. So, on a personal plane, Stalin's position would have to be anti-Comintern in any case.

But there were much more important reasons for phasing out the influence of the Comintern in the mid 1920s. This was 'the greatest disaster suffered by the Comintern', in the words of Claudin, its past secretary. That phrase refers to the failed communist uprising in Germany in 1923. Despite having had a headstart over other left-wing parties in Europe, the German socialist movement had been bitterly split since the war. Its disputes were manifold, and though some were connected with the rise of the Soviet Communist Party and the subsequent split within the Social-Democratic Party and within its extreme left wing, the Spartakist Union,[2] many had to do with the defeat Germany suffered in 1918, with the right-wing policies of the ruling Social-Democratic government and with the general breakdown of German economic and political prestige after 1918.

Some former communists like Claudin, maintain that in any case the German proletariat were firmly controlled by the Social-Democratic Party, and were not easily influenced by the much more radical Spartakists and Communists. However that may be, the split in the left appears to have done more harm to the Communist than to the Social-Democratic cause, and it is said that both Karl Liebknecht and Rosa Luxemburg opposed the Berlin Insurrection of January 1919 as premature, and that Eugen Leviné opposed the setting up of a Soviet Republic in Bavaria in April 1919. That revolution left the German Left without its best-known leaders. The 1921 revolution, the 'March Action' as it became known, was opposed by the Clara Zetkin–Paul Levi leadership, and it was necessary to instal a new leadership, under Brandler and Thalheimer, to lead the revolutionary movement. While Brandler and Thalheimer started the revolution due to Comintern pressure there are suggestions that it was, in fact, instigated by the German authorities in order to crush the Communist opposition. These two viewpoints do not seem to clash, and indeed, what is known of Soviet–German relations at this and later periods may point to the fact that the Soviet government may not have opposed the crushing of the German extreme left at this stage any more than it did at a later stage. The Germans were too undisciplined: the government and the military had too much in common to risk the setting up of an extreme left-wing government in Germany. In any case, since Rosa Luxemburg's opposition to Soviet theories, the Russians had mistrusted the German left to a considerable degree.

Whatever the facts of the case, the 1921 insurrection failed completely and the membership of the party, which stood at 360,000 in 1920, was halved by the end of 1921.[3] The Third Congress of the Comintern confirmed that the 'March Action' had been a mistake but nevertheless ratified the expulsion of Paul Levi from the KPD for opposing it. Yet when in 1923 conditions appeared ripe for yet another German revolution Soviet opinion was divided. Stalin advised caution while Trotsky, Zinoviev and Bukharin seemed to believe that a new revolutionary wave would be successful. This time Brandler was hesitant; having been to Moscow for consultations in the summer, he 'returned to Germany with a set of incoherent and contradictory instructions: he was to organise a revolution against the Social Democrats and at the same time to enter the Social Democratic government of Saxony: he was to start the revolution in Saxony, not in the capital or any other decisive centre . . . . The enterprise ended in a series of unco-ordinated moves and in failure.'[4]

Stalin, who had taken the precaution of stating his views in writing in a letter to Zinoviev and Bukharin, could now be seen to have been justified in his scepticism of the value of the Comintern, and to have shown up the international 'experts' Trotsky, Bukharin, Zinoviev and Radek as hopeless romantics.[5] The revolt, or series of revolts, which occurred in October ended in a complete fiasco militarily, but improved the KPD's electoral chances. In the elections of May 1924 nearly four million electors voted Communist.[6] The German leaders Brandler and Thalheimer who, according to Claudin, had kept strictly to the orders received from the Comintern (with one exception, when they called off the revolt at the last moment, fearing it would fail), were condemned by the executive committee of the Comintern, and bitter recriminations followed. Clara Zetkin declared at the Fifth Congress of the Comintern in June–July 1924 that Brandler 'rendered great service to the party' by calling off the uprising.[7]

At any rate, despite the fact that Brandler, Thalheimer and Radek signed a declaration in March 1925 declaring their agreement to 'bolshevise' the KPD through the inclusion of 'true proletarians', the fate of the leadership was sealed. This had probably more to do with the inner struggle in the Russian Party (though the lines of support were crossed and did not coincide with the left/right controversy) than with the supposed right-wing course which the German leadership were pursuing.[8] The KPD was one of the mainstays of the Comintern, as the figures in Table 3.1 show, but it was sacrificed on the altar of Stalin's struggle for power with his opponents. In the period of 1928–9 Brandler and Thalheimer were purged, together with their supporters. After 1928 Thälmann became the absolute master of the party, carrying out Stalin's orders unquestioningly. Even a financial scandal in which he was involved, and for which he was removed by the Central Committee of the KPD from the General Secretaryship, did not harm him. Stalin merely ordered the presidium of the Executive Committee of the Comintern to veto this decision.[9]

Another ex-communist writer places the rise of Stalin's influence in the Comintern after the failure of the 1923 revolt in Germany, though without defining the exact dates. However, one look at the figures in Table 3.1 of Comintern membership in the period of 1921 to 1931 will show the steady decrease:

Table 3.1[10]

1921	1922	1924	1928	1931
887,745	779,102	648,090	445,300	328,716

This decrease stemmed from the fact that Stalin was carrying out purges in various parties belonging to the Comintern but was unable to dissociate the Russian party from it, partly because of the close ties between the two bodies and partly because of the influence the European communists exerted over the ideology.

Thus, for domestic as well as diplomatic reasons, Stalin could not but extend to the Comintern ... the methods by which he was remoulding the Russian party into a 'monolithic body'. He acted from behind the scenes, mainly through his lieutenants who sat on the Executive of the International; unlike Lenin, who had addressed every Congress of the Comintern and had publicly shouldered responsibility for its policy, Stalin ... never addressed any congress of the Comintern. During ceremonial meetings he sat silently on the platform ... Only the initiated knew that the public debates and votes were of little significance and that no major decision of the Comintern had any validity unless it was approved by Stalin. ... During the four years of Lenin's leadership, four fully fledged international congresses were convened; during the twenty-five years of Stalin's leadership only three: one in 1924, which endorsed the denunciation of Trotskyism, another in 1928, at which the influence of Bukharin and the right Bolsheviks was eliminated, and a third in 1935, which proclaimed the policy of Popular Fronts.[11]

The way in which Stalin exercised his influence was through the Russian delegation, whose voice always prevailed in the Executive Committee. This delegation had to abide by the views of the Russian Politbureau. And Stalin held a permanent majority in the Politbureau. But there were even more important reasons for the predominance of the Soviet view in the Comintern. The Executive Committee was housed in Moscow, and the technical and financial resources were provided by the Russians. So when other tactics, such as calumny and divisiveness, failed, the dissident leaders had subsidies withheld from their party. Deutscher makes an interesting remark in this connection. While maintaining that the effectiveness of financial pressure was only secondary, he notes that the Comintern (and the component parties) had, over the years, become dependent on Soviet financial help and had become careless about collecting their dues. Moscow encouraged large expenditure on propaganda and organisation, and the shortfall had to be met from the Soviet contributions. 'While the role of "Moscow gold" in fostering communism abroad has very often been melodramatically played up, it is true, nevertheless, that the subsidies did much to make the Communist hierarchies amenable to Stalin's guidance.'[12]

The period between 1928 and 1933 was one in which the Social-Democrats (labelled social-fascists at the Sixth Congress of the Comintern in 1928) were considered to be a worse enemy than fascists or Nazis. The understandable reason for this lay not only in Stalin's intensified struggle for power but also in the introduction of Five-Year Plans, in problems created by forced collectivisation and, externally, in the apparent breakdown of capitalism in the run-up to the Great Crash of 1929, in the crash itself and in the following depression. It would be reasonable to suppose that capitalism had reached its final stage, that fascism would follow and that its excesses would quickly push the working classes into a communist revolution. But, in the meantime, 'one Soviet tractor is worth more than ten good foreign communists' was a motto in the Bolshevik party, a motto built into the theory of 'socialism in one country'. This had already been noted by Gramsci in 1926, when he wrote a letter to the Russian leaders stating that: 'You are today destroying your work. You are degrading the party and running the risk of destroying the directing role which the Communist Party of the Soviet Union had acquired under the impulse of Lenin.'[13] The Italian Communist leader, shortly to be arrested by Fascist police, warned the Russians of becoming overabsorbed in Russian affairs and losing sight of the international implications of their actions.

On the other hand, perhaps the internationalists were too hard on Stalin. It would have been very difficult to place all the emphasis on an international revolution which had failed the Russians so many times before. And an international revolution led by a quarrelsome Comintern, more interested in keeping its subsidies from the Soviet state than in keeping its membership, while at the same time demanding complete independence of Moscow, seems hard to imagine. Even assuming that the European working classes were ready for a communist revolution — an assumption which might have had some grounds in the early 1930s, during the worst period of the depression — their leadership would have been poor, irresolute and unprepared. Experience had shown, even at that early stage, that major revolutions take much longer to mature, that they are composed of a variety of reasons and that they are mainly the result of a combination of a loss of hope on the part of the poorest strata of the population (not necessarily the proletariat) and of extreme disillusionment on the part of the intellectuals. The Chinese theory that a revolutionary must have at least two major classes behind him (mandarins and peasants or intellectuals and peasants, or soldiers and peasants) in order to succeed has been proved true in the twentieth century time and time again.

In the circumstances of the early 1930s, with large pockets of extreme poverty but some hopeful signs of recovery here and there, with a relatively free clas of intellectuals, with some dictatorial regimes in Europe (but without their later excesses) and with fresh memories of the war and the revolutions which followed it, the Europeans were not ready for a major international upheaval again. They were much more easily subdued by right-wing dictatorships which sprang up all over Europe, because they did not appear to be revolutionary; and, to start with, at least, they did not change their life-styles radically. Most importantly, they did not appear to be international: an Italian, Portugese or Spanish dissident could seek asylum in other European countries where he could pursue his activities. It was not till Nazism began to oppress far wider groups of population and when there were more and more people seeking fewer and fewer places of refuge that those dictatorships began to be seen in their true light. But in the early 1930s there were few Europeans who had not come across refugees from the Bolshevik Revolution, and few who did not know the hardships and horrors undergone by the Russians in the process of the revolution and for a long period afterwards. On balance, therefore, Stalin's decision to concentrate on Russian affairs — even considered apart from his other problems such as the need to co-operate with capitalist states for economic reasons — does not seem to have been either senseless or as unprincipled as the old communists appear to make out. And Stalin's problems were not limited to European ones; the problems of the Chinese Communist Party were a warning that outside Europe the revolutionary situation was not yet ripe. Hence, whatever blame attaches to Stalin for subverting the Comintern, little blame can be laid at his door for pursuing the 'Russian' rather than the 'international' line of action. Whether seen from the point of view of communists, or from an anti-communist position, there was nothing to be gained from attempting to start up an international revolution at this stage. This would not have stopped the fascists and the Nazis; on the contrary, it might have helped them. Nor would it have undermined capitalism any more than it had already undermined itself through the Great Depression. By and large, Stalin's political instinct was right at this stage, as it had been before and many times afterwards — and despite the distasteful tactics he employed, his policy can only be described as realistic.

The Comintern's By-products

If the Comintern was of little use to Stalin at this stage, would it not have been simpler to dissolve it in the early 1930s? As Deutscher had pointed out, this was not a simple operation, though it proved easy enough later on during the Second World War. Besides, the Comintern had its uses, the most interesting of which was the access it gave Soviet plenipotentiaries to foreign countries and foreign communist parties. The Fifth Congress in 1924 empowered the Executive Committee and its Presidium to send plenipotentiary delegates to individual sections; and the Sixth

Congress in 1928 extended this to the sending out of 'instructions' to individual sections.[14] These Comintern delegates and instructions had the ostensible task of conveying the Executive Committee's policy to national parties and of watching its implementation. There were also numerous Comintern representatives described as 'couriers'. Their task was to take messages from Moscow to national parties and bring back replies, unhampered by police supervision. This applied particularly to countries where communist parties were outlawed but it was also practised in those where they were legal. From time to time lapsed communists would publish lists of supposed Comintern agents. From time to time various revolutionary activities would be ascribed to them. But if the Comintern was so despised, if its leadership was totally subjected to Stalin's rule, and if the Russians did not really care to prolong its existence, why would there be a need for so many travelling emissaries?

One of the stock replies is that Comintern operatives were de facto Russian spies. This seems doubtful. Many of these men were committed members of a revolutionary party. Though some may have been involved in spying, most did not appear to have been professional spies any more than they were professional arsonists. But there is a more interesting theory: that is that the Soviet intelligence forces sent out spies *in the guise* of Comintern agents, particularly to difficult operational areas.

Naturally, it is a difficult task to try to unravel not only the dealings of an organisation which preferred to remain clandestine during most of its existence but of organisations which are clandestine by their very nature — various intelligence networks of various countries. Nevertheless, some accounts seem to confirm the fact that the cover of a Comintern agent was used by various spies recruited by the Fourth Bureau of the Red Army Intelligence. The best-documented (though still puzzling in many respects) is the spectacular case of Richard Sorge. Sorge, a special correspondent of the *Frankfurter Zeitung* in Japan, was arrested by the Japanese police in October 1941. He faced charges of having been a member of the German Communist Party since November 1919 and of having joined the Information Department of the Comintern when 'in January 1925, he attended a congress convened in Moscow by Comintern Headquarters in the capacity of a delegate of the Central Committee of the German Communist Party Secretariat.'[15] The summary of the preliminary interrogation of

Sorge sent to Berlin then goes on to say that Sorge had been sent to China in 1930, then, having received instructions to carry out spying activities in Japan, he became a member of the German Nazi Party and arrived in Japan in September 1933, under the cover of being a newspaper correspondent.

During his interrogation by the Japanese police, Sorge is said to have admitted that he had been recruited by General Berzin, head of the Fourth Bureau of the Red Army, some time in late 1920s, and that he was sent to the Far East as part of the Soviet offensive to create a revolutionary situation in 1930.

The rest of the story is well known. Sorge built up a successful espionage ring with Japanese, German and Yugoslav agents. He went to Moscow once, in 1935, to meet Berzin's successor, Uritsky, who apparently did not distrust him. However, of all Sorge's activity, the most important message which he is said to have sent to Moscow — that the Germans would attack the Soviet Union (apparently on 15 May 1941 Sorge wired the exact date of the attack) — was disregarded. His associate Klausen described the scene:

We were awaiting every hour further information, confirmation, and above all news of the diplomatic and military reactions of the Soviet Government. We were aware of the importance of the message, but nevertheless we never got an answer. When the war really broke out, Richard was furious. He asked in a puzzled way, 'Why has Stalin not reacted?'[16]

Sorge was tried as a member of the Comintern, not as an agent of the Fourth Bureau, thus perpetuating the belief that Comintern agents acted as spies, and incidentally masking the activities of the real intelligence agency. For various reasons, some of them probably connected with the abuse of the Comintern's facilities by undercover agencies, the Comintern lost most of its importance. It was revived temporarily during the Popular Front era. This will be discussed below.

Notes

1. I. Deutscher, *Stalin*, p. 392 and n. 2.
2. The vicissitudes of the German parties of the left are described in P. Nettl's

Rosa Luxemburg: in F. Claudin's *The Communist Movement*: in Deutscher's *Stalin:*, and in R. Fischer, *Stalin and German Communism.*

3. Claudin, *Communist Movement*, p. 133.

4. Deutscher, *Stalin*, p. 395.

5. The letter, which had not been published in Stalin's *Collected Works*, is quoted by Deutscher and Claudin, and is believed to be authentic.

6. Claudin, *Communist Movement*, p. 139.

7. *Inprecorr*, quoted by Claudin, ibid., p. 140.

8. Claudin points out that though the 'right' was the first to be purged, the 'left' would suffer the same fate later. The purge in the KPD which eliminated all former Spartakists and the Independent Social-Democrats coincided with Stalin's fight, first with Trotsky and then with Zinoviev and Bukharin.*Communist Movement*. pp. 142-3. See also Fischer, *Stalin*, and J. Humbert-Droz, *L'Oeil de Moscou à Paris.*

9. Humbert-Droz, ibid., pp. 256-9: quoted by Claudin, *Communist Movement*. p. 143.

10. Figures quoted by Claudin, ibid., p. 112 and A. Kriegel, *Les Internationales Ouvriers*, pp. 112-13, but questioned by some Soviet works in the 1960s.

11. Deutscher, *Stalin*, pp. 395-6.

12. Ibid., p. 397 and n. 2.

13. Quoted by J. Joll in: *Gramsci*, p. 64.

14. Claudin, *Communist Movement*, pp. 113-14.

15. F.W. Deakin and G.R. Storry, *The Case of Richard Sorge*, p. 20. The 5th Congress of the Comintern was held in 1924, not in 1925.

16. Deakin and Storry, ibid., pp. 230-1.

4
European Communist Parties, 1919-33

Socialism or Communism?

'Socialism and communism derive from exactly the same source, a shrewd, psychopathic, neurotic barbarian named Karl Marx, a product of Central Europe which has never known democracy in any form.'[1] The very violence with which Louis Bromfield, usually a mild writer on agricultural problems, attacks the acknowledged father of communism demonstrates the dilemma of historians. This work is merely concerned with reconstructing the events of the period which split the social-democratic movement into communist and socialist parties, and which led to a rivalry between the two which can only be compared to the European religious wars between Catholics and Protestants: both claiming the same God and the same ideology, but with different interpretations.

Socialism, communism and social democracy all grew side by side in a Europe which was industrialising quickly in the second half of the nineteenth century. The terms were often used interchangeably, and rightly so, for they were theoretical ones, without much practical testing. Most European left-wing parties took on the name of Social-Democracy, though there were some exceptions. The British preferred the name 'Labour Party'. The Russians, torn by inner dissent, broke up the Social-Democratic Party into a section of the Majority and the Minority. The German Social-Democratic Party became the parent of various parties bearing different names from the moment Bernstein invented Revisionism. There was no monolithicism among the European Social-Democrats and virtually the only ideology they agreed upon before 1914 was that they were an international movement. Nevertheless, even before the First World War put paid to the myth of international solidarity certain adjustments had to be made in the parties which grew up in multinational empires. The Social-Democratic Party of

Austria–Hungary broke up into national sections at the end of the nineteenth century.[2] This was done in order to satisfy the various nationalities in the Empire that their interests would be treated even-handedly, and though it did not immediately affect the party it did produce a gradual estrangement between the national sections.

In Russia, always more affected by the national question because of the repressive policies of the government, the strongest separatist movement came from the Jewish Social-Democrats, who set up a section known as the *Bund* in 1897; this soon demanded autonomy, and suffered expulsion from the party as a result. Other parties more or less loosely incorporated in the Russian Social-Democratic Party were the Polish Social-Democratic Party of the Kingdom of Poland (1893) and the Social-Democratic Parties of Georgia and Latvia.[3] The situation in Russia was more complicated than in other European countries by the fact that till the setting up of a semi-constitutional regime after the 1905 revolution the Social-Democratic Party was illegal. While this in itself need not necessarily have made it more violent than other Social-Democratic parties, it did have the effect that it broke up into two wings, one of which was much more violent than the other. Besides this split, Russian left-wing politicians had to contend with movements which were even more violent than the most radical social democracy: the anarchists, the nihilists and the radical Social-Revolutionaries, whose ideology embodied the most violent elements from the anarchist and from the socialist programmes.

Hence even before the First World War, the Social-Democrats were split into national sections and into various political groupings. This handicapped them immensely. But there were further handicaps. The Social-Democrats were a party of the 'people', but they professed to care most of all about the industrial proletariat, a relatively new class which had roots in the peasantry in most countries but which was divorced from the peasantry by its life-style as much as by the manner in which it earned its living. Bitterly opposed by the bourgeoisie and capitalists, the Social-Democrats could not really count on the peasants either. Even the landless labourers identified far more readily with the rich farmers than with the city proletariat. One of the reasons for this dichotomy was the way in which the Social-Democrats viewed organised religion. While being a socialist was not necessarily synonymous with being an atheist (and in some countries like Britain the Christian Socialist strain was much stronger than Marxism), Marx did disapprove of religion; and Utopian Socialists before Marx, being direct followers of the eighteenth-century rationalist philosophers, often sided with Deism or some other personal religion rather than with the Churches. The Churches, on their side, did little to encourage Social-Democrats to practise Christianity (again, with the exception of some Nonconformist faiths in Britain). Indeed, for a long period no practising Catholic could become a member of a Social-Democratic party on pain of being excommunicated. In a Europe still largely ruled by strict religious practice, particularly in the countryside, such lack of respect for God created an enmity between the peasant class and the Social-Democratic proletariat which was difficult to surmount.

Social-Democratic parties had, therefore, to contend with class hostility, with clerical hostility, often with government hostility and with internal splits, both of a national and ideological nature. But they were even more handicapped by their ideology. Despite the fact that a large volume of socialist works had grown up by the end of the nineteenth century, 'the Marxist legacy was uncertain, perhaps necessarily so, about the road to power. It insisted only on political rather than economic means. Marx was in no way dogmatic about the socialist future and appeared willing to let tactics reflect circumstances.' Marx died in 1883 and his collaborator, Engels, displayed an even greater flexibility:

> One can envisage that the old society could peacefully grow into the new one in countries where the representatives of the people concentrate all power in themselves, where one can do, constitutionally, whatever one pleases, so long as the majority of the people give their support, in democratic republics such as France and America, or in monarchies like England where the dynasty is powerless against the will of the people. But in Germany, where the government is almost omnipotent and the Reichstag and other representative bodies for all practical purposes powerless, to proclaim anything like this in Germany would be to remove the fig leaf from absolutism and use it to conceal one's own nakedness.[4]

Not only was the socialist tradition uncertain; it was also full of failures. The Paris Commune and the collapse of the First International were body-blows to a young and diversified movement.

When the Second International was founded in Paris in 1889 (on a date which commemmorated the hundredth anniversary of the French Revolution), the Marxist socialists and reformist socialists made sure that the anarchists, who had, in their opinion, wrecked the First International, were excluded. Another difficulty was provided by the French syndicalists, who, though Marxist ideologically, were opposed to a centralised party structure. The anarchists were finally excluded at the Zurich Congress in 1893 and the syndicalists at the London Congress in 1896.[5] In this way the party of the oppressed produced its own undesirables, partly out of fear for its own position and partly motivated by the desire for greater cohesiveness within the International, which would bring about the socialist system quicker.

It was not till the beginning of the twentieth century that the lines of the split began to crystallise into a left- and right-wing split. This split (first evidenced in the German Social-Democratic Party because of Bernstein's revisionist theory, and later in the Russian Social-Democratic Party, when it split into the Menshevik and Bolshevik wings) would from then on surpass any other splits, national, tactical or practical. The personalities on each side, though extremely important in themselves, need not concern us here, for some of them changed sides, others were quickly eliminated. But the theory is of utmost importance for it has produced two movements which are contemporary.

To oversimplify matters somewhat, the left wing of social democracy opted for anti-parliamentarism, revolutionary tactics to reach power and maximalist socialism (nationalisation of the means of production, distribution and exchange) and, in the event of war, for refusal to join in on the side of imperialist governments. The right wing opted for parliamentary systems, evolutionary tactics to attain power and for a mixed economy; in the event of war this wing was prepared to help its government in the name of national interest. The left-wing position became known as communism, and the right-wing position socialism or social democracy. However, such definitions were difficult to establish in theory in 1903, in 1914 and are difficult to establish now. This is because many parties and personalities have adopted intermediate positions, and because radical movements much more to the left and to the right of social democracy as it was understood in 1903 have become commonplace since. It is also because these radical movements are much more sophisticated than were the anarchists and socialists of the nineteenth century, and that they are able to find support among wider strata of population than was the case in the nineteenth century. Hence it is best to look at the split from the point of view of a case study.

Socialism and Communism in Germany

The German Social-Democratic Party was the largest and wealthiest in the world. It had the best leaders, the best organisation and the strongest following in Europe. In 1914 the SPD had over a million members, obtained 30 per cent of the votes and held 40 per cent of the seats in the Reichstag, making it the largest party there.[6] The SPD supported, partly willingly, partly reluctantly, the First World War on its outbreak. But as the war dragged on, previous opposition from the left wing became stronger, the right wing weakened and a split finally occurred in January 1917, when the Independent Socialist Party (USPD) was formed. Another left-wing group, which had existed in the SPD since 1906 and was known as the International Group, adopted the name of Spartakus Bund some time between 1915 and 1916 and announced it on 11 November 1918 — Armistice Day. The Spartakus Bund was led by Rosa Luxemburg and Karl Liebknecht.[7] The Spartakists and the USPD shared only one viewpoint: that of opposition to the war. Nevertheless, when the war ended, the Empire fell and the situation seemed ripe for a revolution, the mainstream of the SPD won the support of the military, of the people and of parliament. An abortive uprising by the Spartakists ended with the brutal murders of Luxemburg and Liebknecht in mid-January.[8] Apart from creating new communist martyrs the only thing which Rosa Luxemburg and Liebknecht accomplished was to split the SPD completely by creating the German Communist Party out of the Spartakus Bund on 30 December 1918 and in unifying the centre and right-wing Social-Democrats against communism. The point has been made that the SPD mirrored the attitudes in Germany much better than the KPD, and that the Social-Democratic leaders, Ebert and Scheidemann, were shocked by the chaos they saw in Russia, and wanted to preserve order in Germany. 'Germany was not revolutionary, although a revolution had occurred . . . . Workers' and soldiers' soviets were not so much engines of revolution as consequences of the disappearance of the Reich.' The error of the SPD's leaders, though, according to some authorities, lay in leaving untouched the structure of the previous regime: the upper administration, the military and the judiciary.[9] However, this is exactly what the left-wing radicals were saying: that without a complete social and political revolution the Germans would be unable to create a democratic system. While it is dubious if the Spartakists would have created such a system, it is undoubted that the docility of the mainstream SPD towards the old ruling classes prevented the birth of a truly democratic republic in 1919, and its duplicity in the early 1930s virtually made Hitler's ascent to power inevitable. Marx's error then was twofold: first, he expected a successful revolution in Germany because of its well-developed industrial system and the strength of the SPD, and second, he expected the SPD to remain the party of the proletariat. Experience has shown (and admittedly Marx could not have known of this) that it is the least-developed countries with the weakest socialist movements that tend to create really revolutionary conditions.

The abortive revolts of 1921 and 1923 merely served to underline the lack of support for radical left-wing politics in Germany. The USPD was unable to survive as an independent party and it split in 1920, one part joining the KPD, another the Majority SPD. But the KPD would have been unable to function if it were not for the constant support it received from the CPSU. In view of the weakness of the KPD it is surprising to see the criticism of the purges which Stalin instigated within it. They led to the catastrophe of 1933, it is true. But would anything else have revived the KPD? It had no roots among the people. The Luxemburgist democratic trend (if it were ever implemented) would hardly have satisfied the people as a whole; German democracy was too weak a plant to thrive without support; the road which the SPD followed was probably the only possible one for Germany at that time.

Without doubt, the main reason for the KPD's weakness in the early years was lack of ideological leadership. The murders of Luxemburg and Liebknecht had deprived the party of natural leaders. They may not have had a larger following than Brandler and Thalheimer had in the 1920s, but ideologically and charismatically they were much better suited for leadership, and they were much stronger characters as well. Hence, it is difficult to blame Stalin for his actions in the 1920s. As he said himself:

We hear the voices of certain intellectuals asserting that the

Central Committee of the German Communist Party is weak, that its leadership is feeble, that the work is adversely affected by the absence of intellectual forces in the Central Committee, that the Central Committee does not exist..... It is said that theoretical knowledge is not a strong point with the present Central Committee. What of it? If the policy is correct, theoretical knowledge will come in due course.... The strength of the present Central Committee lies in the fact that it is pursuing a correct Leninist policy.... Comrade Thälmann, use the services of these intellectuals if they really want to serve the cause of the working class....[10]

Thälmann, whom Stalin put in charge of the KPD, was not an intellectual personality, but then neither was Stalin. Deutscher recalls how the Old Bolshevik, Ryazanov, stopped Stalin short in a theoretical argument in early party meetings, by saying: 'Stop it, Koba, don't make a fool of yourself. Everybody knows that theory is not exactly your field.'[11] But practice was Stalin's field. As early as 1923, after the failure of the uprising, Stalin implied that 'The German Communists could not hope to seize power either in 1923 or in any forseeable future, because they could never obtain backing from the peasantry comparable to that received by Bolshevism, and that, at best, only a German defeat in another war might give them a chance.'[12] The German left was not only broken up and leaderless, it was well known to be so. After Liebknecht's murder, the leadership was taken over by Zetkin and Levi; then by Brandler and Thalheimer; then by Ruth Fischer and Maslow. It may have been the last straw when Stalin imposed Thälmann on the party, but at least Thälmann did what he was told and stayed at his post till he was captured by the Nazis.

One observer finds that

The German Communists, never strong in leaders after the murder of Rosa Luxemburg, were further reduced in wisdom by accepting the leadership of the Communist International; and Moscow, obsessed by the turnip ghost of a united intervention of capitalist states against Russian Communism, cared only to drive a wedge between Germany and the western powers. ... All that the Communists achieved was to increase the unscrupulousness of German political life, and to prepare the way for the truly ruthless and unprincipled. When, in 1933, the moment

came for the Communists to undertake the battle in the street
... it turned out that they were old-style parliamentary talkers
like all the rest.[13]

Another confirms this by saying:

This is not the place to tell the story of the collapse of the
Weimar Republic, the story which ended in the surrender of the
most powerful labour organizations on the Continent to the
Brown Shirts, without a single shot, without a single act of real
resistance. Suffice it to say that after the collapse, one of the
phrases that were current among the men of the German left
was that 'without Stalin there would have been no Hitler'. The
saying should be taken with a grain of salt. Amid the Katzen-
jammer which befell them after 1933, most leaders of the
German left were only too eager to explain away their own
failure and ascribe it to Stalin's evil influence.[14]

Yet another commentator explains it in different terms; he
claims that while both SPD and KPD were mostly composed of
working-class membership, with a quarter of intellectual members,
the Communists were significantly younger. 'In the Reichstag of
1930, over eighty-five per cent of the Social Democrats were over
forty years of age, while more than seventy per cent of the
Communist deputies were under forty.'[15] However the collapse of
the Left in Germany is explained, it must be admitted that while
Stalin and Thälmann did not help its chances, the KPD was as
much to blame for the adoption of the anti-SPD line as the SPD
was for trying to align with the Nazis against the KPD.

The Fifth Congress of the Comintern (in 1924) began to elaborate
the theory that social democracy equated fascism. In April 1929,
Stalin reiterated the need to fight against social democracy, saying
that social democracy was the main buttress of capitalism, 'Hence
the task of intensifying the fight in the communist parties against
the right-wing elements, as being the agents of Social Democratic
influence, was essential.'[16] In July 1929, the Tenth Plenum of the
Executive Committee of the Comintern completed the equation;
social democracy became social fascism: 'The aims of the fascists
and the social fascists are the same; the difference consists in the
slogans, and partly also in the methods.'[17] Thälmann and other
representatives of the KPD declared that they fully agreed with

the theses formulated by Manuilsky and Kuusinen. It may well be that, had the Great Crash not intervened at the end of 1929, the Stalinist line, however faulty its theory, may have proved useful — at least in Germany. However, the Wall Street crash and the Depression which followed it immediately in Germany cut the ground out from moderate parties' programmes. The radicals who gained were the Nazis not the Communists. The reasons for this were many, but most lay in the fact that the Nazis were able to offer money and jobs to the unemployed without a revolution. If one opted for the Communists, one opted for a struggle against the state: on the other hand, opting for the Nazis meant siding with a powerful part of the establishment and receiving an immediate reward. In this way, Stalin did not misunderstand the weakness of the Communists, or the indecisiveness of the SPD; he simply underestimated the support the Nazis would get from parts of the German establishment, and it was this support which enabled them to get mass following at the right time. Lenin might not have made the same mistake.

The KPD was outlawed by Hitler on 21 March 1933; its property was confiscated, its 100 deputies were expelled from the Reichstag and its membership was imprisoned *en masse*. Soon afterwards Trotsky wrote: 'The criminal role of the Social Democracy requires no commentary: the Comintern was created fourteen years ago precisely in order to snatch the proletariat from the demoralising influence of the Social Democracy, if it has not succeeded up to now, if the German proletariat found itself impotent, disarmed, and paralysed at the moment of its greatest historic test, the direct and immediate blame falls upon the leadership of the post-Leninist Comintern.'[18] The KPD, with the exception of those members who had fled to USSR and were not purged by Stalin, was virtually extinct in Germany. It was not till the creation of the DDR and the fusion of the Social Democrats and remnants of the KPD that a party was again created in East Germany. The West German party had suffered various problems which will be discussed later.

Other European Communist Parties

While the German party was the largest in Europe and its influence had been of great importance, other European parties took a share in the policy-making process of the Comintern. A distinction has to be drawn between parties which were legal throughout the inter-war period (like the French, British, Czechoslovak and Scandinavian parties) and parties which were illegal part or all of the time (like the Italian, German, Spanish, Polish and Hungarian parties). Further distinction has to be drawn between parties which had attempted or engaged in armed action in this period (like the German, Hungarian and Spanish parties) and those which, functioning either legally or illegally, were content to stay within the limits of the existing state systems.

Another factor which has to be taken into account is the degree of obedience which national parties exhibited towards the Comintern and Stalinism at various periods. Finally, the last (though not least) factor consists of estimating what support the parties had outside their own membership, how steadfast such support was, and whether the membership itself was sufficiently disciplined both to stay within the party and to obey its frequent changes of policy dictated by Soviet changes of course. Viewed from this standpoint, it can be seen that the communist parties in Europe were by no means large, highly influential or that they had mass support. Moreover, there were other problems as well. The non-European communist parties were either extremely small, or very weak. The Communists had no traditional 'congregations', being a new and controversial party. And even in European countries with sizeable communist parties, their size did not prevent disaster, as had happened in Germany. In 1924 it was said that 80 per cent of the European membership was concentrated in four countries: Germany, Czechoslovakia, France and Yugoslavia.[19] Of these, only the German party appeared to have both numerical and political influence; the Yugoslav party was illegal; the Czechoslovak party was accused, admittedly by one of its bitter critics, that 'From its birth in 1921 through all its vicissitudes [it] adhered unflinchingly to Moscow-made precepts, shifting the line whenever the signals were changed by the Kremlin.' Though the KSC ranked among the country's four strongest parties, even at the peak of its success, its voting strength amounted only to 13 per cent of the electorate. Its membership fluctuated between a high of 150,000 in 1928 to a low of 28,000 in 1930. Also 'all through the first twelve years of its existence the Party was plagued by continuous factional strife and personal rivalries'. Even after the purge carried out at the instigation of the 6th Congress of the Comintern and the installation of Klement Gottwald as the Secretary-General in 1929, the feuding between left and right wings within the party did not stop, and the dissenters were finally expelled from the party.[20]

The French party had different beginnings. It grew out of a vote taken at the 1920 Congress of the SFIO in Tours which decided to support the association with the Comintern. However, it produced a breakaway Communist Party, with the Socialists, led by Blum, remaining in the anti-Comintern faction. 'Those who voted to join the Third International ... had for the most part belonged to the party for only a few years. The sections that rallied were largely new and located in the countryside.'[21] The purges and crises within the PCF made it lose ground; in the 1924 elections the SFIO and the Radical Party won 101 seats, whereas the PCF won only 16 seats. The resolutions of the 6th Congress of the Comintern, which stigmatised the Socialists as Social-Fascists, hit the PCF particularly hard; it lost 80 per cent of its membership, from 131,000 members in 1921 to 28,000 members in 1932.[22]

But numerical strength was not always of such importance as the theory of communism. One of the most persecuted European parties, the Italian Communist Party, produced a major political theorist, whose influence had gone on well beyond his immediate period. This was Antonio Gramsci.

Gramsci came of a Sardinian middle-class family who had fallen on hard times. His background was formed by this misfortune as much as by his observation of the lives of Sardinian peasants and miners. He was further affected by a severe physical disability, which stopped him from joining in the normal social life of a young Italian and turned him towards study. His university studies were pursued in the centre of the Italian 'red revolution' in Turin before the First World War.[23] There Gramsci joined the Italian Socialist Party at the same time as Mussolini, Bordiga and Togliatti. It was from Turin that Gramsci welcomed the Bolshevik Revolution and it was there that he started the 'only Marxist revolutionary organ in Italy with any degree of intellectual seriousness'.[24] This was the journal *L'Ordine Nuovo*, whose first issue appeared in May 1919.

The Italian Socialist Party (PSI) was a different body than the German one. It had been relatively small before the First World War, with only 50,000 members in 1914. It expanded rapidly after the war, with 300,000 members in 1920. The Confederation of Trade Unions expanded from a modest half-million to two million members. The size of the party and its quick growth served to weaken it rather than the opposite: 'The two principal consequences were, on the one hand, a diffuse revolutionary faith based on the blind presumption that this proletarian onrush would inevitably result in final victory,' on the other, in the rise to leadership of demagogues without theoretical background or experience.[25] The splits within the party were manifold, but they seemed to hinge not only on lack of experience but also on the fact that the Italian geopolitical and economic background was very different from that of Germany, and that though Russia, where a successful revolution had happened, was a backward agricultural country, like parts of Italy, it had had a completely different tradition in almost every facet of its life.

At any rate, there was no question of dividing the socialist movement at the start. The PSI Congress in Bologna in October 1919 voted to join the Third International, though it rejected Bordiga's suggestion that the party should change its name to 'Communist'. The split came in January 1921, during the 17th Congress of the PSI in Livorno. 98,000 members voted for the socialist leadership of Serrati, while 58,000 for 'pure' communism. On 21 January 1921, the communists met in the San Marco theatre in Livorno and set up the new Communist Party of Italy (*Partito Communista d'Italia* or PCDI; not the post-war renamed *Partito Communista Italiano* or PCI). The new party was dominated by Amadeo Bordiga: the Central Committee consisted of eight members from his group; Bordiga, Grieco, Fortichiari, Repossi, Polano, Sessa and Tarsia; five left-wing maximalists; and two members from *Ordine Nuovo* — Gramsci and Terracini. The executive committee consisted of Bordiga, three of his followers and Terracini. Gramsci was left out.[26]

Perhaps not unreasonably, the Communists felt that they had been betrayed by the Socialists, who refused to follow their policy. Certainly Gramsci felt extremely bitter about the split, about which he later wrote: 'The reactionary forces intended to thrust the workers back into the state they had known during the early days of capitalism, when they were dispersed, isolated, a collection of individuals without any consciousness of class unity, or any aspiration towards power. The Livorno split [which detached the greater part of the Italian proletariat from the Communist International] was without any doubt the greatest single victory won by these reactionary forces.'[27] As one commentator writes: 'Much of his writing in late 1920 and in 1921 was devoted to a repeated criticism of the Italian Socialist Party.' And further: 'For

Gramsci ... the Socialist Party by now represented all that he disliked most in Italian life: in one of his most bitter articles he compared the Socialists to the figure of Pulcinella in the classical Italian *commedia dell'arte*, a character who never takes anything seriously and flees from assuming full responsibility for his actions.'[28]

It is interesting to note that this period of Gramsci's identification with the official Comintern line, condemning socialists as the real foes of communism while neglecting to pay attention to Fascist danger, won him the praise of the Comintern. He was invited to Moscow in May 1922 not to return to Italy till May 1924. He then took over the post of Secretary-General of the Italian party from Bordiga, ostensibly because of Bordiga's unyielding left-wing line and insubordination to the Comintern, in reality — however much his biographers gloss over the fact — because he was prepared to toe the official Moscow line. Gramsci's main efforts seem to have been devoted to saving the unity of the CPSU, not to finding out which faction in the CPSU and, therefore, the Comintern, held the correct Marxist position. 'The attitude of Bordiga, like that of Trotsky, has disastrous repercussions; when a comrade of the value of Bordiga stands to one side, a lack of confidence in the party is produced among the workers and this results in defeatism.'[29]

Gramsci himself had now changed his attitude; the coming to power of the Fascists had made him reconsider his position towards the Socialists, and the new Communist paper was deliberately called *Unità*. However, the harm of the split, of bitter attacks, of Comintern progaganda over the years had already broken up the left sufficiently for Mussolini to pick them off, one by one, without too much opposition in the country. Gramsci himself was arrested on 8 November 1926 in Rome, and was never to regain his liberty. He died in April 1937. But it was in prison, under appalling conditions and mostly fighting illness, that Gramsci developed his main theories. These theories were for the first time independent of the Moscow line, of the Comintern ideology, and concentrated mainly on Gramsci's own Italian experience.

Almost on the eve of his arrest, and possibly before an abortive attempt to escape from Italy, Gramsci showed that he had begun to reconsider his attitude towards the Comintern line. In a letter already mentioned here, he stated that 'Comrades Zinoviev, Trotsky and Kamenev have contributed powerfully to our education as revolutionaries... they have been our teachers. We appeal to them especially, as the group responsible for the present crisis, because we would like to be sure that the majority of the central committee of the CPSU does not intend to go too far, that it does not intend to abuse its victory and take excessive measures.'[30] This letter earned censure from Togliatti, in Moscow as the Italian representative of the Comintern. A split developed between the two men, who never met again owing to Gramsci's imprisonment. A meeting was arranged between the Comintern representative Humbert-Droz at Valpolcevera, near Genoa, and the executive of the Italian party at the beginning of November in order to explain the expulsions of Trotsky, Kamenev and Zinoviev to the Italians. Gramsci could not get to the meeting; he had been met at the station in Milan by a police inspector and told to return to Rome, where he was arrested within a few days. It may be that had he reached Genoa, with its nearness to the French border, he may have escaped. It may be that, as he maintained, he never intended to escape. It could be that Togliatti had already made sure that he would remain in Italy and be removed from his party post because of his imprisonment. Or it could be that the whole incident was a complete coincidence. At any rate, whatever Gramsci suffered in a Fascist prison — and it was grievous particularly in his state of health — he was at least saved the necessity of supporting the purges of Old Bolsheviks, of becoming a complete Stalinist or of being purged by Stalin.

The incidental effect of his imprisonment was that it made him into a serious communist theorist, where formerly he had been a serious journalist and propagandist. Gramsci developed the theory that, in order to gain power, communists must make an alliance with backward peasantry; an alliance far more difficult in a liberal state which had imposed its own political culture on other classes than was the case of Tsarist Russia, where the government had no consensus. His thoughts on alliance (which unfortunately came too late to prevent the rise to power of fascism) were based almost purely on the Italian experience, and on his subjective experience as a Southern Italian. They provided a basis for the PCI's 'historic compromise' of post-war years, but they did not provide a basis for a non-Marxist solution. Yet one may wonder why a non-Marxist solution should not have occurred to Gramsci, if, as he himself admitted, the proletariat took well to the middle-class, liberal, parliamentary political culture. Throughout his life

His ideology remained one of action; and it was always a

'philosophy of praxis'. Moreover, the basic structure of his thought and the core of his emotional and political committment were undoubtedly Marxist, and it would be wrong to suggest that he ever envisages a non-Marxist road to Socialism . . . . The ways by which Gramsci hoped that people would come to accept the 'philosophy of praxis' as the basis for their lives and the hegemony of the Communist Party as the basis for the state are more humane than those employed by Lenin or Stalin, but one must not think that Gramsci was ever just a democratic reformist Socialist prepared to work indefinitely within the existing political and constitutional framework. His followers talk of the need for a 'historic compromise' with other social and political forces, but it is hard to think of this compromise as being other than tactical.[31]

While Gramsci was influenced by the philosophy of Benedetto Croce he rejected Croce's committment to liberalism, and moved near to the position of Rosa Luxemburg and Lukacs in believing that Marxism would have to become more sophisticated in order to appeal to intellectuals, while the level of popular culture would have to be raised among the masses in order to make them understand its philosophy. In a way, Gramsci's theories could be traced much better to the eighteenth-century philosophy of the 'perfectability' of human nature than to the nineteenth- and twentieth-century theories of adapting human nature to new systems. But many Marxists became much more flexible and subject to doubt when confronted with loss of power or illness; one need only mention Trotsky and Lenin in this connection. Our main interest in Gramsci in connection with this work is that he gave the Italian Communists a basis of theory which they could apply to their own country, and that he was indirectly responsible for the modern phenomenon of 'Eurocommunism'.

There was one European communist party whose fate has had a negative influence on the policy both of the CPSU and of the Comintern. It has also provided an episode which, though revolutionary, is not highly publicised. This is the Hungarian Communist Party in its 'Soviet Republic' period. Soon after the formation of the Comintern, Bela Kun, a friend of Lenin, set up a Communist-Socialist government in Hungary as a result of the provisional government resigning on 20 March 1919 in protest against excessive Entente demands. On 21 March a Hungarian Soviet Republic was proclaimed in Budapest under the leadership of Bela Kun and with Mathias Rakosi, the future Stalinist ruler of Hungary, as deputy Commissar of Commerce. The new government immediately abolished private property of the means of production and decreed the death penalty for anyone who engaged in private trade. The government found it difficult to maintain its power. The Red Army was unable to come to its aid because of the Kolchak and Yudenich offensives. Despite this, Bela Kun launched an offensive to regain Slovakia and parts of Romania which had broken away after the collapse of Austria–Hungary. His assistant, Tibor Szamuely, in the meantime broke up Hungarian opposition by mass murders of opponents. It is said that during the short period of the Soviet Republic some thirty thousand people were massacred. The massacres repelled Austrian socialists, who refused to come to the help of the Hungarians. The Allies, alarmed by the apparent spread of the revolution, blockaded Hungary, and the Romanians sent in an army to overthrow Bela Kun's regime. The Communist government collapsed on 19 August 1919, and the impression of violence it created in Europe was much stronger than that of the Bolshevik Revolution, partly because Hungary was in the centre of Europe and partly because the terror was so concentrated. The Hungarian revolution is mentioned in one sentence in the Soviet *History of the CPSU*[32] and Bela Kun's name is not included. Bela Kun himself was executed by Stalin in 1937 or 1938.[33]

The Hungarian revolution appalled European communists and non-communists alike and annoyed the Soviet government and party. It was a timely reminder that ideological commitment could breed large-scale violence (since the counter-revolution committed atrocities on the same scale as the Communists did); it created the myth of anti-communist martyrs to counter that of communist martyrs in Germany; and it brought to power a reactionary semi-dictatorial regime of Admiral Horthy, which made the Communist Party illegal throughout its existence.

Most communist parties were founded as breakaway movements from Social-Democracy. They were sustained by the Comintern, without whose organisational and financial help they would have been unable to function. Their leaders were in general either approved by the CPSU or in tune with the Comintern's policy. Their main problem was that of separating from the mainstream of Social-Democracy, against the wishes of many of their members. The dispute about who was right in Marxist terms — the Social-

Democrats or the Communists — is one which it would be futile to pursue. Both sides have perfect arguments about the validity of their case. What must be remembered is that both sides have felt uneasy about the split.

However, the situation was made even worse during the 1920s owing to the power struggle which developed within the CPSU and subsequently within the Comintern. This struggle affected the European communist parties most of all; it made them split from within; it deprived them of a large part of their membership; and it made them both insecure and over-aggressive. The episode of 'social fascism', though imposed from Moscow, had its roots in the bitterness European communists like Gramsci felt about the 'treason' of their fellow-socialists. It is quite certain that had there been strong opposition to such a course within the leadership of the European communist parties Stalin would not have dared to impose it at this stage. The later break-up of the left in Germany, and the spectacle of both the Communists and the Social-Democrats trying to trade with the Nazis in order to eradicate each other is another example of such insecurity.

But the best example of the problems the communist parties had in finding their rationale within the European political system is what happened after the Nazi rise to power; the era of the Popular Fronts.

Notes

1. Louis Bromfield, at the height of Cold War, quoted by Norman Thomas in the Preface of M. Salvadori, *The Rise of Modern Communism*, p. vi.
2. I have discussed this problem in *The Green Flag*, particularly Ch. 3.
3. L. Schapiro, *The Communist Party of the Soviet Union*, pp. 22-3.
4. L. Derfler, *Socialism since Marx*, p. 55: Engels quoted from *Die Neue Zeit*, vol. XX, 1, 1901-2.
5. Derfler, ibid., pp. 56-7.
6. Ibid., p. 104.
7. P. Nettl, *Rosa Luxemburg*, pp. 443 and 391.
8. For details of the uprising, see Nettl, ibid., Ch. 15.
9. Derfler, *Socialism*, p. 119.
10. Stalin, speaking at the Sixth Enlarged Plenum of the Executive Committee of the Comintern, quoted by F. Claudin, *The Communist Movement*, p. 144: See also *Sochineniya*, Vol. 12: *O Pravom Uklone v VKP (b)*.
11. Deutscher, *Stalin*, p. 290.
12. Ibid., p. 394.
13. A.J.P. Taylor, *The Course of German History*, pp. 224-5.
14. Deutscher, *Stalin*, p. 406.

15. M. Kolinsky, *Continuity and Change in European Society*, p. 77.

16. *Collected Works*, Vol. 12, pp. 17-18, quoted by Claudin, *Communist Movement*, p. 156.

17. *Inprecorr* (English Edn), Vol. 9., No. 40, p. 848, quoted by Claudin, ibid., p. 157.

18. Trotsky, in *The Struggle Against Fascism in Germany*, pp. 379-80; see also Claudin, p. 128.

19. Claudin, *Communist Movement*, p. 112.

20. E. Taborsky, *Communism in Czechoslovakia, 1948-1960*, pp. 4-9.

21. Derfler, *Socialism*, p. 122.

22. Ibid., pp. 124-30.

23. For a detailed account of Gramsci's early life, see G. Fiori, *Antonio Gramsci: Life of a Revolutionary*; a brief account of Gramsci's life will be found in James Joll's *Gramsci*.

24. Quoted by Fiori, *Antonio Gramsci*, p. 118.

25. Ibid., p. 126.

26. Ibid., pp. 146-7.

27. Quoted by Fiori, ibid., p. 147.

28. Joll, *Gramsci*, p. 50.

29. P. Spriano, *Storia del Partito Communista Italiano*, Vol. 1, p. 441; see also Joll, *Gramsci*, p. 64.

30. Quoted in Fiori, *Antonio Gramsci*, p. 215.

31. Joll, *Gramsci*, p. 115.

32. B.N. Ponomaryov (ed.), *History of the CPSU*, p. 311.

33. See Deutscher, *Stalin*, p. 380, n. 3.

5

The Comintern and European Communist Parties, 1933-41

The Comintern Faces Fascism

Despite the fact that from the outset of his rule in Italy Mussolini set out to destroy the Communist Party, and that by 1926 all its leaders were either in prison or in exile, the Comintern did not appear to be unduly worried. This was not due to stupidity or shortsightedness; on the contrary, it was the result of faith in the future. As Soviet historians of the Comintern point out: 'For a long time .... the Communists persisted in the mistake of regarding the world economic crisis that opened in 1929 as the final crisis [of capitalism], from which the bourgeoisie could find no way out, and the necessary result of which must be the triumph of the proletarian revolution. This thesis often took the place of a rigorous analysis of the extent to which the revolution had matured, on the basis of the development of class contradictions in each country.'[1]

Gramsci's role in the formation of this attitude cannot be overlooked. He was the creator of the Italian Communist Party. He was witness to the fact that, despite a majority vote by the Socialists to accept the Comintern's guidance, the party was split, with the larger part remaining Socialist. He was a colleague of Mussolini's in the pre-war days in the Italian Socialist Party, and had then seen him set up a fascist regime in Italy. Finally, he was in Moscow as the Italian representative to the Comintern in the crucial period of 1922 to 1924. Returning to Italy, he did not expect to be imprisoned; he was working for a speedy communist revolution which would come as a result of the fascist tactics. It is significant that it was at the 5th Congress of the Comintern in 1924 that the formulation equating fascism with social democracy and a ban on communist support for Social-Democratic parties were first proposed.[2] It is also interesting that this formula was never changed. As Deutscher states: 'These words may be said to represent the fullest contribution that Stalin ever made to the understanding of fascism or national socialism. In subsequent years he vaguely repeated his view once or twice, without modifying it.'[3] Could it be that once Gramsci was back in Italy, suffering fascist oppression, subsequently imprisoned and unable to change his formula as he was held incommunicado for two years, Stalin — never strong on theory, as Ryazanov had testified — was unable to change the formula? The suspicion must, at least, be very strong that the theory was Gramsci's; that he formulated it on the basis of specific Italian events; that the leadership of the CPSU, impressed by Gramsci's undoubted intelligence and learning, accepted it; and that after Gramsci's arrest and during the rise of the Nazis in Germany all that the Russian leadership could do was to improve upon the formula, and introduce a further term of abuse for socialists in 1929, that of 'social fascism'.

By the end of 1929 the Italian question was solved by Mussolini, at least for the time being. But there remained the vexed question of Germany. This was much more important from the Soviet point of view, not only for geographical reasons but for political, economic and military ones as well. It is at this point that one is confronted by the theory that Stalin deliberately sacrificed the KPD in order to continue the military and economic co-operation with the Germans which had been started by the Treaty of Rapallo. One authority states that this co-operation was maintained till 1935.[4] It is quite possible that this co-operation continued in secret despite the apparent ideological warfare between the two governments in the period from 1935 to 1939, when it suddenly came out into the open again, after the Molotov–Ribbentropp Pact in August. This would have required the CPSU being advised of such co-operation by the military and economic bodies but remaining unaware of it for political purposes. It would make perfect sense that the USSR as a state would pursue the economic and defence policies which have served it well in the past, while the CPSU and the Comintern started the policy of the Popular Front.

Such theory fits in well with what was happening. The KPD was being weakened all the time by the divisive policies pursued by the Comintern. In January 1931 the percentage of factory committees led by the Communists amounted to 4 per cent, while the Social

Democrats controlled 84 per cent. By the end of 1932 only 10 per cent of KPD members belonged to trade unions. The KPD's electoral results reflected this state of affairs.

> Many years after the catastrophe, Wilhelm Pieck was to admit that one of the worst mistakes of the German party had been to 'struggle for the establishment of a German Soviet Republic', to refrain from 'putting in the forefront the fight to defend democracy and the political rights of the masses', to 'attack the Nazis and Social Democracy at one and the same time' and 'not to have understood the seriousness of the Fascist danger.' ...Pieck said essentially the same as Trotsky, with this difference, that Trotsky was already saying it in 1930....[5]

The rapprochement between the Social-Democrats and the KPD between 1930 and 1932, which brought about a rising left-wing vote in the 1932 elections, shows that, faced by the Nazi danger, the left wing in Germany could have united and fought Nazism through normal political means. Why did this not happen? Various theories have been advanced beginning with the theory that Stalin deliberately led the KPD towards extinction in order to save the Treaty of Rapallo, and ending with the theory of Stalin's 'blindness' to the danger of fascism. It must be pointed out here that Stalin, while not a good theorist, was not blind to danger. Neither can he be accused of treachery towards the USSR or world communism in view of what happened after 1941. An unbiased witness cannot ignore the fact that Stalin must have been acting with two objectives in his mind: first, he was receiving advice from the military and industrial bosses that co-operation with Germany was vital for Soviet economy and defence; second, he believed that fascism was a transitory phenomenon, the highest stage of imperialism, and that its very radicalism was bound to produce a left-wing reaction in the shape of communist revolution.

Objectively speaking, the first statement is impossible to prove (though Soviet policies analysed since then produce similar results); the second statement did eventually come true, though after much more upheaval than Stalin may have expected, and much later. So, basically, Stalin was justified in his opinion of the early 1930s. The amount of suffering he had caused by his policy, the fact that he then blamed the German debacle on the KPD leadership and that this gave him an excuse to purge it at a later stage, and the fact that the cause of left-wing politics had been undermined outside the Soviet bloc, perhaps forever, were merely by-products of a 'correct' policy as shaped by Stalin. The foreign communists and ex-communists who blame Stalin for all that had happened (as he blamed the KPD) are in an invidious situation: they were capable of opposing his policy — but, for reasons mentioned above, they did not.

The period of the 1930s marks a change of emphasis in the role played by various communist parties in Europe. The period of the 1920s was one which witnessed the strongest action and greatest influence from the KPD; and the growth of theory can be mainly attributed to the Italian Communists. In the 1930s, after the virtual elimination of the Germans and the Italians (except in exile), the lead was taken by the French and Spanish Communist Parties.

What seems to have happened is rather different from the accepted facts. The accepted facts are that faced with the Nazi danger, Stalin suddenly changed the course of Soviet foreign policy and the Comintern and the leadership of European communist parties followed him obediently. In this way, the myth of Stalin's dictatorial powers and of the helplessness of European communists is perpetuated. Stalin is dead, and European communists are vindicated in that they only 'followed orders'. This smacks too much of the Nazi defence at the Nuremberg Trials. It is quite true that the European communists were demoralised and isolated after the splits of the early 1920s, and that European governments were basically (and with good reason) hostile to communism. But as had been demonstrated above, much of the communists' isolation was of their own making; much of the Comintern's anti-Socialist policy was planned in Europe; and it must be assumed that the Soviet authorities did rely — though perhaps not totally — on advice of European leaders. This last seems plain from circumstantial evidence set out above. Leaving aside the very serious complication of Trotsky's influence on the European Left and its implications for Soviet policy, one is presented with very strong evidence that the change of course was first mooted by Trotsky in 1930; was then taken up by the socialist leaders in Europe; transmitted to the communist leaders; and finally suggested to the Russians.

Chronology speaks for itself. After Hitler's accession to power in February 1933, the Labour and Socialist International declared its willingness to open conversations with the Comintern to organise joint action against fascism. The only condition made was to end mutual attacks. A conference held by the LSI in August 1933 demonstrated that even the centre Socialists (like Blum and Adler), joined the left wing in declaring themselves for joint action. In the early months of 1934 the Spanish Socialist Party declared itself in favour of the Worker's Alliances and proposed to the Communist Party that it join them. In 1933 the French Socialists suggested that they join forces with the Communists. Other parties in Europe made similar moves.

There were thus, for the first time since the split in 1919, real possiblities not only of united action by Social Democrats and Communists, but also of the unification in a single party of all the different, revolutionary tendencies inspired by Marxism. Yet the year 1933, and half of 1934, went by without the Comintern modifying in any way the ultra-sectarian attitudes that had already caused the destruction of the KPD. ... Four months later, at its Thirteenth Plenum, the ECCI continued to counterpose the united front 'from below' to the united front 'from above' still regarding Social Democracy as a whole as the main social basis of the bourgeoisie....[6]

According to Claudin, the leadership of the Comintern (which after the purge of Bukharin consisted of Manuilsky, Kuusinen, Pyatnitskiy and Lozovsky) as well as European leaders had been aware for some time that a change of policy was necessary but that petrification and fear of Stalin made it impossible to turn away from the 'social fascism' theory. Yet, when Stalin gave the go-ahead, the difficulty ceased to exist. It is far more likely that the communist leaders in Europe were as afraid of joining up with socialists as they were in the 1970s, when we witnessed a replay of the Popular Front theme in France, and that the main reason was a simple human fear of losing influence and power to the socialists. It was not till Dimitrov pressed the European communists to change course in view of the fascist danger that the move was finally made. Soviet historians claim that Stalin did not oppose the move, though he insisted, not unreasonably, that he should not be held to blame for the previous course.[7]

Little need be added here to amplify Stalin's position. A supreme tactician, he 'maintained a prudent silence on the international situation during an entire year, between January 1933 and January 1934. He broke this silence at last on 26 January 1934, when he delivered his report to the Seventeenth Congress of the CPSU.'[8] This was the crucial speech in which Stalin made a reference to Nazism, in an oblique fashion. Good relations with fascist Italy had been possible for the USSR; he saw no reason for good relations not to be possible between Nazi Germany and the USSR. The countries which seek peace would always be the friends of the USSR, whatever their regime, fascist or capitalist. But in the end Marxism would prevail, said Stalin: 'It is said that in some countries in the West Marxism has already been destroyed. It is said that it has been destroyed by the bourgeois-nationalist trend known as fascism. That, of course, is nonsense. . . . . Marxism is the scientific expression of the fundamental interests of the working class. To destroy Marxism, the working class must be destroyed. But it is impossible to destroy the working class. . . . Bourgeois governments have come and gone, but Marxism has remained.' Moreover, added Stalin, the only country in which Marxism had won was the only country without unemployment and economic crises.[9] It is quite clear that Stalin counted on the economic crises in both capitalist and fascist countries to complete the work of the Bolshevik Revolution; in the meantime, the USSR might as well live in peace with all the countries and use this period to build up its strength. Hence to accuse him of sacrificing the Comintern and foreign communist parties for the sake of Soviet foreign policy is to misunderstand both Stalin and the situation. As far as Stalin was concerned, there never was any choice, particularly after 1923. The choice presented by the theory of Trotsky's Permanent Revolution had proved to be as ephemeral as the revolution itself. Stalin, faced with tough economic and political problems within the USSR, had little time and energy to spare for the spread of revolution. Strength within the USSR and weakness in the capitalist world were enough for the time being; they were better guarantees of future communism than any current political action.

It could well be that Stalin may have been vindicated in his attempt to ignore the rest of the world had it not been for the increasing Nazi menace. On the same day on which he was making his report, 26 January 1934, the Polish–German Declaration on Non-Agression was signed, an agreement that was to be valid for ten years. 'The Polish–German agreement met with violent criticism both at home and abroad. . . . The Communist Party claimed that the pact marked the first step towards Polish co-operation with Germany against the USSR. Press reaction in France was violent and the agreement was portrayed as betrayal by an ally.'[10] As Claudin also notes:

> The Quai d'Orsay and the military leaders of France drew the conclusion that the time had come to give serious thought to a return to the traditional strategy of the French governments of the period before the First World War .... Geography dictates. At the beginning of May, Barthou defined the French position, proposing to the government of the USSR a Franco-Soviet pact of mutual assistance ... On 25 May Barthou told the Chamber of Deputies that Russia's entry into the League of Nations 'would be .... a considerable event from the standpoint of the peace of Europe'. Six days later came the article in *L'Humanité*, reproduced from *Pravda*, urging the Communist Party of France to reach an understanding with the French Socialist Party.[11]

The biggest change in the policy of the Comintern, therefore, was not dictated by Stalin or by the European communist leaders, or even by fear of fascism — it came about as the result of the traditional French foreign policy; the policy of pursuing a 'balance of power' in Europe, and of keeping Germany in check. Nevertheless, by then the policy became accepted by the communists as the only one which could save them from a victorious rise of fascism. It is in France that one must look for an explanation of the Popular Front policy and in Spain for its final bankruptcy.

The PCF and the Popular Front

The French Left was ahead of its counterparts in the rest of Europe by reason of having had much longer traditions of radical revolutions and of republican politics. By the same token, however, it suffered the same drawbacks which have beset the British labour movement in the second half of the twentieth century: it was too broken up into factions; it had too many differing demands; and it tended to diffuse its energies by internal feuds. In 1920 the left wing of the Socialist Party split off to form the Communist Party, and a large section of the trade unions split off from the CGT to form the Communist CGTU affiliated to the Third International. This split was reinforced by the strength of the Radicals, whose support came from all classes, and by the strength of the rural vote in the Third Republic. The strength of the Radical–Socialist vote was demonstrated in 1924 when the Cartel des Gauches won an overwhelming majority of the seats (101 compared to the PCF's 16). However, in the urban industrial areas, the Communists were winning a steady following. The PCF followed the Comintern's line faithfully; implementing a purge of Trotskyites in 1923–4; a shift to the right in 1926 and the 'class against class' policy of 1928–34. Maurice Thorez, the Secretary-General since 1929, ranked with Togliatti of the Italian Party in his loyalty to Stalin.[12]

The policy of opposing the Socialists and Radicals in the last period caused many doubts among the Communists and weakened the Left considerably.

> In his report to the Comintern's executive committee, Maurice Thorez, the leading figure in French communism, gave a picture of 'confusion, doubt and indiscipline' in party ranks. He described how some communist municipal councillors had supported a resolution calling for 'the defence of bourgeois democracy'. Communist trade union leaders had negotiated, and in a number of strikes had formed joint committees with their socialist and Christian Democrat counterparts. Following its own investigation, the Comintern agreed that many PCF members wanted a change in the communist attitude to the socialist party.[13]

Nevertheless, till the February riots in the streets in 1934 the Socialists and Communists fought each other bitterly, despite the Nazi threat.

It took a visit to Moscow by Thorez and the article pleading for unity in May to make a start of negotiations even possible. On 11 June 1934 conversations took place between Thorez and Blum, and four days later the Socialists accepted the principle of joint demonstrations. Despite hesitation on both sides (Thorez was reluctant to accept unity with the Socialists and they were unwilling to join a Moscow-oriented party) a Unity of Action Pact was signed on 27 July. In October, before the congress of the Radical Party, Thorez put forward a further idea; that of a Popular Front with the Communists, Socialists and Radicals. How far this was on his own initiative, as he claimed in his autobiography[14] and despite the Comintern's advice, is open to doubt. At any rate, the move coincided perfectly with Franco–Soviet diplomacy of the period. The French–Soviet Pact was signed in Paris on 2 May 1935 and on

31 May Thorez suggested in the Chamber of Deputies that the time was ripe for the Radicals to join the Popular Front.

The Popular Front was produced for the first time on 14 July 1935. Thorez, Blum for the Socialists and Daladier for the Radicals all stood on a platform in Paris and swore a solemn oath to 'remain united to disarm and dissolve the factious Leagues, to defend and develop democratic freedoms and to ensure peace for mankind'.[15] When the Seventh Congress of the Comintern opened in Moscow on 25 July 1935 the French Popular Front was well established. The co-operation between the three parties led to the acceptance of a united programme in time for the 1936 elections. The Socialists received 146 deputies, and the Communists with 70 deputies had doubled their vote from 6.8 per cent to 12.5 per cent. Blum formed the Popular Front government, but, as one author put it, 'at five minutes to twelve'.[16]

The French Popular Front became a model for similar organisations in other European countries. But it has come under criticism from the 'pure' wing of the Comintern. It has been called a betrayal of Marxism, and Dimitrov found it hard to justify the changed tactics at the Seventh Congress of the Comintern, whose central slogan was 'The fight for peace and for the defence of the USSR'. It was left to Togliatti to urge that the French and Czechoslovak Communist Parties — the Czechs had also signed a pact of mutual assistance with the USSR — defend the pacts with the Soviet Union. And the prospects of world revolution, so clear at the Sixth Congress, were postponed, though not abandoned. The centre and liberal politicians regretted that the Popular Front tactics came so late, and appeared to be merely a response to the Nazi threat. They believed that the communists had more in common with the socialists than the Comintern had allowed for in the previous period, and that, given time, these common bonds would reassert themselves. Ideologically speaking, this may have been true. But practice had shown since (as in the case of Italy in the 1970s) that the communists find allies in parties more to the right of the socialists much more easily, and that such alliances have a better chance of survival than those of the Popular Front. The true test of the Popular Front era came very soon after the Seventh Congress of the Comintern, and it was demonstrated to be of very little use.

The Spanish Civil War and PCE

'The Spaniards are the only Latins who are tough.'[17] It was the toughness or intransigence of the Spaniards which led to the practice of the most radical politics in Europe, and to the greatest tragedy since the unification of Spain: the Spanish Civil War. And it was the same traits which made the task of the communists particularly difficult in Spain, because Spanish left-wing politics were traditionally anarchist and not socialist. Any organised communist party would have to struggle hard against the policy of the largest Spanish left-wing movement: 'The Anarchists stressed spontaneous struggle by the workers, eschewed all political action and organization as a bourgeois trap, and encouraged acts of individual terrorism against the representatives of the government.'[18] The principal anarchist organisation was the *Confederacion Nacional del Trabajo* (CNT) founded in 1911, and claiming one and a half million members in 1931. The Spanish Socialist Party decided by a narrow majority not to join the Comintern in 1921, thus making a split into a Communist Party inevitable. The Socialists were split into right and left wings, the right led by Prieto, the left by Largo Caballero. The Caballero wing was much more revolutionary and was in theory in favour of the dictatorship of the proletariat. The Socialists claimed to have several hundred thousand members in their trade union organisation, the *Union Géneral de Trabajadores* (UGT) at the beginning of the 1930s.

The Spanish Communist Party (PCE) founded after the split with the Socialists was isolated and small. It had about 10,000 members in 1922. The PCE remained faithful to the Comintern's policy and reflected its twists and turns throughout the 1920s and the beginning of the 1930s. This line brought about serious trouble within the party, and by 1930 it had about a thousand members; though speaking in Moscow in 1934, Dolores Ibarruri claimed that by 1931 it had only 800 members. Hugh Thomas put its membership at the beginning of 1936 at 10,000, i.e. the number it had at its inception.[19]

In 1930 one of the principal organisations of the PCE, the regional federation covering Catalonia and the Balaeric Islands, broke away and soon afterwards merged with the independent Catalan Communist Party to form a Workers' and Peasants' Bloc. In 1935 this organisation united with the Trotskyite Communist left and founded the Workers' Party of Marxist Unity (POUM).

Though POUM regarded itself as a Trotskyite organisation it was not considered to be such by Trotsky himself, who first urged it to join the PCE and later the Socialist Party (PSOE).[20] POUM was later virtually annihilated by the Russians during a period of executions in the summer of 1937.

In these conditions the Comintern could spare little thought for the PCE except to opine, in the words of Manuilsky in 1930, that 'It is not Spain which decides the fate of the world proletarian revolution . . .'.[21] From the creation of the Second Republic in 1931 till the 'turn' in the Comintern policy of 1934, the PCE was opposed to the Republican government. In April 1935 it proposed the creation of the Popular Front on the French model. In the elections of February 1936 the Popular Front (which embraced Communists, Socialists, Republicans and Anarchists) gained 35 per cent of the votes to 29 per cent gained by the right-wing CEDA (Spanish Confederation of Independent Right groups).[22] However, owing to the peculiarities of the Spanish electoral system, the Popular Front received 278 seats in the parliament against 137 seats for the right-wing National Front and 56 for the Centre parties.

Their majority in the country not being overwhelming one would expect that the Left would proceed cautiously. Caution does not appear to have entered calculations at this stage, or at any other stage, till Franco became the Spanish dictator. Between February and July 1936, a *de facto* state of 'triple power' was established in Spain: that of the legal government, which was very weak; the power of trade union organisations and various left-wing groupings; and finally the power of the Fascist organisations. On 17 July 1936 the Fascist uprising began. It was now the chance for the Left to show its mettle: 'Throughout the existence of the Comintern no Communist Party ever had a better opportunity than was now offered to the PCE to unite with the left-wing of Social Democracy in a single Marxist party' says Claudin. But: 'To [the Communist Party], winning the war meant winning it for the Communist party and they were always ready to sacrifice military advantage to prevent a rival party on their own side from strengthening its position.'[23]

In June 1937 the PCE had demanded that the central government (which had moved to Valencia in November 1936) should outlaw POUM, under the pretext that its leaders were paid agents of Franco. Then the final assault on POUM began in Barcelona, its stronghold. The POUM leader Andres Nin and all his associates were murdered on the orders of the Russian Consul-General, Antonov-Ovseenko. 'From this point on the fortunes of the Republic began a steady decline. The war of attrition was to drag on for twenty-one months, but the revolution was already dead, and with it had passed any hope of halting Franco.'[24]

Trotsky's epitaph on the Spanish Civil War was that: 'The Spanish revolution was socialist in its essence; the workers attempted several times to overthrow the bourgeoisie, to seize the factories, the peasants wanted to take the land. The Popular Front led by the Stalinists strangled the socialist revolution in the name of an outlived bourgeois democracy. ... The Soviet government played the role of hangman towards the revolutionary Spanish workers, in order to demonstrate its trustworthiness and loyalty to London and Paris.'[25] What Trotsky neglects to say is what other commentators have stated many times: in the first place, the Spanish Revolution had no Lenin; in the second it suffered from too many parties of the left; and in the third the Comintern did not assign a leading position to Spain in the creation of a revolutionary Europe. Manuilsky's statement of 1930 applied equally well in 1936: there was no place for a communist Spain in the Comintern's scheme for a proletarian revolution. By the time the Spanish Civil War had ended there was little hope for the exiles, seeking refuge from Franco's vengeance. Out of the estimated half a million refugees, several thousand Spanish communists emigrated to the USSR, only to be met with a lukewarm welcome. Some of them, like Dolores Ibarruri (*La Passionaria* of the Civil War), lived to return to Spain after Franco's death. But the new leadership of the PCE was formed, like Santiago Carrillo, in exile — outside Spain, but not in the USSR.[26]

The Purges in the Comintern

'I believe the Comintern may have made many mistakes, some of which were bound up with excessive centralism. But to say that it did not play a role in the development of the world revolution seems to me to be contrary to the truth, because everywhere (except perhaps in Cuba) the revolution has been carried out by Communist Parties created by the Comintern. In the countries where socialism has become a reality, that has been the achievement of parties created by the Comintern.'[27] In this collection of (sometimes less than frank) interviews, the former official of the Comintern comments on the work of the Comintern, on its role in the Stalinist period, on the imposition of Dolores Ibarruri on the PCE in exile as Secretary-General, when Jose Diaz died in USSR in 1942, and on his essential belief that till 1946 the USSR had to be supported by all communists in whatever it did, as it was the cradle of the revolution.

It was in this belief that Stalin purged the Comintern and its national units of all who might have opposed him; and it comes as a surprise for an ardent Eurocommunist like Carrillo to avoid the question of the purges of communists in the 1930s. Yet even the extremely circumspect *History of the CPSU* sees fit to mention the purges of foreign communists, though in somewhat Aesopian terms:

> In the summer of 1935 the Seventh Congress of the Communist International was held. It was attended by delegates from the Communist Parties of 65 countries. It testified to the growth of the revolutionary forces of the world proletariat and to the ideological consolidation of the Communist Parties on the principles of Marxism–Leninism. The anti-Leninist groups in the Communist Parties of the capitalist countries had been ideologically defeated and isolated. A staunch Marxist–Leninist core had formed in the struggle against Trotskyism and Right-wing opportunism within the Communist Parties. In China it was united around Mao Tse-tung; in Germany, Ernst Thälmann, Wilhelm Pieck and Walter Ulbricht; in France, Maurice Thorez and Marcel Cachin; in Italy, Antonio Gramsci and Palmiro Togliatti; in Finland, Otto Kuusinen; in Bulgaria, Georgi Dimitrov and Vasil Kolarov; in the United States, William Z. Foster; in Czechoslovakia, Klement Gottwald; in Poland, Jerzy Lenski; in Spain, Jose Diaz and Dolores Ibarruri; and in Britain, William Gallacher and Harry Pollitt.

The work then proceeds to discuss the 'Rectification of the Errors' of the Stalinist period.[28] No mention is made of the countless communists from foreign parties who were executed by Stalin, but the reader is left with the impression that the cause of international socialism was seriously harmed by the purges. If the authors of a carefully edited, official Soviet history can at least attempt to rectify the errors, one would expect Carrillo to be more outspoken.

There is no doubt that if the defeat of the KPD in Germany marked the beginning of the catastrophe, that of the PCE in Spain marked its lowest point. The Comintern abandoned every European communist party in its hour of need as the political situation was deteriorating. (The Italian, German and Spanish parties were abandoned in the period of the mid-1920s to mid-1930s, the Czechoslovak Party in the late 1930s.) The normal desire to find scapegoats for the catastrophe probably played as big a part in the purges of foreign communists as Stalin's fear for his own leadership, the Trotskyite heresy and any plots which the foreigners may have been implicated in.

The Spanish Party was already partly purged in Spain during the Civil War. The German Communist leaders, like Thälmann, had been imprisoned by the Nazis. In Italy, Gramsci was nearing his death in prison. But this was not enough. The failure of the communist revolutions, the rise of fascism and the incipient pro-Nazi policy which Stalin had already hinted at earlier, needed sacrifices. As one author puts it: 'Refugee Communists from Nazi Germany, from Pilsudski's Poland and Horthy's Hungary, who had in the past been connected with the one or the other faction or coterie in the Bolshevik party, were automatically caught in the net.' And further: 'Among the best-known foreign Communists who then perished were: Bela Kun, the leader of the Hungarian revolution in 1919, Remmele and Neumann, the most important Communist spokesmen in the Reichstag before Hitler, nearly all members of the Central Committee of the Polish Communist Party, and many others.'[29]

The author of a definitive study on the Polish Communist Party maintains that it was picked out for the most thorough purge and produces a convincing analysis of the process, which is confirmed, though very briefly, by one of the more recent Polish studies of the CPP.[30] The dissolution of the CPP in the summer of 1938 is obviously a dark page in the history of Stalinist purges of communists. As Dziewanowski points out, the anti-communist Polish Government executed about two or three dozen Polish communists for high treason in the period between the wars, whereas the Soviet authorities liquidated several hundred active members of the party, including all the leadership, twelve members of the Central Committee, the party intellectuals and Polish members of the Executive Committee of the Comintern and the

Control Commission of the Comintern. The apparent motive was the 'Trotskyite' tendencies of the CPP, and its dissolution was also based on the same grounds.[31] Dziewanowski analyses the causes as follows: the Soviet authorities were not certain of the loyalty of the Polish party in view of the growing Soviet–Nazi co-operation. The large number of Jewish members and the increasingly nationalist views of the Polish members made the party particularly difficult to deal with should there be a Soviet–German understanding. Further, while Dziewanowski strenuously denies that the party was penetrated by Polish security services, it is undeniable that the party contained many 'refugees' from anti-communist parties; that it did, in 1926, support the Pilsudski coup; and that it did trace its origins to the party of Rosa Luxemburg. All these reasons would have been sufficient to have it eliminated, though, as Dziewanowski rightly states, all these reasons would have been insufficient to 'justify so radical a step'.[32]

The most cogent reason may well have been the fact that Stalin did not trust Polish Communists, considering — rightly as it turned out in 1956 — that they would exhibit unduly nationalistic feelings in any forthcoming war. But perhaps the mystery is simpler. The Polish purges coincided with the supposed abortive military coup by Tukhachevsky, who was executed in June 1937, the period when the first Polish Communists were also said to have been executed. And while Deutscher discusses the Tukhachevsky plot in detail and is very willing to expound at length on the executions of the Soviet Communists and military leaders, he assigns to the Polish purge one small footnote in the chapter on purges.[33] Perhaps there really was a plot, and perhaps the Polish party — not as insignificant as Dziewanowski maintains, because Poland is right on the borders of the USSR and has excellent access to the West — was being used in a way which nobody wishes to divulge. At least Polish ex-communists like Deutscher may have had some idea about its role and may have preferred to keep quiet on this count.

The CPP was rehabilitated in 1956,[34] when it was stated that the accusations were invented by Yezhov and Beria, but the mystery remains unsolved. The victims have no graves; it is not known how they were executed, or even whether they were executed or died in some appalling circumstances. It is not even certain what their dates of death were. For instance, in the case of the German Communist leader, Heinz Neumann, one authority gives his date of death as 1936, another as 1937, though both seem to agree that he was shot in Moscow.[35] It is almost easier to find out the date of the death of communists in Nazi hands; Weber states with some certainty that Thälmann was exterminated in Buchenwald in 1944.[36]

The Turning-point of European Communism

The decade of the 1930s was certainly the turning point of the European communist parties; they were never to be the same again. While their role in the European Resistance movements after the German invasion of the USSR had done much to rehabilitate them, it has never been forgotten that the previous period was one of subordination to the demands of Soviet foreign policy. This has made the task of European communist parties much more difficult in the contemporary period, and may have made the 'Eurocommunist' trend virtually impossible to implement. The effect of the purges was the weakening of all the European communist parties, though the PCF escaped them because it had always followed the Comintern's orders.[37]

But according to some authorities, this was in any case irrelevant because the communist parties had failed in their basic objectives. They and the

Comintern had failed in the main aim it set itself at the outset of its existence — to wrest the working class from reformism and organise it politically and trade-union-wise on revolutionary principles. The Comintern did not succeed in taking a single important step in this direction in the USA ... or in Britain, the country that stood next in importance ... on account of its colonial empire.... But the International failed in 'Germany too, where the objective conditions were at first very favourable and where a positive achievement would have altered the world situation to a serious degree. France was the only capitalist country of importance where the Comintern, seventeen years after its formation, held positions of strength in the working class. When, however, we look at events with the advantage of hindsight, we may wonder whether the rise of communism in France in the second half of the 1930s was not, rather than a victory for revolutionary Marxism, the first step in the Social

Democratic retrogression of the Communist movement in the advanced capitalist countries.[38]

Whatever one may think of the above statement it is clear that the 'internationalist' theme, eroded over two decades, was virtually phased out by the end of the 1930s. The 'national' theme, which had been in abeyance, began to take pride of place, particularly in the next phase of history.

Notes

1. B.M. Leibzon and K.K. Shirinya, *Povorot v politike Kominterna*: quoted by F. Claudin, *The Communist Movement*, p. 685, n. 70.
2. This formula is attributed to Stalin and Zinoviev by Claudin, ibid., p. 152, and by Deutscher, *Stalin*, pp. 406-7.
3. Deutscher, ibid., p. 407.
4. Ibid., p. 407.
5. Claudin, *Communist Movement*, pp. 161-2.
6. Ibid., pp. 171-3.
7. Leibzon and Shirinya, *Povorot*, 1965, pp. 307-9: see also Claudin, *Communist Movement*, p. 175.
8. Claudin, ibid., p. 176.
9. *The Essential Stalin*, ed. by B. Franklin, Report to the Seventeenth Congress, p. 298.
10. A.M. Cienciala, *Poland and the Western Powers 1938-1939*, p. 16.
11. Claudin, *Communist Movement*, pp. 178-9. The *Pravda* article appeared on 23 May 1934 and was reproduced in *L'Humanité* on 31 May.
12. After Gramsci's arrest in 1926 Togliatti became the Secretary-General in exile of the Italian Communist party.
13. Derfler, *Socialism since Marx*, p. 153.
14. *Fils du peuple*, p. 102: also Claudin, *Communist Movement*, p. 179.
15. Quoted by Claudin, ibid., p. 182.
16. D. Thomson, *Democracy in France since 1870*, p. 198.
17. A saying attributed to Hitler, in E. de Blaye, *Franco and the Politics of Spain*, p. 153.
18. L. Evans, in the Introduction to L. Trotsky's *The Spanish Revolution*, p. 27.
19. Figures quoted by Claudin, *Communist Movement*, p. 695, n. 30: see also S.G. Payne, *The Spanish Revolution*, p. 144: H. Thomas, *The Spanish Civil War*, p. 99: and L. Evans, *Spanish Revolution*, p. 29.
20. See L. Evans, ibid.
21. *Inprecorr*, quoted by Claudin, *Communist Revolution*, p. 211.
22. de Blaye, *Franco*, p. 33.
23. Claudin, *Communist Movement*, p. 211: G. Brenan, *The Spanish Labyrinth*, p. 326: see also L. Evans, *Spanish Revolution*, p. 44.
24. L. Evans, ibid., p. 47.
25. Interview with Sybil Vincent, in L. Evans, ibid., p. 347.
26. It is claimed that Carrillo was a paid agent of the Comintern, looking for ways of overthrowing Franco and travelling all over the world. See *The Observer Colour Supplement*, 14 August 1977.

27. Carrillo, *Dialogue on Spain*, p. 83.

28. Ibid., p. 481: also pp. 653-73.

29. Deutscher, *Stalin*, p. 380 and n. 3.

30. M.K. Dziewanowski, *The Communist Party of Poland*: and M. Malinowski, *Geneza PPR*.

31. Malinowski, *Geneza PPR*. pp. 25-7.

32. Ibid., p. 153.

33. Deutscher, *Stalin*, n. 3, p. 380.

34. See *Trybuna Ludu*, 19 February 1956.

35. F. Borkenau, *World Communism*, p. 379, gives the earlier date. Hermann Weber, *Die Wandlung des deutschen Kommunismus*, Vol. 2, p. 233, gives the latter in his biographies of German Communists. R. Conquest in *The Great Terror* gives some dates, but they are mostly based on hearsay.

36. Weber, *Die Wandlung*, vol. 2.

37. Though Thorez was not elected as Secretary-General till July 1930, the previous period was marked by a turnover in leadership which was very quick and by a period of indecisive collective leadership. See R. Tiersky, *French Communism 1920-1972*, p. 31. and n. 12.

38. Claudin, *Communist Movement*, p. 243.

Part two:

National Resistance and Marxism

6
Ideology and Resistance

The Prologue: 1939–41

The Soviet–German Pact of 23 August 1939 was like a bombshell for European communist parties. Though the French Popular Front government resigned in June 1937 the Communists played an increasingly important part in the trade unions. By 1939 they controlled twelve out of the thirty industrial federations, including metals, engineering, building, chemicals and electricity. They also wielded influence in the railway and mining unions. The Nazi–Soviet pact caught the French Communists by surprise, and though they accomplished the changeover in political attitudes with ease, they lost their influence in the unions. At the end of September the government banned the PCF and all its publications, arrested leading Communists and sent several thousand suspects to detention camps. These quick and unexpected events demoralised the CGT and the PCF. By 1940, membership of the CGT fell to under a million, but:

> The illegal position of the Communists was not altogether without advantages in the period of the phoney war. ... The Communist CGT weekly, *La Vie Ouvrière* appeared illegally and stressed that the war was a pretext for the elimination of the 1936 social gains. It appealed to pacifist tendencies by arguing that Russia, in its desire for peace, was right to stay out of an 'imperialist' war. ... In this way the Communists tried to justify their support for the Nazi–Soviet pact and to turn a harsh, tense situation to their advantage.[1]

The situation which was created in 1939 and reinforced after the collapse of France in 1940 produced a state which had been called 'les deux Frances', a term which did not apply to geographical division. It referred to the change in alliances and groupings, as well as changes of allegiance. Many well-known Communists, like Paul Nizan, a talented writer, resigned from the PCF after the Nazi–Soviet Pact and went into the army, only to be killed in action in 1940. At the same time Maurice Thorez was deserting his unit in order to flee to Moscow.[2] One third of Communist parliamentary deputies resigned from the party, and large numbers of ordinary members resigned. The PCF was totally demoralised, and it is a measure of its degradation that after the German occupation of Paris in 1940 the party's first action was to seek permission from the Nazis to publish *L'Humanité* openly. Though this was refused, the underground *L'Humanité* urged fraternisation with the German forces, attacked de Gaulle as a reactionary in the pay of British imperialists and talked of joint Anglo–French war guilt. To repay them for such loyalty, the Nazis released over three hundred Communists who had been imprisoned by the French authorities. The PCF policy in official terms was not 'pro-German'; it was 'anti-anti-German'. The exception to this was the PCF's attitude to the Vichy regime. It was as hostile towards it as the regime was hostile towards the PCF. So in a strange triangle, the PCF was friendly towards the mortal foe who had defeated France, while at the same time, hostile to the French authorities, who, however mistakenly, were attempting to salvage some remnants from the 1940 catastrophe.[3]

If the Soviet–Nazi Pact was a shock to the French Communists it was much worse for the Polish Communist Party; or at least, what remained of it. In fact, most of those who worked on the territory of former Poland, now incorporated in the USSR, were hardly more than fellow-travellers, or, even more often, very recent converts to communism. As one author puts it: 'Several non-Communist writers, who held radical views, gave somewhat reluctant collaboration .... being fearful of persecution by Soviet authorities.'[4] In fact, being a communist in the 'liberated' territories was tantamount to being suspect; and this applied even more to the members of the Ukrainian and Belorussian Communist Parties, who were suspected of nationalism far more than the Poles. The policy of systematic deportation, arrests and mass murders which was carried out on Stalin's orders (and executed in the area of Western Ukraine by Khrushchev) was virtually a prolongation of the purge of the CPP, which had been carried out before the war. According to some sources, the policy of exterminating the Poles was carried out in a concerted manner with the Nazis:

In the German occupied zone the Communists refrained from activity, thereby showing that the Soviets were prepared to stand by their agreement with Germany. In March 1940, my staff received information that an NKVD mission had come to Cracow to work out with the Gestapo the methods they were jointly to adopt against Polish military organizations.[5]

While the Polish underground began to organise almost immediately after the defeat, there was no Communist participation till after the German attack on the Soviet Union. But there were individual protests from Communists. Gomulka openly disapproved of the Nazi–Soviet pact and urged the Comintern to organise a Communist underground in Poland. He also fought against the Germans during the defence of Warsaw.[6] However, the behaviour of Soviet authorities and the passivity of such Communists as remained did not make the CPP's contribution to the later liberation of Poland any more popular. The CPP lost on all counts, and could not be reintroduced into Poland again under its old name. The onus of the underground work fell on the regular army units, the Socialists and Populists, and some National Democratic forces in Warsaw and western Poland.

Only one European communist party found its rationale almost at the same time as its country was attacked. This was the Yugoslav Communist Party, a small and underground party, which kept neutral like the other European communist parties but which was fortunate, because Yugoslavia was invaded by the Germans just before the invasion of the USSR (April 1941).

The Yugoslav Communist Party in Resistance

The history of the CPY is almost simultaneous with the biography of Tito. Born Joseph Broz in 1892, near Zagreb, Tito was the son of a Croat father and Slovene mother. He was conscripted in the Austro–Hungarian army in 1913 and soon became an NCO. During the First World War he became a sergeant and was taken prisoner-of-war by the Russians in 1915 on the Carpathian front. He was sent to a prisoner-of-war camp in Russia. The period between 1917 and 1920 is not very clear. He is said to have escaped to Finland at the beginning of the Revolution, then to have come back to Russia via Petrograd, and then to have gone back to

Yugoslavia via Siberia. Some time during this period he is thought to have joined the Bolshevik Party. He finally came back to Yugoslavia in 1920, with a Russian wife. He joined the CPY, but was forced to hide from the authorities as the party was illegal in the period of 1920 to 1928. He seems to have spent the 1930s partly in Moscow, partly in Paris, and appears to have been sufficiently important to the Comintern not to be allowed to go to fight in Spain directly on Stalin's orders. He went back to Yugoslavia in 1936 and purged the CPY on behalf of the Comintern, becoming the Secretary-General in 1937. The Stalinist purges diminished the already small CPY, which was said to have numbered only 3,500 members in 1933. Tito followed the 'correct' Stalinist line towards the imperialist war in 1939, and was apparently totally obedient to Stalin throughout this period.

It was not till the German invasion of Yugoslavia, on 6 April 1941, followed by the swift collapse of the Yugoslav government (the Simovic government fled from Belgrade on 11 April), that Tito began to act on his own initiative. His first action was, however, not against the Nazis, but against the Ustasi. After the German invasion, the Yugoslav territory was partly allocated to its neighbours and partly made into puppet states. The Ustasi formed their own state in Croatia (so-called 'Greater Croatia') while the Serbs, who continued to carry on resistance to the Germans, organised under the royalist commander General Mihajlovic in Cetnik detachments. The full story of the Yugoslav resistance is well documented.[7]

The main reason why the Tito forces, for long called 'Partisans', came to the fore seemed to hinge on their sheer numerical strength and the early start they had. The exiled King Peter told a British diplomat early in May 1941 (only three weeks after the German invasion) that he wanted to contact 'troops fighting in the Yugoslav mountains'.[8] From July onwards there were reports from a neutral press and from Moscow about guerrilla fighting in western Serbia, Bosnia and Montenegro, sometimes attributed to Communists. In the meantime, the Mihajlovic forces seemed to be more interested in fighting the Communists than the Germans: 'The impressions of an English officer are that the Communists at the head of the Partisans are also opposed to the Axis ... The Cetnik leaders say openly that they prefer to collaborate with Nedic rather than the Communists.'[9] The reason for this early indifference to Tito's forces seems to have been Mihajlovic's conviction that he had the most important position in Yugoslav resistance. On the strength of this, the British authorities advised the Soviet government, which was in constant touch with Tito, to urge the Communists to put their forces at the disposal of Mihajlovic. By November 1941 Eden told the British cabinet, on the basis of a vague message from Mihajlovic, that the differences between the two parties were now settled. As a matter of fact, by then Mihajlovic was already forced to flee the Tito forces, not the Germans, and by early 1942 all reports reaching the Foreign Office and the SOE spoke of the fighting being conducted by the Communists. Not surprisingly, in view of their underground existence and minor importance 'the Foreign Office — and the SOE — were almost entirely ignorant about the Yugoslav Communist Party. In April 1942 Douglas Howard of the Southern Department wrote to Professor Arnold Toynbee, then head of the research department: "We have recently been hearing a great deal about Communist activities in Yugoslavia, and as far as we can make out they are rapidly gaining strength ... and are taking a leading part in sabotage and resistance to the German and Italian forces. Unfortunately, we have very little idea who or what these Communists are ...".[10]

While the British were hesitantly trying to prop up now this side, now the other, the Russians openly began to attack Mihajlovic as a traitor in the summer of 1942, first through a radio station on Soviet territory called 'Free Yugoslavia', and then through neutral communist newspapers. The amount of Soviet military aid does not seem to have been great, but of moral and political support there was no question. As a result, the Tito forces grew: by July 1943 there were said to be 65,000 Partisans and possibly 20,000 Cetniks. In March 1943 the British decided to contact Tito, and by November it was almost decided to drop Mihajlovic. Eden suggested to the War Cabinet in December that the King should go to Tito's headquarters and fight with him; the British should not worry too much about Mihajlovic. The all-important consideration at this stage was the military situation; Tito was much more effective against the Germans than Mihajlovic, and political considerations took second place.

In the meantime, Tito's forces and self-confidence grew. It was clear that he gathered round him all those who wanted to resist both the Germans and the puppet governments of Croatia and Serbia, not just Communists. When the British sent liaison officers to the Partisan units in Serbia in early 1944 it was obvious that the rapid strides Tito made there — in the Cetnik territory — would assure him the control of the whole country at the end of the war. Hence the idea of a government of National Unity, with Tito and Subasic, as the King's nominee, was agreed upon in 1944. Nevertheless, the problem of Tito's allegiance was worrying both the West and the East. The story goes that Stalin warned Milovan Djilas in Moscow[11] that the British might try to assassinate Tito as (he alleged) they had killed the Polish General Sikorski. This, Djilas wrote later, was probably the reason why Tito did not tell the British before flying secretly to Russia in September 1944.

In the meantime, Tito made a great show of retaining an even-handed approach and, as Fitzroy Maclean wrote to Churchill:

> Marshal Tito has, in his reception of the newly arrived Soviet Mission, gone out of his way to emphasise that their status here is to be exactly the same as that of my Mission. Reconstruction and rehabilitation are urgent problems and the Partisans cannot but realise that their country is bound to depend on Great Britain and America not only for material support during the war, but for relief and the means of prosperity after the war . . . there can be no doubt that they have realised the advantages of maintaining good relations with other Great Powers besides the Soviet Union.[12]

Despite this apparent willingness to co-operate with the West, Tito and Subasic drafted the agreement for the National Government in Moscow: the Foreign Office was very chilly, and a head-on conflict developed with the Yugoslavs over Trieste. The Yugoslavs refused to withdraw beyond the demarcation line, until threatened by a joint Anglo–American confrontation. The Moscow agreement between Churchill and Stalin on a fifty–fifty influence in Yugoslavia was set aside and Yugoslavia was consigned to the Soviet sphere of influence.

In March 1945 a new Yugoslav government was sworn in in Belgrade, with Tito as prime minister and Subasic as foreign minister. In April Tito went to Moscow, to be received as head of the Yugoslav government. The monarchy was formally abolished in November 1945. Tito had won power; the British had to acquiesce; the Russians felt sure of their continuing influence. In the spring of 1946 Mihajlovic was tried for treason and executed.

Tito suggested as early as 1945 in a conversation with Stalin that a new communist international organisation should be formed in place of the now defunct Comintern. In June 1946 Stalin asked Tito to take the initiative to found such an organisation, to avoid the appearance of forming another 'Comintern' and alarming the West. But he distrusted Tito, as the plan for a Balkan Federation which Tito had already mooted (a federal state from the Black Sea to the Adriatic, with Yugoslavia playing a vital role and Tito at its head) had made him decide that Tito was too independent.

Hence the idea of situating the headquarters of the Cominform in Belgrade was at once a Soviet attempt to bind Yugoslavia to the Eastern bloc and an attempt to keep Tito in check. But the interesting thing is that Tito actually proposed such an organisation on his own initiative. All known sources confirm this. Yet Tito was first an organisation man, and then a military leader, only to become a politician at the end of the war. Though some of his close associates were theorists, none of them was a rigid Marxist theorist, and most of them became distinguished by rejecting some or all of Marxist theories, most particularly as evolved by Soviet theorists. Therefore one must ask why Tito suggested this organisation, an international communist one, in which he himself would obviously have little interest — except insofar as a Balkan Federation might be part of his plan. An international communist organisation, placed in Yugoslavia where the West had easy access, might give the British and the Americans an insight into Soviet plans. Perhaps this, rather than Tito's undoubted independence, gave rise to the break of relations with the USSR, and to Stalin's dubbing Tito as a 'capitalist traitor'. At the time of the founding of the Cominform, however, the Yugoslavs appeared to be loyal communists and willing supporters of Stalinism. The break did not come till 1948.

The PCF and Resistance

While Tito and the CPY were fortunate in that before the war started he was an unknown leader and the party small and illegal, and that, almost immediately after the Nazi invasion, they could go into action, and collect all anti-Nazi forces around the small nucleus of the party, the French Communists were extremely unlucky. They were found wanting in patriotism between the outbreak of war and the collapse of the Third Republic; they were accused of treason for their collaborationist policies from June 1940 to June 1941. Thorez's defection to Moscow in the autumn of 1940 was hardly compensated for by the fact that his deputy, Jacques Duclos, remained in France. Thorez himself stayed in Moscow till late 1944, only to reappear as a staunch supporter of Stalinism. Thorez's lack of independence has been noted by Stalin himself; in a conversation with Yugoslav leaders he is said to have described Thorez as a dog who cannot even frighten anyone by baring his teeth.[13] The stigma of collaboration with the Nazis might have appeared to be difficult to repudiate after Stalin's call for a 'united front' in July 1941 had it not been for the fact that owing to having been banned by the French government in 1939 and not persecuted by the Nazis, the PCF had retained almost the whole of its organisation intact. This was in contrast to other French political parties. The Socialist leaders like Blum and Dormoy, Radical leaders like Daladier and Socialist trade union leaders like Jouhaux, had been arrested, deported or killed. Others retired from the political scene, or sympathised with Pétain. But the Central Committee of the PCF carried on its organisational work throughout the war. With the exception of Thorez in Moscow, many members of the Central Committee — Duclos, Tillon and Franchon — were in Paris, and Marrane and Mauvais were in Lyons. Duclos reorganised the Party into three-men cells at the end of 1940, thus making it virtually impossible for the whole organisation to be wiped out.[14]

Yet, despite the enthusiastic call for united action, and despite the fact that the Communist underground (the FTP) were created immediately afterwards, in September 1941, the first meeting between Gaullist representatives and Communist representatives is said not to have happened till May 1942, when it was accepted in principle that a unified network of command and communications would be established. In November 1942, under Soviet pressure, the Communists agreed to incorporate their paramilitary forces into the forces of Fighting France.[15] The efforts of Communist propaganda gave modest practical results. In November 1942 the party press accused Communists of 'fence-sitting' and being 'criminally inactive'. By the end of 1943 there were said to be 200,000 FTP members throughout France. By comparison, with a much smaller population, the Polish Home Army numbered some 300,000 members in 1944: some 50,000 members took part in the

Warsaw Uprising alone.[16] According to some authors it was only the Vichy propaganda against Communists that helped the recruitment to the FTP and helped to create the impression that the Communists were the only active resisters against Nazism.

The PCF regained its lost prestige during the period of resistance; its numbers and influence rose, and it planned a general uprising against the Germans before the invasion of Europe. By September 1943 the PCF gained 27 seats in the newly established Consultative Assembly in Algiers and in April 1944 two Communists joined the CFLN. After the creation of FFI in February 1944 the Communist FTP was merged with it. However, almost simultaneously the Communists began to organise Communist militia, which had an apparent insurrectionary aim. This was not dissolved till the return of Thorez from Moscow at the end of November 1944. According to some authorities, the PCF had accepted the Three-Power division of spheres of influence in Europe, which ruled out a Communist government in France.[17]

Nevertheless, 'On the eve of the invasion of France, the Communists were entrenched in all the important centres of Free French political, social, and economic life. For the first time in its history, the Party held cabinet responsibilities. . . . The Party was beginning to recapture its former status in the trade-union movement. Its clandestine press was active and aggressive.'[18] The political wrangling which ensued after the liberation of France need not concern us here. It must be remembered, however, that it was the Socialists' insistence that the PCF disengage itself from the Soviet allegiance, reformulated by Blum on his return from Buchenwald in May 1945, which broke up the left-wing unified front which had been in existence since 1944. Blum concluded that, despite the dissolution of the Comintern on 23 May 1943 and the PCF's declaration that this proved that there was no wish on the Communists' part to 'bolshevise' France, 'nothing had occurred to change the *status quo ante* of the French and Soviet Communist attitudes . . . . Thus, under his influence, by the end of the summer of 1945, the Subcommittee on Organic Unity had been placed in limbo.'[19]

Despite the PCF's participation in government up to the abrupt dismissal of its ministers in May 1947 the party saw that its only way to power would now be through the build-up of trade-union support. While enjoying electoral successes, the Communists never really hoped to gain key positions in government or to vote in a

Communist president, though Thorez stood for the office in 1946 on a platform of moderation and a 'French road to Socialism'.[20] They were aware of the Socialist opposition to this, much more than of the Gaullist or right-wing opposition. Thus, as in the 1920s and the 1930s it was the unwillingness of the left-wing parties to unite that helped to bring a right-wing coalition into power.

The PCF's stand in the resistance and its participation in the government till 1947 did not promote it to the importance of a main party of the government: in this way it differed from the CPY. Similar policies on the part of the CPY led it directly to power in 1945, and the main reason for this must be that there was no serious left-wing opposition in Yugoslavia, as there was in France. The additional reason is that the CPY stood unambiguously on the side of national independence while the PCF was compromised on that count.

The PCI and Resistance

One other European party needs special attention because of its resistance effort. This is the Italian Communist Party, which had been underground in Italy since 1926 and which only kept a skeleton organisation in the country till 1943. However, there were large numbers of Communists in exile, some in France, others, like Togliatti, in the USSR. Throughout the fascist period, the PCI was staunchly anti-fascist and hence it did not make any concessions to the Stalin–Hitler Pact in 1939. In June 1940, when Italy entered the war, the party accused Mussolini's government of selling the nation to German imperialism. In May 1941 it called for the departure of German troops from Italy and for the breaking off of the Italian–German Pact. In October 1941 the PCI made a pact of unity with the Socialists and later with the *Giustizia e Liberta* group, which was soon re-named the Action Party. In the spring of 1943 there were massive industrial strikes in Northern Italy, involving over 100,000 workers. After the Armistice in September 1943 the resistance action grew in the north with a predominance of Communist partisans.

The PCI joined the CLN set up in Rome at the same time, and in the summer of 1944 there were about 100,000 partisans in the north. While the initiative was a joint PCI–PSI–Action Party effort there is little doubt that the majority of the fighting units were made up of Communists or fellow-travellers. The movement was organised by Luigi Longo, the leader of the PCI in the absence of Togliatti. He was, according to every authority, the most important resistance leader in North Italy, occupied by the Nazis. The strength of the left wing, and particularly the Communists, alarmed the Allied authorities, and might have led to repressive steps against the PCI had not Togliatti, on his return from Moscow in March 1944, announced the so-called *svolta di Salerno*, in which he called for a government of national unity which would finish the war against Germany.[21]

The difficulty in the case of the PCI is the volume of works by communist historians, attributing all the credit to their party, only to be equalled by the volume of anti-communist works questioning this. Thus, the *svolta de Salerno* is condemned by Claudin as a pro-Soviet move at a time when the Russians wanted Allied help, while Amendola claims that it was a move which allowed the PCI to come out of the underground to become the party of government and a mass, national party, all at once. As such, the *svolta* was to be highly recommended as an example of a progressive development of the PCI, which allowed a strong voice to its supporters, and which advanced the cause of socialism.[22]

However it is interpreted, there is no doubt that the communist influence in Italy (first in the north, later also in central and southern Italy) was very strong. Unlike France, it was not the Socialists who broke up the left-wing movement. In Italy the Socialists broke up into a left- and right-wing party in 1947, thus strengthening the PCI. But the PCI faced a formidable opponent in the conservative Catholic right; the Catholic Action came to the aid of the Christian Democrats, increasingly under pressure from the left wing, and from 1945 onwards a Christian–Democratic government, sometimes supported by other parties sometimes on its own, has been in power in Italy.

Though there were other communist parties in Resistance movements in Europe, these three parties played the largest and most significant role. It can be seen that in the case of Yugoslavia, the Communists came to power for lack of a real democratic alternative; in France, they missed this aim because of a traditional left-wing split; in Italy, they appear to have missed it far more because of their conciliatory policy, combined with the opposition from Catholic circles. This conciliatory policy may have ensured them the character of a 'national' party as Amendola and other communist historians claim; on the other hand, it may have convinced their possible supporters of a weakness uncalled for in a party only so recently revolutionary. In other words, while the Yugoslav and French experiment did not change the nature of their respective parties (even though the former came to power and the latter did not), the Italian experience seems to have progressed towards the 'historic compromise' as early as 1944.

Notes

1. M. Kolinsky, *Continuity and Change in European Society*, p. 112.
2. R. Tiersky, *French Communism 1920-1972*, p. 102.
3. Tiersky, ibid., n. 15, p. 103, questions the numbers who left the Party. Communist sources estimate that the majority remained in the party.
4. M.K. Dziewanowski, *The Communist Party of Poland*, p. 158.
5. T. Bor-Komorowski, *The Secret Army*, p. 46: see also Dziewanowski, *Communist Party*, p. 340, n. 11.
6. Dziewanowski, ibid., p. 340, n. 13.
7. See, *inter alia*, P. Auty, *Tito*; B. Davidson, *Partisan Picture*; and F.W. Deakin, *The Embattled Mountain*.
8. E. Barker, *British Policy in South East Europe*, p. 157.
9. General Nedic was the head of the German-appointed government in Serbia. *Foreign Office Papers*, quoted by Barker, p. 159.
10. Barker, *British Policy*, p. 161. The SOE was the Special Operations Executive.
11. Ibid., p. 141.
12. The Soviet mission arrived in Yugoslavia early in 1944; Maclean's letter to Churchill is dated 18 March 1944: quoted by Barker, ibid., p. 171.
13. Recounted by F. Claudin, *The Communist Movement*, p. 764, n. 21.
14. A.J. Rieber, *Stalin and the French Communist Party, 1941-1947* p. 81-3.
15. Ibid., pp. 26-7.
16. Figures for France quoted by Rieber, ibid., from Soviet sources, p. 84.
17. Tiersky, *French Communism*, p. 121, and Rieber, *Stalin*, p. 157, n. 96.
18. Rieber, ibid., p. 108.
19. Tiersky, *French Communism*, p. 127.
20. Ibid., pp. 148-9.
21. Claudin, *Communist Movement*, pp. 344-51.
22. Ibid., p. 350: G. Amendola, *Gli Anni della Republica*, pp. 10-11.

7
Communism in South-eastern Europe, 1944-53

The Post-war Period

The development of communist parties and communist-dominated governments in South-eastern Europe is one of the most involved questions of the immediate post-war period. This is due partly to the fact that wartime agreements divided this area into British and Soviet spheres of influence; partly to the fact that some of these states had followed Germany into the war; partly because an internal conflict between communist and anti-communist forces had existed there during part, or the whole, of the war period. Second, one has to take into consideration factors which indirectly contributed to the communist take-over in some countries, those which contributed to the installation of anti-communist regimes, and those which finally made some countries chose their own 'road to Socialism'. Among these factors, the most important are the geographical ones — i.e. which countries were immediately accessible to the Soviet troops or occupied by the Soviet troops during and after the war; and traditional ones — i.e. which nations could be expected to exhibit a degree of sympathy for the Russians (if not necessarily for communism); and third, blood ties — i.e. which countries could claim to have a common racial, linguistic or cultural heritage with Russia, and follow it up with an understanding with the Soviet Union.

If analysed in this way, one can see immediately that of the three German allies during the war, the country which had most affinity with Russia was Bulgaria. Bulgaria had close religious ties with Russia; it had had a close political relationship with Pan-Slavism to be followed by a close personal link with the CPSU and the Comintern in the person of the Bulgarian Communist leader, Georgi

Dimitrov. It was Dimitrov who transformed the Balkan Socialist movement into the Bulgarian Communist Party in 1919. Dimitrov then became the delegate to the Comintern Congresses in 1920 and 1921, and a member of the Executive Committee of the Comintern. In 1923 he had to flee from Bulgaria, apparently after an unsuccessful coup, spending the period of exile partly in the Soviet Union, partly on Comintern missions. The Bulgarian Communist Party was made illegal in the 1920s. Dimitrov was arrested and tried by the Nazis in 1933 for alleged complicity in the Reichstag fire, and was released to the Russians by the Nazis on the personal intervention of Stalin. At the Seventh Congress of the Comintern in July–August 1935 Dimitrov was appointed Secretary-General of the Comintern, a post he held till the dissolution of this body in 1943. He was later to be instrumental in the creation of the Cominform. When Stalin initiated the policy of Popular Fronts he demonstrated a special regard for Dimitrov. Deutscher recounts that: 'Manuilsky, Stalin's mouthpiece in the Comintern, who had excelled everybody in his vituperations against the Social-Fascists, was replaced by Georgi Dimitrov, hero of the Leipzig trial over the Reichstag fire, whose name was now the symbol of militant anti-fascism. Stalin demonstrated his personal association with Dimitrov on every possible occasion — the Bulgarian leader invariably appeared at his side at ceremonies and parades.'[1] In 1945 Dimitrov came back to Bulgaria, occupied by Soviet troops since 1944 (as a result of Bulgaria's occupation of parts of Greek and Yugoslav territory the USSR had declared war on the country and had occupied it in the last stages of the war). He became leader of the Patriotic Front which had been created in 1942 out of anti-fascist parties under a communist umbrella. Dimitrov became the Secretary-General of the party's Central Committee, a post which he held till his death in July 1949.

In 1944 the Communist Party of Bulgaria had only 25,000 members, and was forced to create a coalition government under a left-wing populist leader. The new government comprised four Communists and twelve ministers from other left-wing parties. The prime minister was a member of the agrarian *Zveno* party. Large-scale purges followed the installation of this government, the terror lasting from 1944 till 1947. In 1946 Bulgaria was declared a republic and in 1947 the so-called 'Dimitrov' constitution was promulgated. In the general election of November 1945 the Patriotic Front won an overwhelming majority of the votes, but one author states that the election was 'anything but free'.[2]

Due to his close personal relationship with Stalin, and because of his convictions, Dimitrov had no difficulty in following Stalinist policies throughout his period of leadership. After his death, the leadership was taken over by Vulko Chervenkov, who executed Traicho Kostov, the most obvious successor to Dimitrov, as a Titoist in 1949. Chervenkov became known as the 'little Stalin' of Bulgaria. However, in 1956 he was eliminated from the leadership and became an 'unperson'. Kostov was quietly rehabilitated in 1953, and Chervenkov was purged from the party by his successor, Zhivkov, in 1962.[3]

Bulgaria serves as a model of a new people's democracy, and has so far always followed the Soviet lead without much difficulty. This may have much to do with the traditional patterns of Bulgarian loyalties. The Bulgarians owed their nineteenth-century liberation to Pan-Slavism promoted by the Russian Empire; their inter-war regime was a mixture of feudalism and fascism; their underdevelopment made them perfect material for a socialist experiment; and last, but not least, their religion was Orthodox. The Bulgarian Orthodox Church is the religion of the majority of the Bulgarians, and it was drawn in to support the regime without much difficulty. One author notes that the 'Communists have patronized the church as the traditional national church of Bulgaria, not only to obtain support from the Church devotees, but also to unify national Orthodox Churches under the aegis of the Soviet-controlled Russian Orthodox Church ... Patriarch Kiril clearly demonstrated his attitude ... when he thanked the regime for the re-establishment of the Bulgarian Patriarchate and called on all the faithful to support the Government in its policies.'[4]

Romania shared its religion with Russia, but had a different culture. The Romanian Communist Party was established in 1921 and was outlawed in 1924. It went underground, but at the time of fascist upsurge in 1936 it was virtually destroyed by the authorities. In 1944 its reduced leadership is said to have included a large number of non-ethnic Romanians (Jews, Ukrainians and Hungarians). At that time it is estimated to have had a thousand members.[5] Romania declared war on the USSR, but in August 1944 King Carol abdicated and the new king, Michael, declared war on Germany and brought the Romanian army to the side of the Red Army. In February 1948 the Communist Party and the Socialists merged to form the Romanian Workers' Party (the king was forced to abdicate in December 1947), and in April 1948 a new constitution was promulgated, thus establishing the 'Romanian People's Republic'.

Through a mixture of pressure, violence and promises the Romanian Workers' Party held on to power, always supported by and supporting the CPSU. In the spring of 1952, following the 'Doctors' Plot' and before the Slansky trial in Czechoslovakia, the Secretary-General Gheorghiu-Dej executed two leaders of Jewish origin, Anna Pauker and Vasile Luca, and took over the entire party and state organisation.[6] Gheorghiu-Dej retained power until his death in 1965 and avoided de-Stalinisation by his doctrine of 'national Communism' in the 1950s.

There was some opposition to the Communist government in Romania, but it had no focus. The largely fascist-dominated politics of the pre-war and wartime periods had eliminated any possible political opponents. The Romanians, deprived of the few liberal leaders they had between 1945 and 1948 and without traditions of parliamentary government or a long struggle for independence, and troubled by ethnic problems (those of the Hungarians and Slovaks being the most important) had little heart to oppose the policies of the new Communist-led government. The opposition in Romania grew at the top — the Workers' Party leadership began to oppose Soviet policies after Stalin's death for various reasons but there had been little opposition from the nation. Similarly, after Romania began her independent policy in opposition to Soviet leadership, there was apathy among the people. This is not to say that the people were particularly keen on this government; it is rather that they did not see a viable alternative. Hence Romania has not experienced any uprisings either against its own government or against the USSR throughout its post-war existence. However, this may also be an index of her geographical position. Without an external border with a non-communist country, and with an ongoing quarrel with other communist countries, such an uprising would be very difficult to sustain.

Like Bulgaria and Romania the third country in this area, Hungary, had been assigned to the Soviet sphere of influence during wartime conferences. However, unlike them, Hungary had a longstanding distrust of the Russians (partly owing to Russian intervention in the 1848 Revolution) and tended to be pro-German. The religion of the Hungarians (Calvinist and Catholic) did not bring the nations any closer, and the Hungarians' racial origin and language were alien to the Russians. Further, the communist revolution led by Bela Kun did nothing to make either communism or Soviet domination more palatable to the Hungarians. Most Hungarian Communists stayed in the Soviet Union during the inter-war period and came back to Hungary in 1944. Among them were Matyas Rakosi, Erno Geroe and Imre Nagy. Others stayed in the country and were active in Budapest during the war. These were Laszlo Rajk, Janos Kadar and Gyula Kallai. The party's numbers were said to be 2,000 in 1944 but it grew to nearly one and a half million in 1949 through a merger with the left wing of the Social-Democratic Party.

The Hungarians' well-known resistance to communism and their capacity for taking up arms against oppression led to very careful Soviet tactics from 1944 onwards. The Hungarians had been German allies during the war and they made efforts to surrender to the Western powers in 1944, but in vain. Soviet troops occupied all of Hungary by 1945. Despite their presence, the Hungarian Communists were forced to proceed cautiously and to penetrate the government apparatus by stages. As one author says of Matyas Rakosi:

> With the famous 'salami' tactics, he first went into a coalition with the Smallholders, Peasant and Social-Democratic parties to crush the Conservatives, then annihilated the Smallholders party with the help of the remaining parties. Then he suborned the Peasant party and absorbed the Social-Democrats, killing off or imprisoning their party leadership. Politicians were bribed, blackmailed, driven to exile, imprisoned, or sentenced to death.[7]

The degree of Communist unpopularity was seen in the first electoral results in November 1945, when the Communists received only 17 per cent of the total vote. In the next elections, despite what some authors call resort 'to various kinds of fraud and intimidation' they received 22.3 per cent of the vote. The 'salami' tactics used by Rakosi led to the creation of the 'People's Front for Independence', which produced a single electoral list for the elections of May 1949 and ensured full Communist control. The problems of the government did not end, however. Because of Moscow's alarm over Titoism and Rakosi's complete subjection to Stalin, Hungary was one of the first countries to begin purges of

non-Muscovite Communists. Laszlo Rajk was sentenced to death
in 1949. Rakosi then supplied the Czechoslovak party with a list of
possible Czech and Slovak suspects during the Czech trials. The
Catholic Church was also highly suspect. Cardinal Midszenty was
arrested in early 1949 and sentenced to life imprisonment for
treason. In 1952 the second stage of purges was carried out and
Rakosi had the head of the secret police arrested — this was
Gabor Peter who had arranged the Rajk trial. In March 1953
Stalin's death was announced and in June Beria's arrest was
revealed. The news astounded and dismayed Rakosi and the other
Stalinist Hungarian leaders. Hungary had had a hard winter and
was in a bad economic situation. Rakosi was called to Moscow in
May and was urged to follow a 'new course' and to divide power
between himself and his rival, the 'soft-liner' Nagy. He did not
follow the advice. Following the uprising in East Berlin in mid-June
1953, the Hungarian leaders, including Nagy, were again called to
Moscow, and Mikoyan severely criticised Rakosi's economic policy,
Krushchev and Molotov agreeing. The Hungarians returned to
Budapest and called a meeting of the Central Committee on 28
June. 'The comrades listened in astonishment and with bated
breath to Rakosi's self-criticism and his admission of having
substituted his personal leadership for collective leadership.'[8]
Nevertheless, in the end Rakosi retained the party leadership and
appointed Nagy to the post of Prime Minister. Nagy began to
institute the liberal economic policy which the Russians had urged
upon Hungary, while Rakosi and his chief aide, Geroe, were
sabotaging it. In March 1955 Rakosi managed to oust Nagy and
have him expelled from the Central Committee. Unfortunately for
Nagy, Rakosi and Hungary, in May 1955 the new Soviet leadership
made its trip to Yugoslavia to make amends to Tito and the CPY
for Stalinist abuse. This gave rise to further relaxation all over
Eastern Europe, and made Rakosi's ardent Stalinism even more
anachronistic.

Thus, in Hungary, the situation was rather different from that in
the other countries. It was the zeal of the Hungarian Communist
leadership, their inflexibility and their unpopularity which caused
first, extreme and cruel purges in the party and country, and later,
a rigid economic and political dictatorship which was pursued
against Soviet advice. These events led to the Hungarian revolt
of 1956.

There was one country in South-eastern Europe which had

some affinity with the Soviet Union, despite having had no traditional ties with it. This was Albania, destined to be divided by the Treaty of London in 1915 and apparently saved from it by Lenin's revelation of this clause. An Albanian left-wing government was ousted in 1924 and King Zog maintained an authoritarian regime from then till 1939. No political parties were permitted and though there were Albanian Communists, the Communist Party of Albania was not founded till 1941, under guidance of two Yugoslavs.

In 1939 Albania was seized by Mussolini and the Albanians were divided up into resisters and collaborators. The king was in favour of an alliance with Britain, but the Greeks wanted to partition Albania after the war for collaborating with the Italians. The Albanians broke up into two resistance movements, one royalist, the other communist. First partisan groups were created in early 1942. In the meantime, the British declared publicly that Albania would be partitioned after the war, and the Greeks demanded an official acknowledgement of Greek interest in Albania. So the Albanians had good reason to look for support in the East. By the summer of 1943 the communist resistance movement grew and the British assigned a minor military mission to it. By late 1943 the British liaison officer, Brigadier Davies, suggested helping the resistance movement (LNC), though it was by now almost completely communist, but warned that a civil war could not be avoided between the two groups. Davies was captured and wounded in January 1944 (almost certainly delivered to the Germans by the Communist leader, Enver Hoxha) and the British decision was postponed.

However, in May 1944 the Albanian Communist Party at its congress voted to ban the king's return and asked the Soviet Union and the USA to send military missions to Albania. In July 1944 a Soviet mission arrived in Albania and by October 1944 the British began to support Hoxha, who now had the largest forces (25,000 members, against 2,000 of non-Communist partisans). On 20 October 1944 Hoxha issued a declaration that the first Albanian democratic government had been formed, but this was not recognised by the British, Soviet and American governments till November 1945. Hence, while the Albanians had little tradition of communism they tended to lean towards the USSR for political reasons. The Communist government was established without much help either from the Russians or from the Yugoslavs (though the Yugoslavs had some influence in Albania during the war period and they may have planned to absorb Albania into the Yugoslav Federation); and no army occupied its territory to make communism inevitable. The low Albanian economic standards and its political feudalism did not engender much interest in a liberal parliamentary regime. The Albanians are mostly Moslem, and the clergy did little to oppose the Communists partly out of traditional apathy and partly because of lack of any organised structure.

Hoxha, though he owed his post to the Yugoslavs in the first place, became and remained a firm Stalinist. He carried out purges of Titoists in 1948-9 (when his associate, Koci Xoxe, was executed). When de-Stalinisation was urged by Moscow he held on to party leadership and appointed Mehmet Shehu, who had organised the anti-Titoist purge after 1948, as chairman of the council of ministers in 1954. Shehu was completely loyal to Hoxha and was in favour first of the anti-Yugoslav stand, then of following the Stalinist line, and finally the anti-Soviet and pro-Chinese line. In 1976 Shehu was still the Prime Minister and Defence Minister. In 1955 Albania joined the Warsaw Pact and was one of the chief beneficiaries of the treaty since it gave her a measure of protection against absorption by Yugoslavia. Hoxha refused to rehabilitate the victims of anti-Titoist purges, particularly Xoxe, whom he described as an Albanian Beria. When the pro-Yugoslav elements nearly overthrew Hoxha in 1956 he frustrated the plot, hanged several conspirators and the main leader, Panayot Plakon, fled to Yugoslavia to be given political asylum in the USSR in 1957.

In all the above countries the introduction of communist governments was carried out cautiously and with a limited measure of success. In the process of this, the parties carried out Stalinist policies, which made periodic purges necessary, and could count on the support of the CPSU for most of the period, though this became much more problematic after Stalin's death. There is no doubt that since the introduction of 'collective leadership' in the USSR, the leaders in these countries, though pressured into certain courses of action, were not forced into them. Perhaps the measure of their lack of statesmanship is the fact that most of them made grievous mistakes, took their countries to the brink of civil war, and, in most cases, lost their leading positions. However, these can be blamed much more on their own policies than on the policies of the post-Stalinist CPSU.

There was one party in South-eastern Europe which was in a different position. This was the Greek Communist Party, the KKE.

The KKE played a large part in resistance to the Germans during the war through its guerrilla forces EAM/ELLAS, which were supported by the British. Encouraged by this, the KKE agreed in 1944 to join a government of national unity, which proved to be its undoing. The strength of the KKE in Greece made Churchill press for Greece to be included in the British sphere of influence at the Moscow Conference in October 1944, a request to which Stalin readily agreed. When the Nazi troops evacuated Greece in October 1944 the ELLAS forces could have occupied Athens, where they had 20,000 troops. Instead they agreed to accept the authority of the National Unity government of Papandreou, who immediately began to disarm the ELLAS militia. Alarmed by this, the Communist leaders, Siantos and Ioannides, gave the signal for a Communist uprising on 28 November 1944, with the apparent approval of Tito and covert support from the USSR. By the end of December the Communists drove government forces out of almost every corner of Greece, with the exception of central Athens. The British began to reinforce Greek government troops and a conference was arranged between Churchill, Eden and Field-Marshal Alexander on the one hand, and three Greek Communist leaders (with the inclusion of other politicians) on the other, on 26 December 1944. When the KKE leaders began to make unacceptable demands the conference broke down The British troops began to attack ELLAS positions and the KKE asked for a ceasefire. Finally an agreement which was quite advantageous to the KKE was signed in Varkiza with the British.

At the Yalta Conference which followed the first Greek settlement Stalin is said to have declared that he had 'confidence in the British government's policy in Greece'.[9] Defeated in the first round, the Greek Communists decided to reopen the struggle at the end of 1946, which lasted, on and off, till 1949. The main aid to KKE came from the Yugoslavs and, according to one source at least, the Yugoslav aid made the Greeks so successful that Stalin ordered it stopped at the beginning of 1948. This the Yugoslavs were unwilling to do till their own condemnation by the Cominform, when they had to limit aid to Greece because of their fears of a Soviet invasion. The Greek Communists, who were pro-Titoist (like Markos, a successful commander in the north of Greece) were purged by Zachariades, the General-Secretary of the party. From the end of 1948, after the removal of Markos and the anti-Yugoslav purge, the Communist forces in Greece were weakened and were finally defeated in August 1949.[10]

In accordance with the Cominform instructions Zachariades then embarked on an anti-Yugoslav campaign. Some 25,000 Greek Communists fled to Yugoslavia, others fled to Albania. Though the KKE was decimated, it avoided the self-destructive purges of ruling parties.

The question remains: why did Stalin appear to want the KKE's demise, despite its apparent successes? He had already demonstrated his lack of interest in the Greeks by not inviting them to the founding conference of the Cominform. He then decided that they should be exterminated, either by their own Stalinists or by the Greek royalist forces. The reason may lie in the fact that the Greek Communists were indigenous and had little reason to be loyal to Moscow. Another, in line with the above, is given by J.M. Domenach, whose 'conclusions are that the Soviet leaders were afraid of the growth of a new Titoism in Greece, and also regarded the civil war in Greece as dangerous and inopportune. ... It was for these reasons that the Soviet leaders gave the pro-Soviet Greek Communist leaders the order to reject any aid from Yugoslavia and end the civil war. In this way they achieved two things. They demonstrated their good faith to the Western foreign ministries and at the same time were able to denounce Tito's treachery before the other Communist parties and world opinion.'[11]

None of these arguments is fully convincing. By late 1948 Stalin did not have to demonstrate his good faith to Western governments. He had sufficient support in his campaign against Tito not to be overworried by the KKE. The most likely answer is that he had little interest in the KKE as such, that there were more pressing problems nearer home (Yugoslavia being only one of them) and that when he gave away Greece in 1944 he did so because it appeared to be outside the immediate sphere of Soviet interest. This last hypothesis is supported by Soviet foreign policy since then; at no time did the Russians exhibit a singular interest in Greece, whereas they did and still do express such an interest in other Mediterranean countries. The reason for this must be that they believe Greece could easily become communist should the conditions be right for it. In this case only a pro-Soviet communist party would be appropriate. Till such time it is better to have no communists of any note in Greece. It is perhaps notable that the Chinese were not invited to the original Cominform meeting either; and it is possible that it was done for the same reasons.

If Greece escaped becoming a people's democracy because of the Soviet lack of interest, Yugoslavia, the country immediately on her borders, had a much more stormy history. As had been noted earlier, the Yugoslavs developed their own Communist organisation during the years of war. However, Tito (who had become Secretary-General in 1937 when Stalin liquidated Gorkic his predecessor)[12] was a faithful Stalinist and would have been ready to follow the Soviet lead had Stalin supported him more firmly. The first argument came over Tito's clash with the Western Allies over Trieste, when Stalin did not support Yugoslavia's claim to the area. The second clash is said to have occurred because of the behaviour of Soviet troops which drove the Germans from Belgrade in 1944. The third clash came when the Red Army withdrew and the Russians sent in scores of Soviet advisers, apparently bent on modelling the Yugoslav army on the Soviet pattern, but refusing to help Yugoslavia to build up her own armaments industry. The fourth reason, and according to some authorities the most important one, was the Soviet intention to subjugate Yugoslavia economically, to prevent Yugoslavia's industrialisation and to delay development.[13]

Despite the Yugoslavs' protestations to the contrary, there is ample evidence to think that the Russians treated Tito and Yugoslavia preferentially till the final quarrel. Tito, the foremost communist leader in Eastern Europe, was allowed liberties no-one else would dare to claim. Stalin praised him constantly, both behind his back and to his face.[14] Whether (as Tito seemed to think) this was merely a strategem to gain time and purge him (as Gorkic was purged in 1937) or whether — as appears more likely — Stalin saw in the gallant Yugoslav communist the future leader of the Soviet bloc is immaterial. At any rate, Tito did not trust Stalin, and his own intention was much less ambitious: he saw himself as the leader of a new Balkan Federation. It was on this point voiced by Dimitrov in Romania in January 1948 rather than on collectivisation and economic exploitation that the Yugoslav–Soviet split occurred.

Dedijer describes the interesting episode of the Yugoslav and Bulgarian leaders being summoned to see Stalin in February 1948.[15] Stalin, angry that Tito had not come in person — apparently fearing the worst — arraigned Kardelj, Bakaric and Djilas as well as Dimitrov, about the federal project. He agreed that there should be a federation of Bulgaria and Yugoslavia (with Albania included), another one between Romania and Hungary and one between

Czechoslovakia and Poland, but not a Balkan federation. This was the first time that Stalin had criticised Tito and the Yugoslavs, and spoke darkly of 'conceptions different from our own'.[16]

The split deepened and a series of letters, most of them since published, passed between Tito and Stalin. The accusations and counter-accusations contained in these letters are now common knowledge. What is less well known is the fact that apparently *some* letters were suppressed by the Yugoslavs and that among the accusations levelled at them by Stalin were the following: that the Yugoslav cabinet contained British spies; that the American ambassador in Belgrade 'behaves as if he owned the place'; that American agents in Yugoslavia were becoming more numerous; and that the Yugoslavs were travelling the road of Trotsky and Bernstein. The Yugoslav reply was to arrest the two immediately identifiable Soviet agents in the government, Hebrang and Zujovic. Finally, the Yugoslavs were called to the next session of the Cominform which would consider their case. The Yugoslavs decided not to go to the meeting, because, as Dedijer stated, there was no guarantee that Tito would return alive from such a meeting. Accordingly, the Cominform met in Bucharest in late June and expelled Yugoslavia from the organisation, apparently not without difficulty. According to Dedijer, the piece of evidence which swayed the delegates was Zhdanov's statement that Tito was an imperialist spy. This evidence was apparently the same as that produced at Rajk's trial in Budapest a year later. That evidence was later said to have been false, and Rajk was rehabilitated. Nevertheless, Hoffman and Neal, who piece together all the evidence very skilfully,[17] do suggest that, even if Tito was not an imperialist spy, it must have appeared to Stalin that he was. if only on the basis of his supposed friendship with Churchill and because he needed Western economic help, having refused to follow the Soviet economic line. The Yugoslavs still hoped that by outwardly adhering to the Soviet policy they might be forgiven. But by January 1949, when Moscow refused their application to join the Comecon, it became clear that the break was finalised.

The results of the split were far-reaching. By the summer of 1949 the Russians were actively considering armed invasion of Yugoslavia. They are said to have been halted by the unity of the Yugoslavs, and their well-known military capability. The reasons why the USSR did not invade Yugoslavia may have been manifold: but the most likely possibility is that the Russians remembered the wartime agreement about a 50/50 division of spheres of influence. Did they think that the West would intervene because of this agreement? Or that it would intervene because Tito was acting for the Western Powers? This is a fascinating problem. While there is no direct evidence for such a scenario some oblique evidence does exist.

The Soviet Bloc after 1948

The Soviet–Yugoslav split occurred between January and June 1948. The open rapprochement between Yugoslavia and the USA did not occur till August 1949, to be completely cemented only in 1950.

At the same time as Tito was demanding that the Russians moderate their influence over Yugoslavia on the other side of the Mediterranean another event occurred: the creation of the state of Israel in 1948. The Soviet Union had been supporting the Israeli cause and Czechoslovakia, with Russian approval, had supplied the Israeli army with small arms and ammunition as well as fighter planes.[18] There were two separate Communist Parties in Palestine: a Jewish one and an Arab one. 'The divergent positions of the Jewish and Arab Communists were reunited under strong pressure from the Soviet Union at the creation of the Israeli State, and the two factions merged on October 22, 1948, in Haifa to form the Communist Party of Israel (Maki).'[19] Yet soon afterwards, in 1949, the Soviet Union had begun to cool its relations with Israel, having realised 'that the influence of American Jews, and through them the United States government, had prevailed in Israel over that of pro-Soviet elements'.[20]

On 15 June 1949 the Hungarian Communist Party announced that Laszlo Rajk had been expelled from the party as a spy and Trotskyite agent. On 10 September the trial of Rajk and several other defendants opened. After the trial Rajk and three others were hanged and two military leaders were shot. Other defendants received heavy terms of imprisonment. At Rajk's trial the prosecutor said: 'This trial is not, strictly speaking, the trial of Laszlo Rajk and his accomplices. It is Tito and his henchmen who are in the dock ....'[21] The Rajk trial opened the gates of a flood of purges: the defendants implicated Tito and the CPY as much as the American secret service and other European communists. Soon after the Rajk trial came the turn of Bulgaria. Kostov, the co-founder of the party, was accused of similar offences, of contacts with the British intelligence and of a plot with Tito. Despite protestations of innocence, Kostov was sentenced to death and executed in November 1949. Between January and June 1949 there were purges of the highest party officials in Albania, in Romania and in Poland. The period came soon after the Communist coup in Czechoslovakia (and the Tito–Stalin break), where there were immediate purges of Titoists. Everywhere the charges were the same: the accused were the agents of the Western secret services, they were Titoists, they had worked to break away from the Soviet alliance.

But the biggest and most notorious trial was that of Rudolf Slansky, Secretary-General of the Czechoslovak Communist Party, who was finally tried in late 1951. The charge was that he 'had been urged by American espionage to defect to the West'. Fourteen defendants stood trial; eleven of them were Jews. Eleven were executed on 3 December 1952. The prosecution tried to show that Jewish communists were told by American colleagues that it was the duty of every Jew to support the American policy, even if he did not agree with it. 'The Jews, an international people, rooted in the young state of Israel, were playing a key role in the vast American conspiracy against the Soviet Union.'[22]

After all the trials, it was only in Poland that executions of main defendants did not take place. All the executed and imprisoned leaders were rehabilitated after 1956. It has been accepted that they were innocent. And yet, one cannot help painting a different scenario: perhaps Tito really had been inclined to turn to the West right from 1944 onwards? Perhaps he was encouraged to stay in the Soviet bloc in order to provide first-hand information on Stalin's plans. Perhaps the West, worried by the left-wing stance of the new Israeli state, had gone out of its way to bind it to the West, rather than to the East. And perhaps these two strands had produced these results: on the one hand, Tito was to found a Balkan Federation, which would be independent of the USSR; on the other, the Jews in the Soviet bloc would be encouraged to help the Israeli state by helping Tito.

The only possible evidence is as follows: Tito did not go to the *first* Moscow conference, when Stalin was still full of praise for him. Why not? Second, of all the accused, the Poles were the only ones not to be executed. Poland did not figure in the Balkan Federation at all, while Czechoslovakia, only recently turned communist, did. Third, as Deutscher maintains, before the 1930s purges in Russia there had been an anti-Stalinist plot, though the evidence was distorted by the show trials and mass prosecutions. If there had been some grounds for trials in the 1930s, perhaps there were some in the late 1940s and early 1950s. Such evidence as there may be has yet to come to light. In the meantime, one can only conjecture. One thing, however, is certain — as early as 1948 one could see the clear development of a 'national' brand of communism not only in Yugoslavia but throughout the Balkan area. That brand was to spread and thrive in the later period.

Notes

1. I. Deutscher, *Stalin*, p. 420.
2. R.F. Starr, *Communist Regimes in Eastern Europe*, p. 35.
3. According to Starr, ibid., Chervenkov was readmitted to the party in 1969.
4. L.A.D. Dellin (ed.), *Bulgaria*, p. 187: quoted by Starr, *Communist Regimes*, p. 45.
5. Starr, Ibid., p. 165.
6. F. Fejto, *A History of the People's Democracies*, p. 21. P. Lendvai, *Eagles in Cobwebs: Nationalism and Communism in the Balkans*, maintains that Luca had his sentence commuted, while Pauker was never tried and died in 1960. See pp. 288-9.
7. G. Paloczi-Horvath, *The Undefeated*, p. 246: quoted by Starr, *Communist Regimes*, pp. 107-8.
8. Quoted by Fejto, *People's Democracies*, p. 39.
9. Claudin, *The Communist Movement*, p. 381.
10. Ibid., pp. 512-13.
11. Ibid., pp. 769-70, n. 36.
12. See Starr, *Communist Regimes*, p. 196.
13. V. Dedijer, *Tito Speaks*, pp. 267 and 289: quoted by G.W. Hoffman and F.W. Neal, *Yugoslavia and the New Communism*, pp. 116-17.
14. See Hoffman and Neal, ibid., pp. 121-4.
15. Ibid., pp. 316-23.
16. For an interpretation of the conference see Hoffman and Neal, ibid., pp. 124-6.
17. Ibid., Ch. 9.
18. Fejto, *People's Democracies*, pp. 18-19.
19. D. Nahas, *The Israeli Communist Party*, p. 25.
20. Fejto, *People's Democracies*, p. 19.
21. Claudin, *Communist Movement*, p. 517.
22. Fejto, *People's Democracies*, pp. 16 and 18.

8

Central and Eastern Europe, 1944-53

East Germany

While after 1948 Yugoslavia developed its own 'road to socialism' and the other countries of South-eastern Europe pursued a Stalinist course, the situation in the Central and Eastern European countries was rather different. This hinged on two factors: one of these countries, East Germany, was divided and under occupation; the two others, Poland and Czechoslovakia, had been allies of the West and USSR throughout the war, and were under special protection of the Western Allies for various reasons. In the final analysis, the East Germans perhaps had fewer traumatic experiences than the Slav countries, probably because of Russia's desire to neutralise Western aid to West Germany, and also partly because they were less inclined to resist Sovietisation than Poland or Czechoslovakia.

East Germany has to be considered first, because this is chronologically correct, but also because the solution tried out there was later used in other East European countries. When the German Communists came back to Berlin (Ulbricht and his subordinates came to Berlin on 2 May 1945, Pieck and others in early June) they were shocked to the core. 'The former capital of the Reich existed no more. Heaps of rubble, burning buildings, shells of gutted houses, which resembled rotting black teeth projecting into the blue sky, carcasses of animals and humans alike, famished civilians in rags seeking shelter and food, stunned, exhausted German soldiers, carousing, inebriated Soviet Army men celebrating victory, a total breakdown of all public services ...' greeted them on arrival.[1] The Communists soon set about re-establishing the KPD (in June 1945) and other democratic parties. The Christian Democratic Party, Liberals and Social Democrats were established. Apart from sheltering the Stalinist German Communists since

1933 the Russians had very wisely fostered other German interests. In July 1943 the National Committee for a Free Germany was set up in Moscow. A little later the League of German Officers was established. These bodies, which appeared to have embraced the old belief in 'national bolshevism' either out of conviction of out of necessity, served as a nucleus of the new German government, administration and future army.[2] The officers were also later instrumental in setting up the National Democratic Party in East Germany.[3] Some of those officers were later to train the East German army, like Field-Marshal von Paulus, the defender of Stalingrad.

Despite such careful preparatory work, the Germans were not too enthusiastic about Soviet occupation or German left-wing parties. Most Communists and Social Democrats had been eliminated by Hitler after 1933, the Germans had been nurtured on violent anti-Bolshevik propaganda for many years and the problem of the Eastern territories, occupied by the Poles with Russian support, was of extreme importance to both Prussia and Brandenburg — the two main components of what was to become East Germany.

On the other hand, as one historian points out, the Communists and Social Democrats in Berlin and in East Germany, remembering the disunity which led to Hitler's rise to power, and having forged their links in Nazi concentration camps, were convinced that unity was essential for the future of Germany.[4] Hence the merger between the KPD and the East German SPD which occurred in April 1946 was by no means as forced as some authorities maintain.[5] However, the merger was opposed by the Social Democrats in the Western Zones of Occupation.

The new party of unity (SED) gave full parity to the Communists and Social Democrats and professed to follow a 'German way' to Socialism. The transformation into a 'Leninist' party did not occur till July 1948, when the Cold War was already in full swing and — significantly — after the Cominform resolution condemning the Yugoslavs (in June 1948), and several months after the beginning of the Berlin Blockade (this started in the summer of 1948 and was called off nearly a year afterwards in May 1949). Similarly, the German Democratic Republic was proclaimed only after the Allies established the Federal Republic in West Germany (September 1949, West Germany; October 1949, East Germany). Further, though 'the whole period from 1948 to 1953 was one of spy hysteria and mutual suspicion', it is pointed out that 'for all its alleged Stalinism the East German revolution has devoured few of its children, far fewer than the other East European regimes did during the purges of 1948-53'.[6] Despite the setbacks, the new constitution of East Germany 'looked like a remarkably liberal document and it could have provided the basis for a stable and representative government'.[7] The Constitution resembled that of the Weimar Republic, and was written for the whole of Germany. It is also notable that East Germany, alone of all the Eastern bloc states, was called a 'democratic' not a 'people's' republic.

Whatever the intentions of the Soviet Union, the East German Communists and the Western Allies may have been, the Yugoslav defection, the Berlin Blockade and the general worsening of the world situation soon ended — though not completely — any attempts at unification. In February and March 1952 the DDR and USSR sent notes to Western Allies proposing a united, neutral Germany with its own defence forces. Some commentators called it 'a clear if dignified and partial offer of retreat', which met with a 'haughty and intransigent Western reaction'; others maintained that the Western policy of negotiations from strength was producing results, and the West German Chancellor Adenauer believed that the USSR would abandon East Germany if faced with massive rearmament and the Federal Republic would take it over.[8]

The rejection of the Soviet offer led to the intensification of Sovietisation measures in East Germany and a deterioration of economic and political conditions. The death of Stalin in March 1953 did not soften the German line. A complicated situation connected with a decrease in pay and increase of output norms led to a strike on 16 June 1953. About 300,000 to 400,000 workers (out of a total workforce of five and a half million) went on strike in 274 localities. On 17 June the East German security police were sent in. There were twenty-one deaths, and the revolt spent itself almost spontaneously. The Russians had been advising the Germans on a new economic course since the death of Stalin, apparently understanding the situation better than Ulbricht himself. When the revolt occurred, the East German government finally conceded that it had been wrong to continue economic pressure, but Ulbricht saved his position, partly because Zaisser, his main opponent, was the immediate subordinate of Beria, who fell on 26 June.[9] The East Germans suggested that the strike and disorders which followed it were fomented by Western agents. This may be partly true; Berlin was the acknowledged spy centre of Europe, Adenauer was very keen to regain East Germany and Stalin's death made the situation propitious from the Western point of view. On the other hand, the East German workers had genuine grievances against the regime which, once expressed and conceded to, seem to have removed their reasons for protest. The situation in East Germany in 1953 was that there was little political opposition to the Communist government among the masses; that protests were isolated and spontaneous; and that such protests as there were tended to be economic rather than political. Political protest in East Germany has been the preserve of the very few Communist intellectuals who have little in common with the mass of the people. This may not mean that the East German government is popular. On the other hand, it means that it is not particularly unpopular. The rise in the standard of living after 1953, the East German 'economic miracle' which matched that of West Germany, has persuaded many that they are doing rather well. The disaffected managed to find their way to West Germany in large numbers till the erection of the Berlin Wall. East Germany may not have found a 'national road' but it has certainly found the road to a measure of economic prosperity.

Poland and Communism

Unlike East Germany, Poland never found that the Soviet brand of socialism was acceptable. Poland has had a long history of enmity with Russia and the USSR. It was dismembered in 1939 by the Nazis and the Soviet Union. Diplomatic relations between the Polish Government in Exile and the USSR were broken off in the spring of 1943 in the aftermath of the Katyn massacre revelations. In the summer of 1944, during the Warsaw Rising, the Red Army stood on the other bank of the Vistula while the insurgents, following orders from the London government, fought alone. Polish Communists themselves had little reason to like the USSR. Their party had been dissolved and leaders decimated before the war. A new party was re-established in January 1942 under the name of the Polish Workers' Party (PPR). It was founded on the initiative of two old Communists, Nowotko and Finder. According to one authority, the party was seriously weakened 'by the brutal liquidation of the German-established Jewish ghetto in Warsaw.

The Gestapo seized the PPR's chief press organ, *Liberty Tribune*, and arrested many leading party members.'[10]

All these factors and the ongoing dispute over the territories known as Western Belorussia and Western Ukraine made it difficult to set up a Communist government. The National Council of Poland, recognised in June 1944, had to wait till one of the chief Communist leaders (and its chairman) Boleslaw Bierut was transported out of Warsaw and into Lublin, by then occupied by the Red Army, on 20 July 1944, and joined by leaders of the Moscow-sponsored Union of Polish Patriots, before the Polish Committee of National Liberation (PKWN) could be set up on 21 July 1944. It must be pointed out that though Dziewanowski states that seven out of the fifteen members were 'avowed Communists', some were either fairly new Communists, others were 'fair weather' Communists. The rest of the Committee were members of splinter groups of some left-wing movement, though they were either Soviet sympathisers or opportunists. From then on, the Committee was treated by Soviet authorities as an incipient Polish government, and considered itself in this light. It issued a manifesto which called for a peaceful settlement on the eastern borders and for the return to Poland of western territories and parts of East Prussia.[11]

The ill-fated Warsaw rising[12] weakened the anti-Communist forces in Poland, and from September 1944 Mikolajczyk, the prime minister of the London-based Government in Exile, was in negotiations with the Soviet government. Finally, after the liberation of the rest of Poland, a government of national unity was set up on 28 June 1945, consisting of the PPR, the Socialists, the Populists and two smaller parties, the Democratic Party and the Labour Party. The post of prime minister was taken by the Communist Osobka-Morawski, that of vice-premier by Mikolajczyk. On 6 July 1945 this government was recognised by Britain and the USA, and during the Potsdam Conference (17 July – 2 August 1945) the German territories which the government demanded were provisionally ceded to Poland, pending the decisions of a future peace conference.

The problems of Polish politicians were not confined to the split between the Communists or fellow-travellers and other parties — though this was important. The main problem was that within the small PPR (20,000 members in 1944, 30,000 members in 1945) there was a serious and deepening split between the 'Muscovites' like Bierut and the 'natives' like Gomulka. This split was emphasised by the very brief party standing of many members. This became much worse after the party's recruitment drive in 1945; by December 1945 the membership rose to 235,000 while the leadership was calling for a million members. The main governmental posts went to the 'Muscovite' faction, under the leadership of Bierut, who became the Head of State.

The first parliamentary elections were held in January 1947 (having been postponed several times) and, while they were undoubtedly falsified, they produced an 80 per cent vote for the Democratic bloc, dominated by the PPR. This led to the flight of Mikolajczyk in November 1947, which was followed by two events of the greatest importance to the future of the Polish Communists: the 'native' faction under Gomulka was purged in the second half of 1948 and the PPR merged with the Socialist PPS at the 'unification' congress in December 1948. This immediately increased the membership of the new Polish United Workers' Party (PUWP) to one and a half million members.[13] The two key men removed in the first purge were Gomulka himself and Spychalski, to be followed by further purges lasting till late 1949. In 1951 Gomulka was placed under house arrest and remained there awaiting trial which never occurred. He may have been saved by Stalin's death from a long prison sentence or execution. But there was a marked difference between the Polish party purges and those in other Eastern European countries: not a single one of the dissidents was executed or prosecuted on charges of treason; the charges were milder ones, of 'harbouring spies' or 'lack of vigilance'. Dziewanowski states that the main reason for Gomulka's dismissal was the fear that unless the PPR and the PPS (which was purged simultaneously) were cleared of the 'nationalist' elements, 'the Gomulka faction of the PPR might combine with the like-minded PPS elements and consequently create a bloc difficult to manage.'[14] The Socialist–Communist merger was followed by the merger of the independent Populist Party with the Communist-sponsored Populists,[15] and the way was open for the introduction of Stalinist measures in Poland. A new constitution was promulgated in July 1952 and according to all authorities it was closely modelled on the 1936 Stalinist Constitution, though it did not give the monopoly of power to the Party.

The Polish road to Stalinism was so long-drawn out and relatively cautious that it was overtaken by events. No sooner had Stalinisation been completed than Stalin himself died. 'That event and the ensuing jockeying for power caused a great deal of confusion among Polish party leaders. At the Eighth Plenum of the Central Committee [held in March 1953] the Polish party promptly accepted "the collective leadership" of the Communist Party of the Soviet Union and, fearing to back a wrong horse, refrained from more outspoken political pronouncements.'[16] In the meantime, the Stalinist measures which had been pursued by the leadership after the purges had had such disastrous economic consequences (mostly owing to the policy of forced collectivisation which brought agricultural production down to below the 1950 level) that the government was forced to introduce the 'new course' in October 1953. The policy was mainly aimed at improving the standard of living and inducing the farmers to grow more food.

Simultaneously, with this, however, the agreement between the Church and the State, signed in 1950, broke down and the Primate of Poland, Cardinal Wyszynski, was arrested in September 1953 for speaking out against a decree of February 1953, which allowed the state to interfere in all clerical appointments. By the beginning of 1954, nine bishops and several hundred priests were held in prison, and Cardinal Wyszynski himself was not released till late 1956, after Gomulka came back to power. It is clear that the Polish 'Muscovites' were more cautious, more conservative and less flexible than any other leaders in Eastern Europe, even including the East Germans. On the other hand, they also avoided the bloodbath of their own supporters in which most of the other parties indulged. The reason for this may lie in the relative insecurity of the Polish Communists compared with other Eastern European countries and the difficulty which the leadership had in attaining its goal of socialisation. This will explain why it was in Poland that the most thorough 'thaw' was instigated in 1956.

Czechoslovakia

The third country which one must consider in this chapter is Czechoslovakia. This country had a completely different tradition of communism from either Germany or Poland. While in Germany the KPD was a mass party before the advent of the Nazis, was almost totally eliminated during the Nazi rule and hence had of necessity to rely on 'Muscovites', and whereas in Poland the

Communists were few and far between, as well as inclined to nationalist tendencies, in Czechoslovakia throughout the inter-war period the party was both legal and relatively popular. It was also a loyal ally of the CPSU in all the changes of course. Formed in 1921, it polled almost a million votes in 1925, and gained 41 seats in the Chamber of Deputies out of 300. Party membership fluctuated between a high of 150,000 in 1928 to a low of 28,000 in 1930, but at the peak of its success it drew 13 per cent of the electorate.[17]

The Czechoslovak party followed the Soviet policy throughout the 1930s only to go into hiding when Czechoslovakia was dismembered by the Nazis in March 1939. Some leaders fell into Nazi hands, like Zapotocky; others fled to the West, like Clementis, but the Secretary-General, Gottwald, and his close associate, Slansky, went to Moscow, to prove an embarassment to Stalin, first during the period of friendship with Germany and then, after 1941, when Stalin was placating the Czech government in exile led by the President, Dr Benes. According to Taborsky, it was not till January 1945 that Stalin specifically mentioned Gottwald in a letter to Benes.[18] The Czechoslovak government returned from London in March 1945 and, according to the same source, the Communists were by then so powerful and the Red Army was so well placed in the country that they could have attained power immediately. The Communists were not unpopular: in the first elections in May 1946 (which were completely free) the party polled 38 per cent of the vote and gained 114 out of 300 seats in the Constitutent Assembly. As a result, its leader Klement Gottwald became the prime minister.[19] In 1946 the registered party membership was well over a million members.[20]

The explanation why the party did not take over immediately but waited to do it very messily in 1948 is, according to Taborsky, that the USSR hoped for a Communist victory in France and Italy and was waiting for a parliamentary co-operation between the Socialists and the Communists. This may have some basis, but the reasons were much more complex. In the first place, as one authority points out, 'while the strength of the Slavophile tradition in Czechoslovakia should not be exaggerated, feelings of friendship for the Russians did exist, in contrast to the historic anti-Russian sentiments prevailing in Poland and Hungary'.[21] Since in Czechoslovakia both communism and the Russians were popular there seemed to be no reason why the Russians should not play a friendly 'Big Brother' role to Czechoslovakia's 'small Slav nation' role. Further, there was a sense of guilt, tinged with regret at the consequences of abandoning Czechoslovakia in 1938. This made the Russians even less willing to resort to harsh measures against the Czechs. The situation may have continued in this way indefinitely but for the problems of international relations.

The American offer of Marshall Aid to Europe was the straw that broke the camel's back. On 4 July 1947 the Czech cabinet voted in favour of participation in the Marshall Plan conference in Paris. Two days later the Czechs were summoned to Moscow (two non-Communists, Masaryk and Drtina, went along with Gottwald). But it was Gottwald alone who went to see Stalin. As he recounted to the others later: 'I have never seen Stalin so furious. He reproached me bitterly for having accepted the invitation to participate in the Paris Conference. He does not understand how we could have done it. He says that we acted as if we were ready to turn our back on the Soviet Union.'[22] The Czechs were ordered to reject the offer of Marshall Aid, which they did immediately. But the harm had been done: first, they had acted without consulting Stalin; second, they proved that they could be disloyal.

Some objectivity must be brought into the analysis of the Marshall Aid offer. It was a very generous offer, made to a Europe which had ruined itself in a war. There is no doubt that Europe was saved by the injection of Soviet troops and American technology from a fate which few have dared to contemplate. Both the major powers expected gratitude. When this was not forthcoming neither the Americans nor the Russians could understand it. George Marshall acted from the highest humane motives; but the American businessmen who supported this offer spoke of opening up new markets. To the Russians the situation was equally clear: they could not offer any economic aid; they expected this to come from Europe, particularly the conquered nations, like Germany. The eastern half of Europe had been allocated to their sphere of influence by wartime agreements. If the western half of Europe in the American sphere of influence received generous aid, this would retard revolutionary movements. But they could do little about influencing this development save trying to stop it through the national communist parties. It was different in the east: any American largesse in Eastern Europe would immediately undermine Sovient influence; it would undo the effect of having won the war; and it would make the smaller nations in the Soviet sphere much more restless. Neither would Stalin contemplate accepting the aid for the USSR itself; in wartime, the need was pressing; in peacetime, he hoped to make up the losses from reparations, and accepting aid from the Americans would have meant loss of face. Any country in the Eastern bloc which accepted such aid would also involve the USSR in a loss of face, apart from a loss of political influence.

All these things considered, therefore, little else could have been expected. The Czech lapse had particularly upset Stalin as he would have expected Czechoslovakia to be the most loyal of all.

The mounting tension between the former Allies, which eventually culminated in the Korean War in 1950, also forced Stalin to consider Czechoslovakia as a key state in his armaments plans. Not counting East Germany (which was at that stage almost denuded of industrial potential), Czechoslovakia was the only country in the Eastern bloc with a capacity to produce heavy industrial goods and armaments. As an economist comments:

> Stalin personally demanded a shift in the orientation and structure of Czechoslovakia's production and export trade 180 degrees toward the East, a rapid increase in the output of its heavy industry, and massive deliveries of heavy industry products to other socialist countries (in particular, the USSR). . . . In implementing this decision, the regime rapidly accelerated investment in heavy industry. The share of investment in the three major branches of heavy industry alone accounted for almost one-half of aggregate industrial investment in Czechoslovakia for the years 1948–53.[23]

These events and the expectation that the Communists might lose ground in the next elections may have pushed the Russians into rash action. The Czech Communists were to take over power. On 12 February 1948 twelve non-Communist ministers resigned in protest when Nosek, the minister of the interior, kept replacing high police officials with Communists. Nosek was backed by Gottwald. Benes was undecided and at first insisted that the new government had to be formed from all the parties in the People's Front. The Communists paraded detachments of workers' militia through Prague streets. In Prague and other cities 'action committees' run by Communists were formed, and public officials were ordered to co-operate with them. Benes, unwilling to offend the Russians and realising that Gottwald still had the support of the majority of the cabinet, yielded, and on 25 February a new government was formed in which the key posts were held by Communists and their allies, the break-away wing of the left Social-Democrats. The only other member was the foreign minister, Jan Masaryk, who was found dead in the courtyard of the ministry on 10 March. A series of purges followed the takeover and in the elections held in May 1948 on a single list the government received about 90 per cent of the votes. On 6 June President Benes resigned, and was succeeded by Klement Gottwald, while Zapotocky became Prime Minister. In the summer of 1949, the breakaway Social-Democrats merged with the Communist Party.

The new government began a rapid process of industrialisation and collectivisation. As a result, the food situation worsened and workers resisted the increased production norms. The government was forced to find scapegoats for the problems. According to some sources, this should have been Gottwald, who had already been in disgrace once, after the Marshall Aid fiasco. The reason why Slansky, a hard-line Stalinist unlike Gottwald, was chosen is attributed to many factors. One is advanced by Taborsky:

> One conjecture which seems to have much credibility is that Slansky's eclipse and ultimate fall were caused mainly by the fall of Andrei Zhdanov. Indeed, the death of Zhdanov led to a ruthless elimination of a number of his protegés from the Soviet Party apparatus. While it is difficult to prove that Slansky was Zhdanov's protegé, the two had been in frequent contact in Cominform affairs. Since Slansky was also the KSC's main representative in the Cominform he was probably closer to the Soviet Cominform boss than any other high-ranking Czechoslovak Communist. One may also note that the sudden rehabilitation of Klement Gottwald coincided with Zhdanov's eclipse in the summer of 1948.[24]

It is suggested also that Slansky may have been chosen because he was a Jew, and while Taborsky confirms that 'his Jewish origin did not do him any good', he suggests that this was merely a marginal matter, though it did help to construct an anti-Zionist case against the Jewish accused, who were treated as 'cosmopolitans', while the non-Jews were treated as 'bourgeois nationalists'.[25] The most important lesson from these show trials was that they appear to have originated in Moscow, not in Prague (this is confirmed by everyone who survived the trials and by all writers, whether communist or non-communist), and that, strangely enough, the country was convinced that they were the work of the Czech hardliners. In fact, it appears to be true that real hardliners were those who were executed, like Slansky, whereas Gottwald had never been classed as such, and did not even wish to have the blood of his former comrades on his hands. The trials, the ill-treatment of the accused and their executions are said to have broken Gottwald and driven him to alcoholism. When he died on 14 March 1953 he was succeeded by Zapotocky, while Antonin Novotny became the First Secretary of the party in September 1953. The new prime minister was Siroky, a Slovak.

Instead of relaxing the economic policy the leadership introduced a fiscal reform which deprived the population of a large part of their savings, and abolished the rationing of foodstuffs and industrial goods on 1 June 1952. This monetarist policy produced a great shock, and there were disturbances in industrial areas. The new Czech leadership was in a quandary: their loyalty to the USSR had to be upheld but they also wanted to retain power. In the event, Zapotocky argued in favour of the 'new course' while Novotny was in favour of retaining the Stalinist measures. In 1954, after a joint meeting of the Soviet and Czech leaderships in April, Khrushchev decided in favour of Novotny.[26] The Czechs continued on their Stalinist course, even erecting a giant statue of Stalin in Prague in May 1955, and continuing the quarrel with Tito as much as was possible. In December 1956 Novotny rejected 'national communism' as practised in Poland and Yugoslavia and identified it with imperialism, and the events in Hungary in 1956 convinced the Czech leadership that they had been right to resist liberalisation.[27]

Thus Czechoslovakia developed differently from the other countries in the Eastern bloc and it retained a separate way after Stalin's death. It did not go into a hostile camp, but it did not follow the Soviet lead on de-Stalinisation. It retained its hardline leadership and policies and it pursued them till the 1960s. Of all the Eastern European countries, Czechoslovakia presents a unique and untypical example of a country which was pro-communist, pro-Soviet, pro-Russian; one which purged its party with a tremendous zeal, and which resisted liberalisation, despite Soviet urging, managing at the same time to retain Soviet trust.

As we have seen, there is no general model to be drawn from the 'sovietisation' of Eastern Europe. Stalinsation was neither as sure nor as consistent as had been assumed earlier, nor was it inevitable. There is no doubt that the underlying motives were, initially at least, the security of the USSR and the undeniable wish to foster communist governments outside the USSR. But there does not seem to have been a general plan of takeover other than that which was already assured by the Soviet armies. It is also possible that, had circumstances turned out differently — for example had the Americans not appeared to intervene in Europe, had they not developed an anti-Communist policy on the one hand, or had Stalin died in 1948 and not in 1953 on the other — the 'intermediate' countries may have been allowed to develop their own brand of government, though one which would be nearer to 'Finlandisation' than to West Germany. It may well have been a tragedy both for the Soviet Union and Eastern Europe that the undeniably backward countries like Bulgaria and Romania could not have been allowed to develop some form of 'modernised' economy; while the more advanced countries, like Czechoslovakia, Poland and Yugoslavia, could have become examples of mixed economy, multi-party states. In the Soviet equation the only country which would have had to be occupied for a long time was East Germany. In the context of a peaceful relationship with the USA the Russians might have been content with just that. Outside that context, even without Stalin, one cannot see that anything else could have happened.

Notes

1. M. McCauley, *Marxism–Leninism in the GDR*, p. 3.
2. D. Childs, *East Germany*, pp. 118-19. On 'national Bolshevism' see A. Spencer. *National Bolshevism Survey* (October, 1962).
3. The NDPD, set up in 1948, apparently to create a party both for ex-Nazis and non-Socialists who were prepared to support a more 'national' orientation in East Germany: see Childs, ibid., pp. 117-22.
4. For this assessment, see Childs, ibid., Ch. 1.
5. R.F. Starr, *Communist Regimes in Eastern Europe*, pp. 82-3, calls it a 'forced merger'.
6. Childs, *East Germany*, pp. 27-8, and p. 16.
7. Starr, *Communist Regimes*, p. 84.
8. Childs, *East Germany*, pp. 29-30; quoting S. Haffner in *Survey* (October, 1962) p. 44.
9. McCauley, *Marxism–Leninism*, p. 74-9; see also Childs, *East Germany*, pp. 31-5.
10. M.K. Dziewanowski, *The Communist Party of Poland*, p. 169. This author suggests that the PPR had found its main supporters in the ghetto and that the

arrests were the result of inter-party struggle, as was the capture by the Gestapo of Finder in the autumn of 1943.

11. Dziewanowski, ibid., pp. 175-7. See also A. Polonsky and B. Drukier, *The Beginnings of Communist Rule in Poland*.

12. See J. Ciechanowski, *The Warsaw Rising*.

13. For the figures and other information see Dziewanowski, *Communist Party*, Ch. 10 and 11, and Starr, *Communist Regimes*, p. 133.

14. Dziewanowski, *Communist Party*, pp. 217-8.

15. I have discussed this in Ch. 10 of *The Green Flag*.

16. Dziewanowski, *Communist Party*, p. 231. Dziewanowski incorrectly describes it as the 8th Plenum. This was held in October 1956.

17. E. Taborsky, *Communism in Czechoslovakia*, pp. 6-7.

18. Ibid., p. 11. As Taborsky was Benes's secretary, his evidence may not be unbiased. But there is confirmation that Stalin preferred to deal with non-communist leaders in general.

19. Ibid., p. 17.

20. Starr, *Communist Regimes*, p. 64, quoting official party figures.

21. G. Golan, 'The Road to Reform', *Problems of Communism*, May–June (1971), p. 12.

22. Taborsky, *Communism*, p. 20, quoting H. Ripka, *Le Coup de Prague* (Paris, 1949), pp. 58-9.

23. O. Sik, 'The Economic Impact of Stalinism', *Problems of Communism*, May–June, 1971, p. 4.

24. Taborsky, *Communism*, p. 106.

25. Ibid., pp. 106-7.

26. F. Fejto, *A History of the People's Democracies*, p. 45.

27. Taborsky, *Communism*, Ch. 6.

9

Communism in Western Europe, 1944-56

Initial Moves

While in Eastern Europe the newly established People's Democracies were eradicating non-communist parties the position of the communist parties in Western Europe was very ambiguous. During the war some parties (most notably the French and the Italian) had gained great prestige through their participation in the Resistance movements. Others gained influence by association, like the British Communist Party which, while numerically insignificant in comparison with the Labour Party, almost took the mantle of Soviet victory in the war on its own shoulders. Some communist parties were encouraged by their own governments to increase their membership in order to prove loyalty to the Soviet Union — this was the case of Finland. In the Iberian Peninsula the survival of the fascist dictatorships after the war meant that the Communist Party of Spain and of Portugal were still illegal. In West Germany the KPD was reinstated under Allied influence in 1945 as an anti-fascist party (it was made illegal as incompatible with the 'fundamental and democratic order' in 1956. and re-established in 1969), but it never regained the following it had had before Nazism. In 1932 it ranked as the third largest party, after the Social-Democrats and the Nazis. Hitler's massacre of German Communists, swiftly followed by Stalinist purges, removed the majority of the leadership and a great many rank-and-file members. Natural wastage did the rest. Post-Nazi Western Germany, still dominated by Nazi officialdom and affected by Soviet policies towards Germany, had little wish to vote Communist. In the 1949 elections the KPD gained 5.7 per cent of the votes; in 1953 this declined to 2.2 per cent.[1] The revival of the party in 1969 did little to improve its electoral chances, for by then the far Left had already gained a large following among the disaffected. In a way, the banning of the KPD during the crucial years of West German development probably also helped the growth of violent left-wing radicalism, and may have been counterproductive. In Greece a desperate struggle between the Communists and non-Communists had ended the possible chance of a Communist regime on Yugoslav lines.

After the abortive Soviet attempt to set up a socialist republic in northern Iran in late 1945 and the defeat of the Greek Communist Party (both in line with the division of spheres of influence decided upon by the great powers during the war), the position of communist parties outside the Soviet bloc was completely subjected to the diplomatic moves on both sides. There would be no war — that was influenced by the fact that the USA had the ultimate weapon, which the USSR had not yet developed — but every effort was made, short of a war, to engage all political bodies in a propaganda effort to ensure a final victory. Such victory had never been achieved by either side, but it produced a series of diplomatic conflicts known as the 'Cold War' and a series of 'minor' localised military conflicts, such as the Korean War as well as non-military conflicts, like the Berlin Blockade. Stalin's speech in February 1946, in which he spoke of a possible danger of a new war, was quickly followed by Churchill's 'Iron Curtain' speech of March 1946, and by the Truman doctrine of 'containment' formulated in March 1947. This was followed by the offer of Marshall Aid in June 1947 and its almost inevitable consequence: the tightening of the Soviet grip on Eastern Europe without a compensating economic policy which would have helped Eastern Europe to develop as swiftly as Western Europe was doing with American aid.

The first shot in the Soviet campaign was the founding of the Cominform in September 1947. All Eastern European communist parties with the exception of Albania were invited. The Greek and Chinese Communist parties were not asked, in line with the Soviet adhesion to the 'spheres of influence' agreement. Only the French and Italian parties were invited from Western Europe. At a meeting in a Polish mountain resort, Zhdanov, then in charge of Soviet ideological policy, outlined the position. He stated that the world had solidified into two blocs; the democratic camp, headed by the USSR, and the imperialist camp, headed by the USA. The USA, in an effort to avoid an economic crisis, had embarked on a policy of economic imperialism (a reference to the Marshall Plan) and would aim at establishing world supremacy. The Italian and

French communist parties would have to stand up for national independence. While the dissolution of the Comintern had proved that the Soviet Union had no wish to interfere in internal affairs of any countries, it was a mistake to think that it had withdrawn from international affairs: 'Some comrades understood the dissolution of the Comintern to imply the elimination of all ties, of all contact, between the fraternal Communist Parties. But experience has shown that such mutual isolation of the Communist Parties is wrong, harmful and, in point of fact, unnatural.'[2] Only the Yugoslavs were enthusiastic about the new body, particularly as they had proposed it in the first place, and as its site was to be Belgrade. (Apparently Prague was suggested in the first instance, but this was vetoed by Stalin.) Zhdanov became the Secretary-General of the Cominform and began to use methods of repression, which eventually led to the expulsion of Yugoslavia from the organisation, to Zhdanov's sudden death and to the failure of the Cominform itself. But the scene was set for a repetition of Soviet policy of the 1920s and 1930s: a mobilisation of public opinion in Western Europe and elsewhere in the world against the USA, against Marshall Aid and in favour of the peaceful and democratic policy of the Soviet Union. The French and Italian Communist parties were chosen to be the main spokesmen for this policy, participating willingly, as they were still smarting from the insult of having been deprived of their share of government.

The PCF and post-war policy

The bitterness in the PCF in 1947 was understandable. In 1944 the Communists may have been on the verge of acquiring power, possibly through the ballot box. The leadership under the direction of Thorez ordered extreme moderation. This was opposed by some local leaders; in 1952 Charles Tillon and André Marty were accused by the Central Committee of planning to seize power in France in September and October 1944. Marty denied this and 'claimed that the Party had not properly exploited the favourable conditions to destroy the power of Fascist remnants in France'.[3] It would have been perfectly legitimate for the Communists, once in government, to come to power with the help of 'anti-fascist' elements. Had power been gained by legitimate means there would have been little that either de Gaulle or the Americans could have done to oppose it, short of using force.

The PCF while relying for its main support on the urban proletariat — its traditional ally — was also keen to win the support of the farmers through an agrarian reform, of the armed services through supporting their claims to more participation in government and to become a mass party. In a drive for new membership between January and April 1945 the membership increased from 400,000 to 600,000. Nevertheless, the PCF suffered many obstacles in its policy. Its FTP organisation was dissolved on direct orders from de Gaulle, and so was the Communist militia, this time on orders from Thorez. Its policy of exacting vengeance[4] seemed to hit out more at former Communists than at collaborators with the Nazis or Vichy. Even more damaging may have been the Communist support for nationalisation of trusts and monopolies. While the leadership underlined its support for private property on a smaller scale, it had a difficult task to assure the small French proprietor that his property was safe.

In the elections to the National Assembly held in October 1945 the Communist candidates, adopting a programme of separation of Church and State, with a powerful parliament and local assemblies, received more than a quarter of all votes cast. Together with their allies, the united resistance groups (MURF) they held 159 seats in the new Assembly. The next few years saw the usual spectacle of several missed chances of creating a Communist–Socialist government. The Communist lack of credibility did not become apparent (despite the efforts of the MRP and the Socialists to make it so right from the start) till the problem of Vietnam occurred in late 1946. Under the dual pressure of establishing its position on Vietnam (patriotism would dictate the acceptance of a war, Soviet policy demanded opposition) and of adopting a position on wage-fixing, the Communists were unable to maintain their policy of co-operation within the government. In May 1947, after hesitation and refusal to resign, the Communist ministers were dismissed by the prime minister. Their period of participation lasted three years and one month.

Having been excluded from the French government, the PCF then had to suffer condemnation from 'fraternal' communist parties. At the meeting to set up the Cominform in Szklarska Poreba, Duclos and Fajon, the PCF delegates, were accused by Zhdanov on behalf of the new body of having committed grave errors, of being infiltrated by right-wing revisionism, of having allowed de

Gaulle to eliminate the French Resistance movement and of being outmanoeuvred by the Socialists. As these measures were apparently taken by the PCF after consultation with the CPSU, the accusations (if true) were clearly formulated with a view to a change in course.[5] At a meeting of the Central Committee of the PCF in October 1947 Thorez announced that the PCF would embrace the Zhdanov line.

While the PCF suffered almost immediate setbacks in the next municipal elections, it gained power in a much more important organisation: in April 1948 the trade union organisation, the CGT, split, and the Socialist minority created a splinter group: the CGT–FO. The Communists now became the main element in the sydicalist movement in France and critics such as Raymond Aron remarked in 1948 that: 'The force of the Communist Party is not so much the number of its membership … as the authority it exercises through the intermediary of the CGT, upon the working masses.'[6] A wave of strikes which occurred in late 1947 solidified the support of the urban proletariat for the PCF without the PCF gaining much tangible profit from it.

In the meantime, the PCF was beset by internal problems. Thorez had to go to Moscow for treatment for a stroke in October 1950 and did not return till April 1953, soon after Stalin's death. His post was taken by August Lecoeur who had made himself unpopular, and was first denounced in 1952 and then removed from leadership in March 1954. The Marty–Tillon affair shook the party leadership in December 1952. The return of Maurice Thorez from Moscow helped to close the party ranks, but under the circumstances of confusion arising out of the death of Stalin the PCF's actions were unconvincing. This hesitant policy, now of supporting the ailing Fourth Republic, now of abstaining in a crisis, was well in line with the cautious Soviet policy emerging from the Stalinist era. So was the abandoning of the hardline policy in 1956; this was not so much in response to the obvious failure of the Fourth Republic as in response to the new Soviet policy of co-existence. However, the Communist support for the Fourth Republic came too late; in any case, it was not wanted. Most other parties insulted and ignored the Communists on purpose in order to avoid the epithet of 'fellow-travelling'.[7] In May 1958, the Communists defended the Republic together with Mendes-France and Mitterand, but it was of no avail. On 1 June 1958 329 deputies voted for de Gaulle, while only 229 voted against. The opponents included

Communist deputies and 49 Socialist deputies. The rationale for the assent was that if de Gaulle did not come to power there would be a military coup. However, the Communists were the only French party which was not split at this juncture – having failed on policy and on strategy, they still won on unity of action.[8]

The electoral law was modified by the Gaullist government to damage the PCF. In the 1956 elections the Communists got 25.7 per cent of the vote and 24 per cent of the seats; after the first elections in the Fifth Republic, they received 18.9 per cent of the vote and 2 per cent of the seats.[9] But there were other corollaries to the apparent weakness of the PCF in the Fifth Republic. The first concerns the fact that the PCF, unlike the PCI, refused to de-Stalinise. It supported the Soviet invasion of Hungary. It refused, at first, to accept the authenticity of Khrushchev's 20th Congress speech. It continued its cult of Thorez's personality. As Tiersky argues, it was the very fact of the continuity of leadership in the PCF, unparalleled in any other European party, which made it both Stalinist and immobile. The numbers of the membership fell from a high of 800,000 in 1946 to about 300,000 in 1956, and stabilised at this figure.[10]

The second is more important from the international point of view. The relegation of the PCF to the level of a conservative party was not distasteful to the Soviet leadership when it became apparent that de Gaulle wanted to disengage from the pro-American policy of the previous governments, when he ended the war in Algeria and when he withdrew from active participation in NATO. De Gaulle in power accomplished more from the Soviet point of view than the PCF would have done. Hence, Soviet relations with the Fifth Republic became cordial, and led both to the repudiation of former PCF policy and to the establishment of France as a 'neutral' power. In these circumstances, a strong and vital PCF would prove to be more harmful to Soviet policy than an old, conservative and discredited one. This led the Soviet government to soft-pedal its support of the PCF and to turn its attention to another major European party — the PCI.

The PCI after the war

While both the Italians and the French were invited to the founding meeting of the Cominform it was clear that the Italians were the 'younger brothers' in any considerations the Soviet Union may have had of a communist take over in Western Europe. First of all, the PCF was by far the older and more trusted than the PCI. Its leaders were well known to follow Soviet policy. It owed much of its growth to Soviet help, and geographically speaking, France was an easier and more realistic target than a Mediterrenean country. The PCI had had a long history of dissent; its leaders were 'intellectuals'; it was much more under the influence of historical and geographical factors (the Catholic Church and the US Fleet in the Mediterranean being only some of them); and finally, Italy's economic situation was much more chaotic and weaker than France's. In addition, the PCI had a following which was very localised; as Amendola points out, in 1946, 73 per cent of the party's support came from the centre and the north of Italy; 62 per cent of members came from the north; and 61 per cent of the members were of working class origin (45 per cent industrial workers and 17 per cent agricultural workers). In contrast, in the elections to the Constituent Assembly in Naples the PCI received only 8.1 per cent of the vote.[11]

The Communists left the Italian government in May 1947 and there followed what Amendola calls 'years of hard struggle'. The PCI was outside the government, without many resources, and had to impose particularly unpopular policies on its unwilling membership. The PCI's rejection of Marshall Aid was most unpopular in Italy, weakened economically to the point of no return. The propaganda against Italy joining NATO was opposed by all the other political parties. Thus the PCI had to contend with the Church, most other political parties (with whom it had worked harmoniously during the war) and with many sections of the population, whose reliance on Marshall Aid had little to do with politics and everything to do with necessity. On 14 July 1948 there was an attempted assassination of Togliatti. In the aftermath of bitter accusations, the trade-union organisation split into several sections, making it much less effective.

One major success could be claimed by the PCI: that it supported the workers' demands for higher wages and organised sit-down strikes in factories in the north at the time of de Gasperi's deflationary policy, and that it organised and supported the landless peasants of the south in their land seizures in the period of 1949-50.[12] Otherwise the prospects were not very good. The 1948 elections held in April were disappointing. Fighting on a common

Socialist–Communist programme under the name of Popular Front, the Communists and Socialists received 31 per cent of the vote to the Christian Democrats' 48.5 per cent. Various interpretations have been read into this defeat: the elections came soon after the Communist coup in Czechoslovakia, which frightened the voters; the Catholic Action mobilised all its resources against a Communist victory; the subsidies which the Christian Democrats received from America were bigger than those which the Left received from the Cominform; and so on. One writer even maintains that voting was influenced by a flood of letters from Americans of Italian origin writing to their relatives advising them to vote for Christian Democracy against Communism.[13]

However, the PCI was in a better position than the PCF in many respects. As Claudin points out, in the first place, it could rely on the support of the majority Socialist Party; second, while 'Like the PCF, the Italian party devoted all the attention demanded by the Cominform to campaigns for peace and the banning of the atomic bomb, against the Marshall Plan and the Atlantic Pact; it was nevertheless able to view the specific problems of Italian society with a certain rigour, even while retaining the reformist outlook of the previous period'.[14] Togliatti even tried to distance himself somewhat from the Cominform, stating at the 6th Congress of the PCI in January 1948 that the party had a purely consultative relationship with this body.

The defeat of the Greek Communists in August 1949 probably helped to moderate the PCI's stance; the Greeks were totally ignored by the Cominform and the USSR in their struggle against royalist forces while the royalists had massive support from the West. If Greece was outside the Soviet sphere of influence, the Italians may have reflected, where does it leave Italy? Nevertheless, Togliatti's stand had some ambiguities in it. According to Claudin, in February 1949, a few weeks before the signature of the Atlantic Pact, Thorez was asked what would the PCF do if the Soviet army invaded Paris, and replied: 'More or less .... that the French workers would welcome them with open arms. A few days later Togliatti was asked a similar question about Italy, and gave the same answer.'[15]

On the other hand, while Thorez and the PCF took a. leading part in the anti-Tito crusade after 1948 the PCI expressed a more muted view of the Titoist phenomenon and the purges in all Eastern European parties which followed Yugoslavia's expulsion from the Cominform. One may assume that the PCI's policy was both ambiguous and unclear, and that in the main it was opportunistic. On the other hand, the policies of the successive Christian–Democratic and coalition governments were becoming extremely sterile and the corruption, which was increasing, put many voters off their 1948 choice. The result was that in the 1953 elections there was a decided swing to the left, with the Communists increasing their share of the votes over the Socialists by almost 4 per cent. In the period of 1946 to 1953 the PSI lost more than 1,330,000 votes and the PCI gained about two million.[16]

The Basic Differences between Eastern and Western European Communist Parties

It is well worth considering at this point what made the situation so different in the attitudes of communist parties in Western and Eastern Europe. The obvious reason — the presence of Soviet armies and active encouragement of communism in the Soviet sphere of influence — is quoted by many Western historians as the main factor in the introduction of 'people's democracies' in Eastern and South-eastern Europe, whereas the presence of American troops and influence in Western Europe impeded such a process.

This explanation is too simplistic. It does not allow for the continuation of communism in Albania, for the development of a Socialist Federation in Yugoslavia, and for the continued growth of communist parties in Italy and France, despite many political setbacks. On the other hand, it assumes that the Eastern European countries have become totally subservient to the USSR, and that their people were enslaved by the system. While it has been demonstrated that during the early period after the war, and at the height of Stalinist oppression, a great deal of force had been used in Eastern Europe, it is also clear that with some exceptions (as in Poland, where more force was used to eliminate the political and military supporters of the London government in exile than the opposition within the party itself) most of the tactics were directed at the communist parties themselves. The violent tactics employed against internal dissenters surpassed by far tactics used against any opposition. Indeed, in some countries, the opposition parties, e.g. large sections of the Socialists, were incorporated into the new united left-wing party without much struggle.

It would be more realistic to concentrate on other factors. The main one which appears to have made the difference in attitudes is that in Eastern and South-eastern Europe there was a classical situation of underdevelopment combined with strong national trends. The student of history is well acquainted with the fact that most of the countries created or recreated by the Treaty of Versailles were unable to manage their economies under the new conditions and were forced to stress the national factor to account for the existence of their states. This condition, variously described as 'fascism', 'chauvinism' or 'dictatorial tendencies', was really the index of impotence. The gap between the classes in those countries, while not as great as that in Russia in 1917, was big enough to create a feeling of two nations. The wartime eradication of large sections of the middle classes, together with the elimination of the Jewish population, created a new social situation which, together with the economic privations, prepared the ground for radical changes.

It is safe to say that, had the Soviet armies not intervened in those areas, a new social and economic system would have been essential in any case. It may well be that the system which was imposed was not in any way better than the previous one, but it seemed to offer two things — a radical economic and social adjustment and the bolstering of national pride — which those countries badly needed after the war. Therefore in Eastern and South-eastern Europe the adoption of socialist systems had much more to do with the failure of previous systems than with Marxist doctrine. It also came at a time when the USSR was at its most nationalistic stance after the victory in the Second World War, and it is notable that nationalism became the vogue in all the countries in the Eastern bloc, particularly during the period of the purges. The re-allocation of wealth appeared to come at an appropriate time, the shake-up of the social classes had already happened and the nationalist policies pleased a large majority of the population. It is very likely that had the economic side of the system worked, and had religion been tolerated, these governments would have encountered much less opposition than was the case. Unfortunately, they came to grief on those very points, and their problems stemmed from them, rather than from political illiberalism or pro-Soviet policies.

On the other hand, in Western Europe there was a classical situation of developed economies combined with a dislike of the

nationalism which had produced Mussolini and Hitler. As there
was a distrust of Soviet intentions in Eastern Europe so in Western
Europe, and particularly in Latin countries, there was a distrust of
American motives. There was little chance that the Soviet armies
would intervene to support the introduction of communist
governments; but there was a strong suspicion that the Americans
would endeavour to stop any growth of communism. This
combination of economic and political development, disenchantment with nationalist policies of previous governments, and the
distrust of US intentions, virtually encouraged the growth of
communism.

The communist parties in Western Europe were in effect a
protest vote, but a protest vote with a difference: realism dictated
that Western Europe was better off than Eastern Europe, but
idealism and a hankering for radical change suggested that support
for the USSR would improve the situation. This explains why the
communist parties all over Western Europe refused to see the
harm of Stalinism: the USSR was the only power capable of
opposing the USA, and the USA was the epitome of chauvinistic
capitalism which the European Left had come to dislike so much.

Hence, in Western Europe the communists were, at this stage of
development, very much in the Marxist mould: in favour of
socialist economic measures, internationalist-minded and devoted
to the ideology of a disciplined vanguard party, which would bring
about the dictatorship of the proletariat. The nationalist trend
which was so fashionable in the USSR and Eastern Europe had
little appeal to the Italian and French Communists. Directions
from Moscow were followed not because they came from Moscow,
or even because of financial subsidies but because these parties
honestly believed that there was no alternative. Stalinist purges
and trials were taken at their face value not because the Communists
practised self-delusion but because questioning them would
undermine the very basis of their ideology. Anyone who disbelieved
Stalin denied Marxism, and there was no room for such people in
the communist parties.

To sum it up, therefore, in the period of 1944-56 a strange
phenomenon occurred in Europe: in the Socialist bloc a brand of
radical nationalism was practised under the name of communism,
whereas in the West, Stalinism was accepted as the theoretical
mantle of Marxism. Neither the practice in the East nor the theory
in the West had much to do with socialism as Marx had envisaged

it, but then Marx had not envisaged a Europe such as had emerged from the Second World War. In this way, conditions of the moment had reshaped a theory, and necessities had modified practice. One constant factor in this situation were the human attitudes: both in the West and in the East, the quest for power or for perfectability of human nature was as operative as it had been in the nineteenth century. It is to this factor that the further developments must be attributed.

Notes

1. M. Salvadori, *The Rise of Modern Communism*, p. 104
2. Quoted by R.F. Rosser, *An Introduction to Soviet Foreign Policy*, p. 250: full text in A.E. Adams (ed.) *Readings in Soviet Foreign Policy*, 1961.
3. A.J. Rieber, *Stalin and the French Communist Party 1941-1947*, p.152.
4. Ibid., p. 166 and pp. 177-83.
5. E. Reale (ed.), *Avec Jacques Duclos*: quoted by R. Tiersky, *French Communism 1920-72*, p.164
6. R. Aron, *Le grand schisme*, p. 191: see also Tiersky, *French Communism*, p. 171
7. Tiersky, ibid, p. 178 and note 38.
8. Figures from D. Pickles, *The Fifth French Republic*, p. 23
9. Tiersky, *French Communism*, p. 185.
10. Ibid., pp. 181-3.
11. G. Amendola, *Gli Anni della Republica*, pp. 134-5.
12. Ibid., pp. 105-6.
13. G. Mammarella, *L'Italia dopo il Fascismo*, p. 184
14. F. Claudin, *The Communist Movement*, p. 478.
15. Ibid., p. 585, quoted from *La Nouvelle Critique* (1953) and the Russian edition of *Togliatti's Speeches* (1965).
16. Mammarella, *L'Italia*, p. 283.

Part three:

The New Regional Dimension

10
Communism in Asia: the Far East

Introduction

In a book written in 1938-9, an American analyst wrote the following: 'Communism professes to aim at a world-state; but can one consider a unified world Communism as even remotely possible? Efficient bureaucratic planning of the economy of the entire world; subjection of all races and nationalities to a single international dictatorship; equalization of living standards throughout the world: countries with rich natural resources and developed industries being placed on a level with the poverty-stricken population of Asia: this is what a Communist world-state would involve.' And he added further: 'As long as different parts of the world differ from each other in their natural resources and in the living standards of their populations, the inhabitants of poorer countries would ... have economic motives for war. As... the mineral resources of the world decrease, the struggle to obtain control over them will become more intense. A Communist Germany would have the same economic motives as a Fascist Germany for acquisition of the natural resources of southeastern Europe. A Communist Japan would have the same economic motives as a Fascist Japan for expansion into China.'[1] This author further points out that Marx himself did not expect the richer nations to surrender their wealth for the benefit of poorer ones any more than he expected the capitalists to surrender their wealth to the proletariat without a struggle.

However, in some societies or nations, the element of choice had never entered into consideration. This applies, in general, to the areas which are poor in natural resources, which do not enjoy an equable climate and where population tends to be too large for such resources as exist. The relation of climate to government has only been explored to a limited extent; very often an attempt was made to relate racial characteristics to types of government rather than to resources available. Yet in historical studies examples abound of the same nations or tribes being ruled savagely and behaving in a savage way when poor and becoming mild and pacifist when they became rich. In this equation, the Asian nations must figure very importantly. While some areas of Asia were always very rich others were poor or had become poor through a population explosion or diminution of resources. These countries which were still rich, but had a small or un-warlike population, usually succumbed to the onslaught of the poor but desperate. The examples of Chinese incursions into the Indo-Chinese Peninsula or of Japan attacking China in search of resources are only some instances of this. One keen observer propounded a theory of 'hydraulic civilisations' which need a wide network of irrigational systems and which must be supported by a well-developed bureaucracy with strong powers in order to distribute the scarce water. The priest–king, with his hierarchical priestly bureaucracy supported by a large military force, enforces such distribution in the name of a religious belief.[2]

Marx himself recognised this when he applied his theories to developed, industrial countries of the West, and treated agrarian countries, like Russia, as a separate category. But he did treat the colonial trends of Western European states very seriously, and foresaw the colonial trend as the final stage of capitalism. Without questioning Marx's undoubted historical perspective, one must point out that this was limited, both in time and in space. The nineteenth century did not provide sufficient examples of the future trends, both in mobility and in development, to revise his theories. One can speculate, however, that, had he lived in the twentieth century, he would have seen that this theory, while correct in itself in the context of the nineteenth century, would need to be developed to allow for post-colonial stages in non-industrial countries. Lenin did begin to see the need for adding (if not revising) to Marxist theory, when he turned his attention, after the acquisition of power in Russia, to colonial peoples. But he did not see far enough.

Towards the end of the twentieth century the issues are clearer. 'Revisionism', somewhat as Bernstein foresaw it, is not dead. On the contrary, it has become established both in the mixed economy countries of Western Europe and in state-socialist countries like the USSR. But the terms of 'dictatorship of proletariat' and 'eradication of the exploiting classes' could be transferred very easily to those countries where poverty was rife, where the masses were ruled by a small elite, and where discipline was inculcated through the operation of the 'hydraulic system'. In the twentieth century this applied particularly to China, where formerly the ruler was 'the supreme authority both in secular and religious matters'[3] and where European, American and Japanese colonialism made savage, though fractionated, inroads into an ancient and rigid system.

Nevertheless, in the absence of an easy means of communication, such as a simple written language which everybody could read, and in view of the large distances as much as the rigid social and religious systems (stemming from isolation within the country and its separate provinces), Marxism was not easy to propagate. Similar obstacles prevailed in other Asian countries. For this and related reasons, the introduction of socialism and communism in Asia was in the hands either of European organisers or of those native communists who had acquired the knowledge at first hand in Europe, or by way of transfer of knowledge through a European-educated Asian. Hence Asian communism has always suffered not only from the distortion of Marxist theory, which was developed for industrial countries, but also from the application of such theories by people who expected it to work in the same way in Sri-Lanka as in Germany. To say that the industrialisation which communism would promote would do away with these problems is to neglect the many centuries of an agrarian theocratic civilisation which had formed these nations.

To take but a few examples: in China, the Communist Party was founded in Shanghai, the most foreign of all cities, in July 1921 by agents of the Comintern, who were mostly Russian. The party secretary, Mao Zedong was under the influence of his teacher and father-in-law, a 'Westerniser', who wanted to do away with most of the Chinese tradition. His colleagues, Zhou Enlai and Chu Teh, were educated in Europe. In Indonesia (then Dutch East India), the first Asian communist party was founded in 1920 by a small group of Dutchmen, but it never took root. In Sri-Lanka (then Ceylon) the first formal Marxist movement was founded in 1932, when a mill workers' union was formed, and was in the following year joined by Western-educated intellectuals to become in 1935 the *Lanka Sama Samaja* Party, which embraced socialists, communists and nationalists. Examples such as these can be quoted throughout Asia.

Communism, as expounded by the Comintern in the 1920s and 1930s, was inexplicable to the Asian masses and impossible to impose. Mao himself wrote in 1928: 'Wherever the Red Army goes, the masses are cold and aloof and only after our propaganda do they slowly move into action.'[5]

Its successes only came after the theory had been applied to specific conditions in each Asian country, when it was allied to a struggle to take away land from the large landlords, to equalise wealth and, perhaps most importantly, to repel the invaders (as with the Japanese in China), or to expel the colonial powers (as in the Indo-Chinese Peninsula). Hence, Asian communism had never had the purity of even Russian communism, its growth was sporadic and unnatural in Marxist terms, and was only assisted by the traditional patterns of obedience and the disruption of these into new patterns of discipline. The main moving force of Asian communism was not to increase international relations between the proletariat and improve the standard of living of the proletariat — it was to remove colonialism, to distribute land and to raise the standard of living of the peasant masses.

There are further differences in Asian communism. Though the early communist leaders in Asia were usually Westernised intellectuals who could be described as 'cosmopolitan', they were, as one writer has noted, not only 'marginal intellectuals' but also removed from the mainstream of their own intellectual community. 'And such an intellectual heritage as did exist in the earlier days began to decline almost uniformly as Asian communism moved from the salon and the university into the streets, and from the urban centres into the countryside.'[6] This author also comments on the fact that lack of consensus-based politics, very localised politics and the urban–rural gap have all contributed towards making Asian communism far nearer to nineteenth-century American populism, whose leaders were 'a figure born out of the mixed, contradictory strains characteristic of a vast region in rapid transition, where the frustrations caused by low levels of "progress" combine with the tensions resulting from an uneven and differentiated process of development favouring the urban over the rural regions.'[7] Other problems upon which Scalapino focuses include the need for guerrilla operators to depend both on peasants and on frontier minority tribes; the inherent Asian tradition of violence; and the dilemma facing the Communists on accession to power:

whether to urbanise the peasant masses — to make them resemble the Marxist pattern more — or to 'socialise' the peasants through the armed forces, at least till such time as industrialisation would complete the process.

While none of these problems are totally alien to Soviet and Eastern European conditions (and indeed some of them are very similar to those which faced the Bolsheviks in 1917), the difference of dimension comes in one factor — colonialism. If communism were alien to the Asian masses, so was nationalism as understood by the Europeans. The Chinese suffered from xenophobia, which is not to be confused with nationalism. The Japanese were isolationist from fear, not from nationalism. The Indians were used to invaders for centuries, and had absorbed them without trouble. Similarly, the Indo-Chinese Peninsula had been invaded by neighbours over a long period of time. Just as communism could only be made interesting for the urban proletariat so nationalism, the second arm of the Comintern propaganda, could only appeal to the urban intellectuals. In rural areas, the propaganda could only be directed at local grievances, something the peasants would understand. In its efforts to create a new political culture, the communist party in any Asian country was faced with all those problems. What seemed suitable for nineteenth-century Europe (and proved difficult to operate in twentieth-century USSR) was difficult to apply to Asia.

On the other hand, one may ask whether these Asian societies, often incorrectly described as backward, had an alternative to communism if they wished to modernise rapidly. While modernisation need not necessarily take the shape of rapid industrialisation it must be pointed out that the older communist governments — such as the Chinese — have attempted to play it from 'both ends', so to speak, and to introduce at times rapid industrialisation, at others a return to the land; and that this has in turn been taken up by new regimes (such as the Pol Pot government in Kampuchea , where the return to the land was both massive and compulsory) and that in both cases the results have been, by and large, appalling. It may well be that communism could be accepted by the Asians and could be adapted to an agrarian culture. It may even be that in form it is a more suitable system for the 'collectivist'-minded Asian peasants than for the individualist European workers. It may be the only system which would, in the end, remove the spectre of death from famine or violence from the majority of

Asian peasants. But so far, appropriate conditions in Asia have been missing. The continent suffers from the results of de-colonialisation, and its corollary: a disastrous population explosion. This, coupled with the breakdown of traditional patterns of government, religion and continuous military conflicts has not produced conditions for testing such a system.

It seems certain that Marx's assertion that colonial countries must first undergo a nationalist period before becoming communist was perfectly correct. What has been witnessed over the last thirty years is the imposition of military regimes which profess to a variety of Marxist beliefs onto a traditional peasant society. In such conditions, it is impossible to assess success or lack of success. A country may be 'ripe' for a nationalist revolution and totally 'unripe' for a communist one. Hence the criticisms of all the aspects of Asian states where a form of communism is said to have been introduced have a totally false basis. And from there spring the disasters not only of the 'cultural revolution' in China and of 'de-urbanisation' in Kampuchea, but of the whole problem of instability in Asia. The longest established communist regime is that in China. It is with China that this chapter will now deal.

The rise of the Chinese Communist Party

It may be appropriate to begin here with the fact that even the setting up of the CPC is not well documented. One source states that 'It was founded in China in 1921, and almost simultaneously in France among the Chinese students in Paris. The first leader, Ch'en Tu-hsiu, was a well-known man of letters and Professor of the Peking National University. ... Among the founders were Mao Tse-tung, then a library assistant in Ch'en's university, and, among the Paris group, Zhou Enlai. Chu Teh, an older man ... had ... gone abroad and, in Germany, became a Communist.'[8] On the other hand, Schram, Mao's biographer, maintains that early in 1920 the first emissary of the International, Voitinskiy, arrived in Beijing, received an introduction to Ch'en Tu-hsiu in Shanghai, and the result was the creation in March in Beijing of a Marxist society. The nuclei of the Communist Party were established in Shanghai in May and in Beijing in September. However, he adds: 'There is some dispute over whether the Shanghai group was merely one group amongst others (seven in all by the beginning of

1921) or *the* Chinese Communist Party in embryo, and consequently over whether the founding of the party should be dated May 1920 or July 1921, when the First Congress was held."[9]

However, the Bolsheviks were not very interested in the Chinese Communists in any case. From 1918 onwards, Lenin had been making efforts to establish relations both with the conservative government in Beijing and with the revolutionary government of Sun Yat-sen. Lenin had realised the importance of Asia after 1905, when he wrote:

> Following the 1905 movement in Russia, the democratic revolution spread to the whole of Asia — to Turkey, Persia, China. Ferment is growing in British India. A significant development is the spread of the revolutionary democratic movement to the Dutch East Indies .... World capitalism and the 1905 movement in Russia have finally aroused Asia ... The awakening of Asia and the beginning of the struggle for power of the advanced proletariat of Europe are a symbol of the new phase in world history that began early this century.

In 1921, referring to Sun Yat-sen's revolution, Lenin asked:

> Does that mean that the materialist West has hopelessly decayed and that light shines only from the mystic, religious East? No, quite the opposite. It means that the East has definitely taken the Western path, that new hundreds of millions of people will from now on share in the struggle for the ideals which the West has already worked out for itself. What has decayed is the Western burgeoisie, which is already confronted by its grave-digger, the proletariat. But in Asia there is still a bourgeoisie capable of championing sincere, militant, consistent democracy, a worthy example of France's great men of the Enlightment and great leaders of the close of the eighteenth century.[10]

Lenin then added that in China the revolution led by Sun Yat-sen was nearer to the Populist programme than to the Bolshevik one and that a long period would elapse before the abolition of the bourgeoisie would be possible.

After the Bolshevik Revolution the Chinese welcomed the Soviet envoys in China. Of these, the most important were Leo Karakhan, the assistant Commissar of Foreign Affairs, Adolf Joffe, an established Soviet diplomat, and Michael Borodin. The issues between Soviet Russia and China were complex and related to the Chinese Eastern Railway, the Trans-Siberian Railway, the status of Outer Mongolia and the problem of Manchuria. There were also other matters either related to the above, or to long-standing grievances. On top of these problems, revolutionary China was being ignored by other European countries and the USA, who refused to give up their extra-territorial privileges.

The Bolshevik envoys performed the following services for Sun Yat-sen's new republic: Karakhan signed a treaty with China in March 1924, recognising each other's governments, abrogating Russia's extra-territorial rights, settling the status of Outer Mongolia as in Chinese suzerainty and ceding the Chinese Eastern Railway to China. Joffe had long conferences with Sun Yat-sen, assuring him that the Russians had no intention of introducing the Soviet system into China and 'that the chief and immediate aim of China is the achievement of national union and national independence'; and finally, Borodin became the 'instructor and re-organizer' of the Kuomintang, making it into a party organised on the lines of the CPSU, but without its political content. He also organised the training of Chinese officers, setting up a military academy with the help of Soviet finances and officers. Sun Yat-sen was particularly pleased with Borodin's achievements, and when some 'Americans once asked Sun Yat-sen what was Borodin's real name, "His name is Lafayette" he replied'.[11] Sun Yat-sen died in 1925 and the relations between China and USSR lost their previous cordiality.

However, the Russians scrupulously avoided the mention of any 'sovietisation' of China and the CPC co-operated with the KMT forces till the revolution of 1926, after which Chiang Kai-Shek who took over from Sun, organised an anti-Communist coup in Shanghai. On 26 March 1927 Chiang had as many Communist leaders killed as could be found. One who escaped, by chance, was Zhou Enlai: 'The Communist party was cast out, driven from power and proscribed; the Russian advisers sent back to Moscow'. The Communists seemed to be finished: 'The workers of the great cities could be, and were, suppressed. The Communists were driven from power, but on 1st August 1927, a part of the Fourth Army, one of the best fighting units, mutinied at Nanchang and, led by its Communist officers, formed the Red Army. The revolution was not over, it had taken to the hills.'[12]

This account overlooks a great many problems which the

Communist forces were facing both *vis-à-vis* the KMT and the Soviet leadership. The chaotic situation in China will probably never allow us to know every detail of the abortive uprising, and Soviet sources are ambiguous. The problem was that the Left Opposition, with Trotsky and Radek at its head, had been opposing the support for the KMT for a long time; after Chiang's eradication of the Communists they felt that they had been justified in their stand. The Stalinist faction, on the other hand, felt that the KMT was a much stronger party, and that even if support for it was ideologically unjustified, the admission that it had been wrong to support it would weaken Stalin considerably. Hence the Russians continued to play an ambiguous role for a long time to come, which had two distinct results: it laid down the basis for Mao's distrust and dislike of the USSR and it led him to develop his own theory of communist power in China. Both were to be of utmost importance for the future.

While the Nangzhang revolt was going on, Mao had been sent to Hunan, to organise the September 'Autumn Harvest' uprising. On its failure, he assembled a remnant of his forces (about a thousand men) and led them to the mountains of Chingkangshan, where he allied with two bandit chiefs and added more men and rifles to his forces.[13] By 1928 Mao joined forces with the main body of the army under Chu Teh and on 20 May 1928 the First Party Congress of the Border Area was held at Maobing near Ninggang, when Mao was elected as the secretary of the Special Committee (executive committee of the party).

From 1929 onwards Mao developed a new strategy in regard to promoting communism in China. Although there is some mystery about his actual involvement and his responsibility for this strategy in the first instance[14] there is no doubt that at a later stage Mao himself claimed that he had devised the new tactics. Indeed, this seems to be very likely in view of the circumstances in which the Communist forces found themselves dependent on local peasants for support and separated from the city proletariat, which was, in any case, not particularly interested in the Communist cause after the failure of the Communist uprisings in 1928.

The strategy had been described by Liu Shaoqi in 1946 and in 1949 in the following terms:

Mao Tse Tung's great accomplishment has been to change Marxism from a European to an Asiatic form.... China is a semi-feudal, semi-colonial country in which vast numbers of people live at the edge of starvation, tilling small bits of soil . . . . In attempting the transition to a more industrialised economy, China faces . . . the pressures . . . of advanced industrial lands. There are similar conditions in other lands of south-east Asia. The courses chosen by China will influence them all.

And in 1949 he re-asserted that: 'The way which has been followed by the Chinese people . . . is the way which should be followed by the peoples of many colonial and semi-colonial countries in their struggle for national independence and people's democracy'.[15]

The strategy was simple, though it appeared to be un-Marxist: the party began to look for support among the villagers instead of the urban proletariat, it changed itself from a party of theoretical Marxists into a party of rural revolutionaries and it committed a sin in Soviet eyes — it rose from success to success on this new policy. As a first stage, the new agrarian policy developed in 1929 provided that land should be confiscated only from large landlords and not from middle and poor peasants. In the period of 1937 to 1945 in order to strengthen resistance to the Japanese invaders land was confiscated from landlords who co-operated with the Japanese. After the defeat of the Japanese in 1945 the situation had changed. Mao wrote that 'today two big mountains lie like a dead weight on the Chinese people. One is imperialism, the other is feudalism.' By feudalism he meant the power of the landlords over the peasants, and by imperialism the penetration of China by foreign forces and commercial and industrial interests, and the power of the foreign countries to dictate to China.

Therefore in 1945 a new land reform movement was introduced in areas controlled by the Communists. Communist work teams were organised, which consisted of party members, peasant leaders and students, teachers and office workers from the cities. These teams were sent to the villages to guide the movement. The peasants were divided into the categories of poor, lower-middle, upper-middle and rich peasants. The first three categories comprised landless labourers and those with land but without surplus. The rich peasants were in the same category as the Russian 'kulaks'; they leased some of their land and lent money at a profit. Once this designation into classes was accomplished, the division of land was carried out on the following principles. The middle peasants retained their possessions and the rich peasants before 1949 (in the north, north-west and north-east) lost surplus land. However, in the fertile south this policy was modified after 1949 and the rich peasants were allowed to retain most of their land, as well as their homes and livestock. Large landlords had all their land confiscated and poor peasants were endowed with land according to their needs. The Chinese land reform had been described as 'tempestuous and uneven'. The number of victims who died as the result of the land division is unknown, but it runs into tens of thousands at the very least. It did have the effect of making the poor peasants the staunchest supporters of the Communist government. Not only had they been given land for the first time, but the Communist work teams lived in the countryside and became acquainted with the harshness of the peasants' lot for the first time. On their side, the peasants willingly embraced the creed which gave them a new status of full citizens.

Problems arose, however, after the CPC came to power. A demand was made in 1953 to grant the Four Freedoms: to rent land, to sell land, to hire labour and to lend money. Mao refused to accede to it and insisted on the creation of co-operatives. These were small at first, but they tended to benefit the richer peasants, while the poor peasants were no better off. In addition, there were constant arguments over the rights to water, which was essential in Chinese agriculture, and the problems of the upkeep of the irrigational canals. In keeping with the demands of 'hydraulic civilisation' in 1957 Mao ordered the amalgamation of small co-operatives into large ones. The old system of retaining private livestock, equipment and land was abolished and vested in the co-operatives. By the end of 1957 the whole of China was, at least nominally, totally collectivised and private property abolished.[16]

The CPC Seizes Power

The turning point in the fortunes both of Mao and the CPC was the 'Long March' of 1934, in which the Communist troops numbering some 100,000 men and cadres were led to the north-west of China, the Shensi-Gansu Provinces, in an attempt to evade both the KMT forces and the Japanese, whose invasion of mainland China had started in 1931.[17] In the autumn of 1935 Mao was given the newly created post of Chairman of the Politburo and was in control of the party, though the dissentions continued for a long time.

From then on till 1945 the war against the KMT troops and against the Japanese continued.[18] The Communist forces made their name by continuous and uninterrupted opposition to the Japanese, while Chiang and the KMT forces behaved in an ambiguous fashion.

While the CPC formed its own government, administration and armed forces in Yenan, and acquired battle experience and the admiration of the Chinese for its exploits, the KMT forces became weakened both through internal dissension and by lack of action against the Japanese. Yet when the Second World War ended, even Stalin did not ascribe much importance to their weakness within the country, and told Harry Hopkins 'that he did not regard the Chinese Communists as a serious factor and recognised only Chiang's government as that of China'.[19]

The reasons for the KMT's defeat between 1945 and 1949 have been interpreted variously. The KMT held on to the most fertile areas in China, they were supported by the Americans through their Japanese bases and they had ample armaments and supplies. Some authors point to the fact that the Americans had no trust in Nationalist forces — as witness George Marshall's advice in 1946, after the end of his abortive mission in China, to end the civil war. Others demonstrate that the Communists had cut China in half, controlled the routes between the north and the south and disabled the Nationalists in this way. Yet others point to the corruption of the Nationalists, compared with the honesty, devotion and hard work of the Communists. There is also the theory that the combination of Communist commanders forged during the Long March, and consisting of Mao Zedong, Lin Biao and Zhou Enlai, was so formidable as to preclude a Nationalist victory in the long run. No doubt all these theories have some basis in fact. But perhaps the most credible one is that developed by Fitzgerald, because it stems from experience of Chinese tradition and history:

In this last phase of the Chinese Revolution the ancient rule of Chinese history had been once more proved true. Only with the support of both the peasants and the scholars can revolution in China succeed . . . . The scholars were lost to the Kuomintang through its corruption, nepotism, misgovernment and inefficiency. They were won by the Communists, who in a long period of exile and hardship had learned to practise moderation, to govern honestly and to build a disciplined army. The Kuomintang had lost the road to democracy, and the Communists had travelled far from the pattern of the Russian Revolution. Thus the scholars and the peasants found they could give support to the Communists, and could not survive under the Kuomintang. Neither party offered the Chinese people democratic government. The ideals of 1911 were forgotten. The Chinese people looked now for a government which could govern ... in fact a modern version of the government under which they had lived for so many centuries.[20]

On 3 February 1949 the Communist army entered Beijing in full battle array; later in the spring the KMT forces evacuated to Formosa (renamed Taiwan) and the CPC formed its first national government on 1 October 1949.

The CPC may not have owed its victory to the Russians, and its Marxism may have departed from orthodoxy. Nevertheless, its initial period of power, and the period up to the Cultural Revolution, owed much to the Soviet example. The effect of land endowment on poor peasants had already been discussed above; it was not unlike the Soviet programme, though adapted to Chinese conditions. Similarly, the Communist attitude towards industry was very much modelled on the Soviet experience. In 1949 the government proceeded very carefully because of the need to start up production after the war. Only industries formerly owned by the Japanese and the KMT were nationalised. This was also extended to industries owned by foreign companies and by the Taiwanese emigrés. However, that sector comprised almost all heavy industries and those concentrated in the north-east. But other industrialists were allowed to retain their factories, and in Shanghai, which accounted for most of the industry in the south, about 50 per cent of industry remained in private hands.

Once established, the Communists began to change policy. Very much in the way Stalin had proceeded in 1928, the government started the 'Five Antis' campaign in 1952 and began to deprive industrialists of control over their enterprises, though they retained part of the profits and property rights. In 1953 the first Five-Year Plan was launched and the new constitution adopted in 1953 announced that there would be 'planned economic reconstruction and gradual transition to socialism'. However, the stress remained on gradual change, at least in theory. Again on the Soviet model, the FYP aimed to develop heavy industry but without Soviet excesses. Nevertheless, the industrialists were gradually deprived of their factories, though those of them who were not purged were retained as employees or directors of their former enterprises, again very much as in the Soviet Union.

The policy remained relatively steady till the 'Great Leap Forward' of 1958. The GLF was partly necessitated by the Sino–Soviet split and partly by Mao's sudden realisation that the Chinese people must be reshaped quickly, because their present poverty and ignorance would make it easier to effect their transformation towards socialism — again, very much in the vein of Soviet reasoning that 'the worse the better'. Some authorities claim that it was the conjunction of Khrushchev's 20th Congress speech, the revolution in Hungary, the withdrawal of Soviet technical help, the Chinese population explosion and the failure of previous collectivisation campaigns which made Mao opt for the GLF.

It is most likely that Mao's insistence on the GLF was not the result of considered calculations but the action of a man annoyed that it was easier to win a military victory than to win economic prosperity. Mao's actions from that period onwards fully confirm that he was becoming ever more erratic in judgement as he was becoming more powerful within the government. At this stage, some years after Mao's death, it can safely be said that many of China's economic and political problems have stemmed from the whims of an elderly man, unable to deal with the complexities of governing in the modern world — yet again a parallel with the last phase of Stalinism in the USSR.

The Great Leap Forward was intended to amalgamate agricultural co-operatives into much larger communes which would be self-contained units of production not only of agricultural products but also of manufactured goods. The accent was on the production of pig iron in small units, and these sprung up all over the countryside as well as in towns. In the cities, the inhabitants were encouraged to grow as much of their own food as possible and communal living and work were encouraged as much here as in the communes. The stress was on communality and the break-up of the family unit — still the strongest organisation in China. The GLF proved to be a complete failure, and by the end of 1958 was being quietly reversed while the 6th Plenum of the CPC in December voiced disapproval of its policies. In early 1959 a much more cautious economic policy began, but the harm had been done. The combined effect of irrational economic policies, bad harvests, peasant resistance to the communes and further Soviet withdrawal of economic and technical aid in 1960-1 dealt a traumatic blow both to the Chinese economy and to Mao personally. There was famine in large areas of China, malnutrition in others and only the application of military measures pacified the countryside. It was Lin Biao's leadership of the armed forces and his personal loyalty which managed to quell the disorders and restore order in the country.[21]

It was now necessary to find the culprits for the disasters. The propaganda machine was geared to persuade the people that the Great Leap Forward failed because of deliberate sabotage by class enemies. The campaign against class enemies was the direct precursor of the Cultural Revolution.

Maoism, Terror and the Cultural Revolution

Although much of the success of the CPC depended on Mao's charisma and the good reputation of the Communists, total control was not achieved without terror. In the first collectivisation campaign landlords were beaten up or put to death in order to show the peasants their powerlessness and, by implication, the power of the party. In 1950, with the beginning of the Korean War, China found herself at war with the USA against her will. The war brought about a large terror campaign against counter-revolutionaries, followed by the 'Thought Reform' movement. This was followed by the 'Three Antis' and 'Five Antis' campaigns.

In March 1951 large rallies were called in the cities at which counter-revolutionaries were sentenced to death; long lists of those executed appeared every day in newspapers. It is unknown how many were executed, as the figures vary from 135,000 executions to ten to fifteen million, though the generally accepted figure is about three million. The 'Thought Reform' campaign was directed against intellectuals to make them at one with the masses, to transform them through labour and to reshape their personalities. The Three Antis and Five Antis campaigns in 1951 and 1952 were more constructive: they put a stress on social utility rather than spiritual transformation. The Three Antis were corruption, waste and bureaucracy, and the campaign intended to purify the party cadres and state officials. Mass rallies were held where the guilty were denounced: some were purged, others merely warned. The Five Antis were bribery, tax-evasion, fraud, theft of government property and theft of economic secrets. This was directed against merchants and industrialists who were still operating their enterprises; they often had to confess to crimes in public and to pay large fines. Many committed suicide, others were executed or imprisoned.[22]

There was a slight relaxation during the first 'Hundred Flowers' campaign in 1956 and 1957, but at the end of 1957 another violent campaign started, directed against all intellectuals, teachers and university professors, many of whom were set to work in humiliating jobs or expelled to the countryside. Soon afterwards, the Great Leap Forward started and took its own toll of opponents, and as soon as this ended, the way was clear for the Cultural Revolution.

Some authors trace the origins of the Cultural Revolution to the criticism of Mao and the Great Leap Forward made by Marshal Peng Dehuai, the minister of defence, in mid-1959, an attack which apparently had the endorsement of a number of China's top economic and political leaders. At the Central Committee Plenum held in Lushan, the minister of defence suggested a large-scale programme of Soviet economic and military aid in place of self-help. Mao is said to have experienced a sense of shock and betrayal, and to have begun to doubt his old comrades-in-arms.[23] Other authors trace the origins to Lin Biao's struggle for succession,[24] or to Jiang Qing's pretensions to leadership.[25] There are also theories attributing the Cultural Revolution to the developments in Vietnam or to the sharpening of the Sino—Soviet conflict. No doubt all these had some basis in fact. However, it seems certain that the main reason was the failure of the Great Leap Forward and the growing criticism of Mao which followed it.

The disaster of the GLF created a great deal of dissidence within the party and criticisms of Mao. A second 'Hundred Flowers' campaign of liberalisation had to be introduced in 1961–2 to placate the intellectuals and technicians who had criticised the setting up of the communes and who now had to dismantle them. The campaign grew into numerous criticisms, although mindful of earlier purges, the critics clothed their complaints with historical allegories, the beloved 'Aesopian language' of Soviet critics.

One such critic, Deng Tuo, the secretary of the Beijing municipal committee, was later accused of criticising Mao in the Beijing press under a pseudonym, in the following terms: 'In the guise of recounting historical anecdotes, imparting knowledge, telling stories and cracking jokes . . . he launched an all-out venomous attack on our great party using ancient things to satirise the present, reviling one thing while pointing at another and making insinuations and oblique thrusts'. The gist of the criticism was as follows: Mao's foreign policy was riduculed, reconciliation with the Soviet Union was advocated and in domestic policy there were jibes at the GLF calling it 'indulging in fantasy' and 'substituting illusion for reality'. Deng insinuated that Mao himself was responsible for the tragic failures of China's domestic and foreign policies, alluding to him as boastful and conceited, and saying he was suffering from amnesia which could only be cured by hitting the patient over the head with a club.

The conclusion was clear: Mao was incompetent and should be replaced. Mao surveyed the scene and decided that a mass campaign of thought control would be necessary if he were to hold power for much longer. The first stage was the Socialist Education Campaign, launched at the Tenth Plenum of the CC in September 1962, when he emphasised the need to guard against intellectual dissidence ('writing novels to criticise the party'), the need to educate youth to follow in Maoist tradition ('revolutionary generation') and finally the need to re-establish socialist controls over the economy instead of going back towards private enterprise ('giving in to the bourgeoisie'). In May 1963 a campaign to eliminate harmful phenomena in literature was launched, and Mao stated that few writers and artists wanted to popularise socialist art, preferring to support reactionary art forms instead.

The problem of youth, particularly educated youth, was the greatest, as the failure of the GLF curtailed their job opportunities. The young were told to study the works of Mao as a corrective to their disillusionment. This campaign failed like the others, and persuaded Mao that coercion would be necessary. In the country-side the Poor and Lower Middle Peasant Committees were revived in order to prevent lapses towards individual farming. In December 1963 urban organisations began to be formed to stimulate socialism and to learn from the People's Liberation Army, in order to stimulate the revolutionary spirit of the urban proletariat. Thus the organisational work was laid down well before the start of the Cultural Revolution.

Finally, Mao imported political commissars from the People's Liberation Army to revitalise the party and government apparatus.

By 1965 some 200,000 political commissars were drafted into the civilian apparatus. And by September 1965 the Great Cultural Revolution began. This seemed to have been undertaken on the advice of Lin Biao, Zhou Enlai and Jiang Qing, and was launched by an attack on Beng Zhen, the Mayor of Beijing. While Beng and his associates resisted and gained temporary respite, a full-scale purification campaign against the party and PLA was launched early in 1966.

In April 1966 Lin Biao's military journal carried a full-scale call for the Cultural Revolution, emphasising the army's leading role in this. All intellectuals, artists, writers, teachers, scholars, professors and right-wing opportunists within the party were to be exposed. The first target of this campaign was again Beng Zhen, who was dismissed from his post in June. By June there was also a massive purge of journalists, writers, composers, publishers and editors, as well as the entire Party propaganda apparatus.

The main task, however, was to purge the educational system, particularly the universities, which Mao considered the breeding ground for discontent. A six-months' vacation was declared and the purge began, against professors as well as non-revolutionary students. Violence of the most crude kind was a basic ingredient of the campaign, with teachers being physically assaulted and often beaten to death by 'work teams' directing the purge. As there was little direction to this work, most people were attacked without much reason. As a result a new organisation, the Red Guards, was created in July with the 'right to rebel in order to oppose a revisionist leadership'. This provided the pattern for the whole of the country and for the rest of the Cultural Revolution.

In August Lin Biao was officially appointed Mao's successor and was put in charge of the Red Guards. The Red Guards were to be unknown young people, who would crush those in authority who had a capitalist mentality, who would criticise reactionary university authorities and who would transform all education to a socialist pattern. Membership of the Red Guards was confined to workers, poor peasants, revolutionary cadres and revolutionary martyrs. At the end of August, bands of young people began to attack individuals and institutions in a systematic way, ransacking homes and offices in search of incriminating evidence. Then the Red Guards were sent out to seek out dissidents among the party leadership, first in Beijing, then in the provinces. It was this step which broke up the Red Guards, for they were acting totally without leadership. 'The masses liberate themselves, and any method of doing things on their behalf must not be used.' The directives were passed directly to mass meetings of Red Guards in Beijing's main square by Mao, Jiang Qing and Zhou. Thus the party apparatus was bypassed and total anarchy initiated by the leaders.

In the provinces this resulted in a civil war when local organisations began to defend themselves against the onslaught of the newly arrived Red Guards. By mid-September a measure of control was reimposed, and Zhou announced that terror had gone too far. By early 1967 the campaign entered a new phase: power had to be handed over to the Army's revolutionary committees. In other words, anarchy was being eradicated, though it took a long time and was not always successful.

By January 1967 the campaign of the Red Guards had managed to antagonise almost everybody, and workers in many cities, particularly in Shanghai, went on strike, partly in opposition to the Red Guards and partly for better conditions of work. Widespread disorders and clashes followed almost everywhere. In February the army was ordered to take over from the Red Guards and they were ordered to go back to school. The PLA was also ordered to purge the Red Guards when they returned to schools. While there was a resurgence of leftist movements in April and May, by the end of May the PLA took over almost all the government and party offices and was running the country. Through the summer of 1967, however, disorders, renewed left-wing attempts to take over power and army and party attempts to introduce order continued. At the end of August foreign diplomats were manhandled in Beijing and the British mission was burned. This dramatic event spelled the beginning of the end of the Cultural Revolution.

Jiang Qing made a speech at the beginning of September calling for an end to violence. The purge of the party during this period was very extensive. About 80 per cent of CC members and provincial party secretaries had been purged. Their places were taken by army commanders. However, with or without support at the top, violence persisted. As late as the summer of 1968 there were reports of large-scale local civil wars and this was the time when hundreds of dead bodies were flowing into Hong Kong harbour, presumably victims of factional violence. Whole cities were reported to be in flames. Finally Mao put an end to violence by purging the Red Guards in late August 1968.

The cost to China in human life, misery and horror as well as in industrial and agricultural production will probably never be estimated. Yet it now seems that the Cultural Revolution was started merely to eliminate Liu Shaoqi and his supporters in order that Lin Biao might be a clear successor to Mao. In view of this, it is ironic that Lin Biao was to die soon after in an air accident, while Mao lived on for several years.[26]

Notes

1. H.B. Parkes, *Marxism, An Autopsy*, pp. 143 and 145

2. K.A. Wittfogel, *Oriental Despotism.*

3. Ibid., p. 95

4. C.S. Blackton, 'Sri Lanka's Marxists', in *Problems of Communism* (January-February, 1973).

5. S. Schran, *Mao Tse Tung*, p. 136.

6. R.A. Scalapino, 'Patterns of Asian Communism', in *Problems of Communism*, January-April (1971), p. 4

7. Ibid., p. 5

8. C.P. Fitzgerald, *The Birth of Communist China*, p. 59.

9. Schram, *Mao*, pp. 62-3

10. Quoted by F. Claudin, *The Communist Movement* p. 50: from Lenin, *Collected Works* (English edn), Vols.18 and 19.

11. L. Fisher, *The Soviets in World Affairs*, p. 461

12. Fitzgerald, *Communist China*, pp. 67-8.

13. Schram, *Mao*, pp. 126-7. Schram gives a detailed account of the dissension within the CPC, of its reaction to conflicting Soviet orders, and of Mao's disregard of such orders. He also comments on the inclusion of bandits in Mao's forces, which assured his survival, as they had built up traditional support in the country-side.

14. Schram, ibid., questions this closely, but finds it impossible to give a definitive opinion because of conflicting accounts.

15. Ibid., p. 254

16. For land reform, see J. Collier and E. Collier, *China's Socialist Revolution*, pp. 25-30.

17. The Long March and its reasons are well analysed by Schram, *Mao*, Ch. 7.

18. The campaigns are described by Schram, *Mao*, Ch. 8 and Fitzgerald, *Communist China*, Ch. 3.

19. Fitzgerald, ibid., p. 88.

20. Ibid., p. 118.

21. For the GLF see Collier and Collier, *China's Socialist Revolution*, Ch. 3.

22. For details, see Schram, *Mao*, pp. 266-74.

23. P. Bridgham, 'Mao's Cultural Revolution: Origin and Development' in R. Baum (ed.), *China in Ferment*, pp. 17-18.

24. See J.van Ginneken, *The Rise and Fall of Lin Piao.*

25. See Collier and Collier, *China's Socialist Revolution.*

26. On Lin Biao's death, see J.van Ginneken, *Lin Piao*: for various aspects of the Cultural Revolution, see Baum, *China.*

11

The CPSU in 1956

The State of the Party between 1945 and 1956

The Chinese experience of communism was not being conducted in a vacuum. As has been seen above, the Chinese followed the Soviet model in many ways, even if adapted to Chinese conditions. Basically, it was a model of an agricultural economy in a large territory with a poor infrastructure which, pressed by the dual needs of a growing population and foreign exploitation, chose to adopt a system which, though illiberal, appeared to serve the aim of rapid modernisation and redistribution of wealth. The Chinese, like the Russians before them, could hardly have missed liberalism, having not experienced it. Similarly, they had been used to very violent periods during their historical development. The Russian 'Time of Troubles' and the Stalinist period were enacted in Chinese history with at least as much violence and often on a much larger scale. Another reason why the Chinese experience was not dissimilar to the Russian one was that the majority of the population had had centuries of hard times, which included major famines, major natural disasters and major wars, weakening the resistance of the nation. Also similar was the general apathy of the population with regard to the system of government: with the exception of a small minority of Western-educated intellectuals, the Chinese middle classes consisted, like the Russian middle classes, of merchants and civil servants, all steeped in the traditions of the Empire. It was the majority which assured a future for the Communist Party and government: the peasants were offered a modicum of help and land, the industrial proletariat, mainly derived from the peasant class, had little experience of self-government, and the upper classes, rigid and afraid of change, were hardly in a position to oppose the revolutionaries.

In China, as in Russia, the revolutionaries appeared to have much to offer in the first instance: endowment with land, employment in industry, emancipation of women, better educational and health care facilities, new housing and improved farming methods, and other concomitants of modernisation. The fact that these benefits had to be attained through compulsion, through periods of terror, and that they precluded the setting up of a parliamentary system of government was meaningless to the hungry, illiterate Chinese peasant just as it had been meaningless to the Russian peasant in 1917.

But by the late 1940s, as the CPC came to power and inherited a situation not dissimilar to that of Russia in 1917, the position in the USSR had changed. Whatever cataclysmic effects the Stalinist policy of forced collectivisation and industrialisation may have had in the 1930s, and however catastrophic the Second World War had been in its results, the way in which the Soviet Union had survived the war, the way the people had fought the invaders and the way Stalin's soldiers had conducted their campaigns had produced a new spirit both of pride and of confidence which was markedly different to the spirit of apathy which had prevailed in the 1930s. Released from the terror of purges and the secret police, left to their own devices in their fight against the Nazis, victorious and respected by the world, the Soviet people had developed a new Soviet identity. This was helped by two factors: the pre-revolutionary elite had by then been virtually eliminated, and the extension of Soviet power to the borders of what had been the Russian Empire, and even beyond them in some cases, had convinced many that the Stalinist way had been the right way and that the price not too high. In any case, after several years of Nazi atrocities in Russia the purges began to pale in popular memory.

If the Soviet people were more confident and assured, Stalin, the chief (though not the sole) creator of this new spirit, was not. The war had been difficult, the hold on new territories was tenuous and his ascendancy over the party and government was less certain as he grew older and relaxed vigilance. Bitter lessons of previous anti-Stalinist plots (or presumed plots) could not have been far from his mind as he surveyed the scene after 1945. Nor was all well with the party. Because of the logistics of the war each territorial party organisation had to develop its own techniques in resistance. The industries were allowed freedom in order to boost production — hence terror had to give way to ability and scientific knowledge. Nor were the people unchanged: the war had forced Stalin to resurrect not only patriotism but the Russian Orthodox Church. The faithful had reverted to religious practice, and the

Church (together with sectarian denominations) began to acquire new, young faithfuls — a galling phenomenon to a party which had done so much to allow one cult only, that of Stalinism, for some twenty years. There were further problems: the armies which had pushed so far into Europe were not oblivious of the fact that, in the capitalist countries, even ravaged by war, the standard of living of the working classes and peasants was often very much higher than in the Soviet Union. Many soldiers on coming back after the occupation were 'quarantined' in camps. Worse still, even those who had not visited foreign countries now expected the reward traditionally expected in Russia after a victory: some relief from oppression and an improvement in their living standards.

Therefore instead of feeling that he could sit back and reap the fruits of a well-deserved victory, Stalin felt he had to redouble his vigilance. Besides, the war had ruined much of Soviet agriculture and industry which could only be rebuilt with a great deal of effort. Had Stalin been willing to relax he may not have been allowed to do so in any case by his clique. As one authority points out, the party as a whole had lost its collective influence at the expense of the ministerial and secret police apparatus;[1] no party congress was held between 1939 and the 19th Congress in 1952. The people surrounding Stalin were Beria, Malenkov and Zhdanov. There was bitter rivalry between the last two, and the position of Beria was ambiguous. Some historians ascribe the excesses of the post-war period to Beria's ascendancy over Stalin; others claim that Beria was merely a tool, used by whoever happened to be in power. The clarification of this situation would require an archival search, and since it is unlikely that any records are extant, one has to rely on hearsay evidence, which is not very satisfactory. But circumstantial evidence which has since emerged points to the fact that Stalin was the dominant force in the clique and that Zhdanov became too powerful and was eliminated in 1948, whereas Malenkov and Beria survived Stalin, Malenkov to become for a short period the First Secretary of the party as well as Prime Minister. He was quickly deprived of the first post, but he retained the latter till 1955. On the other hand, Beria was shot very quickly after Stalin's death; his arrest was made public on 10 July 1953.[2]

The arithmetic of the power struggle after Stalin's death provides a degree of insight into Stalin's position in the 1945—53 period. If Zhdanov was eliminated in 1948 it must have been because he had become too powerful. It is assumed that Malenkov helped to eliminate him as a rival; but on assuming power Malenkov was soon deprived of it. Hence his position, both in the party and in the government, must have been weak. The conclusion is that Zhdanov was the real menace, and that he threatened Stalin rather than Malenkov. Similarly, Beria without Stalin's support was but a cipher; hence, even if it is true — as Schapiro suggests — that Beria was to have been eliminated in the 'Doctors Plot' it simply means that he had outlived his usefulness like the previous secret police chiefs, and that he knew too much, not that he was too powerful.

The hypothesis being presented here is not so much that Stalin was the omnipotent, omniscient bloodthirsty monster before whom all trembled but that he was the moving spirit of a clique which he reshuffled from time to time; a position he held partly because of the instruments of terror he commanded and partly because he was the strongest and most able of them all. This had been obvious as early as 1928.[3] But without his clique Stalin could do little; and individually they were powerless without him. Hence it was a situation of mutual support which helped Stalin and his clique to hold on to power for too long — too long, because the situation in the USSR had been radically changed by the war and because Stalin himself was too old to cope.

The result was that while in the 1930s Stalinist purges went on without many hitches, when the purges of the late 1940s and early 1950s began there was strong opposition both within the party and within the technocratic elite. The early victims of the purges were mostly Jewish,[4] and while Stalin may have been hoping to use anti-Semitic sentiments in Russia he had not reckoned on one factor: his colleagues were frightened for their own lives. The Jews had acquired positions in the technocratic elite which had made them much more powerful than the Old Bolsheviks had been, and he himself had misjudged the temper of the times and of the Soviet people. His death, whether natural or not, was hastened by the purges he had instituted.

The leadership was now — after Stalin's death had been announced on 5 March 1953 — free to undo some of the harm. As Schapiro states: 'Of one thing there is no doubt: for many members of the party, both highly placed and less eminent, the death of the Leader came only just in time.'[5] But the difficulties were considerable. The Soviet people had been used to the Stalin cult for so long and — rather like the people under the Empire — had been conditioned to believe that the atrocities committed against them were the fault of the underlings (whereas Stalin was deified in the Kremlin) that a sudden unmasking might well have produced a civil war or, at the very least, serious disorders.

The New Leadership

The changeover had to begin with a change in leadership. By September 1953 Krushchev, having eliminated all but three members of the Stalinist Presidium, was appointed First Secretary of the party. On 8 February 1955 Malenkov resigned from his premiership to be replaced by Bulganin. The new leadership was faced with serious internal and external problems. Internally, Soviet industry was a lossmaking, heavy-industry orientated enterprise. Soviet agriculture was unproductive, its machinery faulty, its management poor and its labour underpaid or even not paid at all. The fall of Beria had necessitated a rethinking of the role of the secret police, its separate empire within the USSR and the economic status of prison camp labour. Externally, the problems were even more serious: the ongoing and bitter quarrel with Yugoslavia, the status of 'satellite' countries, the Cold War with the West and the war in Korea were the legacies Stalin had left.

Internally, the NKVD, hitherto most powerful in security and economic matters, was disbanded and broken up into a Ministry of Internal Affairs (MVD) and a Committee of State Security (KGB) in March 1954. A large number of prisons and labour camps were closed, and the majority of political prisoners released.[6] Therefore the worst features of the system were eliminated, terror laws phased out and 'socialist legality' introduced.

The new developments in agriculture and industry are fully treated by many authors.[7] They aimed at improving the system, producing more consumer goods, making agriculture more efficient and developing new agricultural regions, as in the 'Virgin Lands' scheme in Kazakhstan. Whatever the drawbacks of the changes, and even given their limited success, they were the most revolutionary developments for the people of the USSR. The effect was both economic and psychological. Economically, the Soviet citizen became a consumer for the first time in Soviet history, even if consumer goods were not always or not easily obtainable. It was no longer unpatriotic or criminal to want to improve one's standard of living. Large imports of foreign goods (from the Eastern bloc in the first instance, from the capitalist countries at a later stage) gave the middle classes a standard of living not dissimilar to that in capitalist countries. The new housing programmes and relaxation on private building produced a new class of house-owners and two-home occupiers, which gave the Russians a real stake in the economy of their country. The planning system was revamped and then changed again: it never really managed to take off to the level of the capitalist system (for reasons connected with the unchanged basis of the aims of Soviet industries, and not because of central planning, in this writer's opinion), but it created more productivity and, after the introduction of Libermanism, the economy was attuned to the profit motive to a certain extent, which meant that desirable consumer goods had to be produced. In the countryside, the relaxation on private agriculture, coupled with the injection of capital into collective schemes, raised the Soviet peasants above the level of serfs for the first time since forced collectivisation; they were now able to travel more freely, to sell more produce on the private markets and they were allowed a say in the collectives. The system became less oppressive, more subject to criticism and more ready to listen to the grass roots — this change was often erratic, but was immediately felt in many areas of Soviet life. This in itself produced a better psychologicl climate.

But perhaps the greatest change was in the behaviour of the new leadership. Stalin, obsessed with plots against his life, was never seen in public outside the Kremlin. His complex about his short stature and his Georgian accent when he spoke Russian made him cautious about being seen by crowds and about addressing them, either in meetings or on the radio. He was less accessible than the Russian tsars had been, for they had, in theory at least, retained the right of access to them by everyone with a grievance. Lenin had carried on the habit of being seen and addressing the people, but Stalin had phased it out almost immediately, and after the disaster of the 1930 winter he was probably right not to appear in public.

Malenkov immediately set a new tone and was seen in public and made public speeches. After he was phased out, Khrushchev developed it to a degree not seen in Russia probably since the days of Peter the Great. As his biographer says:

His endless travelling about the Soviet Union was paying off. It had taken him into regions he had never visited before and where his character was unknown. The world heard all about his public speeches, in which he addressed himself to the lower echelons in mass audiences, bullying, cajoling, exhorting, explaining with obsessive detail how collective farmers should go about their cultivations. This created the public image. But his talks behind the scenes were even more to the point. There he addressed in private the Party workers and with his extraordinary persuasiveness and authority convinced them that he was the man to win. He was fighting the chair-borne Ministerial bureaucracy; he was fighting for Party rights, for the very careers of those who listened to him.[8]

Crankshaw's account deals with Krushchev's power struggle with Malenkov: but his approach changed far more than the leadership; it changed the attitudes of the people towards their leaders. The direct appeal to the people, the apparent openness of Krushchev's methods, gave another boost of confidence to them. They were now free of the worst excesses of the security forces; better fed, better clothed and better housed than they had ever been; and, to top it all, they were, for the first time since the Revolution, actually wooed by the leadership. The new generation would never again be cowed into the same kind of submission which Stalin had created; and it is doubtful if the atmosphere of fear, hate and bitterness which Stalin had created could be re-created soon, if at any time. But one must not make the mistake of imagining that these attitudes made the Soviet people into anti-socialists; on the contrary, they came to believe in the ultimate power of socialism to conquer everything, to improve the world and to regard the Stalinist period as an exception to the rule, rather than the rule. Hence, internally, the new leadership, particularly after Krushchev ousted the remaining Stalinists, commanded confidence and produced a new spirit of Soviet unity which had been absent even in the war years.

But externally the situation was different. Stalin had produced too many international disasters to mend them without major upheavals. The leadership tackled the most important one immediately: the war in Korea. The Chinese leader Zhou Enlai discussed the Korean war with the Russians during his stay in Moscow for Stalin's funeral. After his return to Beijing the Chinese and North Korean governments agreed to exchange wounded prisoners, and to repatriate all prisoners of war. An armistice was signed on 27 July 1953. In the spring of 1954 a conference was called in Geneva to settle Korea and the war in Indo-China, where France was being defeated by the Communist Viet Minh. Against American protests, the Chinese Communist government was invited to participate. On Korea no progress was made, and the *status quo* of partition was retained. But Vietnam was partitioned between the Communist forces in the north and the French territory in the south, along the 17th Parallel; Laos and Kampuchea were neutralised, and the Soviet Union and China were said to have sacrificed Ho Chi Minh for the consolation prize of North Vietnam. This conference brought Communist China for the first time into the orbit of global politics, and one author suggests that it may have been worth the sacrifice of Korea and Ho Chi Minh for the time being in order to achieve the role of a peacemaker.[9]

To follow up the Far Eastern policy, Krushchev went to China in December 1954 to fulfil the Soviet promise that troops would be withdrawn from Port Arthur and the Chinese Eastern Railway at the end of the war. This Stalin refused to do, and it was now left to Krushchev to remove the insult (as the Chinese saw it) to the Communist government. He also signed an agreement which provided for a supply of capital goods to China, allowing it to develop its industries on a more rational basis. In April 1955 the USSR recognised the neutrality of Austria and agreed to withdraw occupation troops. But similar agreement could not be attained on Germany or on NATO. The Americans wanted West Germany to join NATO; the Russians were strongly opposed to the move. However, Germany joined NATO on 6 May 1955 and on 14 May 1955 the USSR and its Eastern European allies signed the Warsaw Pact, which has been called an Eastern equivalent of NATO. The failure on this point, which was crucial to Europe, has been blamed variously on Soviet or on American intransigence, and their mutual unwillingness to trust each other. Here one must note that the Stalinist period was still fresh in the minds of the Western governments. Of all the Western countries, only France appeared to be willing to listen to the USSR, and this more because of fear of a re-militarised Germany than because of trust in the USSR; and none of them were willing to take risks, or indeed to return to the concessions of Teheran or Yalta. One may question whether the Russians were serious in their proposal to demilitarise Europe, a proposal to which they have reverted many times, particularly in periods of an international crisis. In the absence of first-hand documentary information the answer is difficult; nevertheless, certain pointers seem to show that they were. The USSR had serious political and economic problems with the Eastern bloc. The military effort in Eastern Europe was, and still is, very costly, and acts detrimentally to the Soviet economy. There are also other problems: though the USSR is partly a European power its greatest wealth and its biggest development areas lie in Soviet Central Asia, in Siberia and in the Far East. And though in the 1950s the oil in the Middle East did not yet figure in Soviet calculations to a great extent, Soviet foreign policy, like the Imperial policy before it, always paid great attention both to South-West Asia and to the Middle East, both for traditional reasons and because of access to the Mediterranean. Hence one should not discount Soviet overtures on Europe.

However, it is possible that, given the degree of mutual distrust created by the Cold War, no amount of concessions on either side would have sufficed. One must merely point out that attempts were made by the new leadership to soften the Soviet foreign policy; that they were rebuffed by the Americans, with the best of motives; and that the period of Co-existence and Detente which was to follow was coloured to a great extent by these events.

On one front a partial success was attained. This was the mending of the quarrel with a socialist state: Yugoslavia. In May 1955 against bitter opposition by Molotov, who was still the Foreign Minister, Khrushchev, the First Secretary and Bulganin, the Prime Minister. visited Belgrade. Tito, at first sceptical about Soviet moves, became convinced that they were genuine: 'The days when the USSR could be considered a 'highly menacing, aggressive power,' Tito announced, 'are now over.' The Yugoslavs would meet the Russians half-way he said, adding: 'We are not a people who brood ... We have said, let bygones by bygones.'[10] On the arrival of Soviet leaders in Yugoslavia on 27 May Tito did not, however, relax his guarded responses. They were presented with a theoretical programme of the CPY, drawn up by Tito's theorist, Kardelj, which demonstrated the Yugoslav system of democratic socialism. The Soviet leaders accepted the Yugoslavs' 'independent path to socialism'; and Tito, on his part, did not reject their approaches. After the visit he stated that the Russians 'convinced themselves that Yugoslavia was independent and that she wanted to remain independent, both of the West and East, that she had her own road of development, that she could not permit any interference in her internal affairs. . . . They agreed with this position and we were consequently able to find a common language.'[11]

To complement his reconciliation with Yugoslavia, Khrushchev dissolved the Cominform on 17 April 1956. The Cominform, never a very successful tool, had been the main instrument of anti-Yugoslav propaganda. It was only fair that the Yugoslavs should resent its continued existence, and it was a measure of Khrushchev's concessions that he agreed to do this. All these changes were dramatic. To those who had experienced Stalinist policies, either in the USSR or elsewhere, they proved that the new Soviet leadership had decided on a complete change of course. Tito had been convinced. But the Americans remained sceptical, and the Eastern European governments worried by the sudden changes. Communist parties outside the bloc were non-commital and awaited further developments. These were to come like a bombshell.

Twentieth Congress of the CPSU and its Immediate Repercussions

The Congress met in Moscow between 14 and 25 February 1956, some weeks earlier than necessary. There were some indications that there would be changes because of the trials, in September 1955, of Georgian security officials who were Beria's subordinates. It also seems that on his way back from Belgrade, Khrushchev stopped in Sofia, in June 1955, and made an open attack on Stalin, though in a secret Party speech, bringing out some of the charges which he later elaborated.[12] Opening the Congress, Khrushchev made a fairly orthodox report on internal matters, though he stressed the change in Soviet aims: the transition to communism was now in the pipeline and the USSR would overtake the capitalist countries industrially.

The part devoted to foreign affairs was much more interesting: here Khrushchev suggested that peaceful co-existence with non-socialist countries was now possible, because the social and political forces which favoured peace were now strong enough in capitalist systems to make this a viable proposition. He also stressed that there were different forms of socialism, and no single formula was applicable to all countries, making a specific reference to Yugoslavia.[13] But no more emerged in the Opening Report. On the third day of the Congress, Mikoyan made an economic report, in which he criticised Stalin openly. He asserted that there had been no collective leadership for the past twenty years but a personality cult of Stalin. He criticised Stalin's economic theories and even his famous 'Short Course' of party history.[14]

However, the real shock did not come till 20 February, when the Congress went into a secret session to hear a second speech by Khrushchev entitled 'On the cult of personality and its consequences'.[15] The speech was very long, some 20,000 words, and very well arranged to reveal only what could no longer be concealed. Stalin was denounced as the enemy of the party, as the instigator of torture and murder within the party, but little was said about the victims of collectivisation or the purge of the army, nor were the Trotskyites or Bukharinites rehabilitated. Nevertheless, 'With a frankness which had long disappeared from party life he sketched Lenin's conflict with Stalin at the end of his life and retold the long forgotten story of the "Testament". He described, with full facts and figures, the assault which had been made during the period of Ezhov's office on party members and leaders, forced by torture to confess to crimes which they had never committed.'[16]

The impact of this speech was phenomenal, but it is interesting to consider the reasons which Khrushchev had in making it. He was, after all, himself implicated in some of Stalin's crimes. Two theories had been suggested: first, that it was an attempt to force old Stalinists out of the party. It is quite true that on 29 June 1957 a communique was issued which stated that Malenkov, Kaganovich and Molotov had been expelled from the Central Committee for anti-party activities. However, Khrushchev hardly needed to create a worldwide scandal in order to do this; the few elderly Stalinists did not provide such a menace. The second theory is even less probable: that Khrushchev was forced by other members of the Central Committee to make the speech, possibly in order to implicate himself. Crankshaw analysed this and came to the conclusion that Khrushchev had been dropping more than hints of Stalin's wrongdoings for some time, and was hardly likely to be forced into a major, well-prepared speech just to oblige his other colleagues. It is possible that the reasons were twofold: Khrushchev had been humiliated (often publicly) by Stalin for many years; he had also been unjustly persecuted by him. It would have been in his character to take his vengeance in such a dramatic manner — after Stalin's death. The second motive is in line with the Russian habit of confession, much in use throughout history. Khrushchev and the rest of the leadership simply could not continue in power, and could not present a new policy, without confessing to at least some of the former misdeeds. The confession had to be limited, for they did not want to lose power; it had to be sufficiently complete to show that a new course had started; and it had to be dramatic, in order to prove their good faith. It must be remembered that since the speech was intended for the party faithful only and for foreign consumption, the leadership's credibility was severely tested: to say nothing would mean to approve of Stalinism; to say too much would condemn the whole leadership of the Soviet Party. A third, possibly incidental, effect of the speech had an even better result: it found the familiar whipping boy. Economic, political and international affairs of the USSR were in bad shape: it was all Stalin's fault. The new leadership could not be blamed, because they had to obey the dictator. They were fully justified in blind obedience, as they did not want to be tortured and executed. It all made a very convenient package, and the beauty of this package was that, by and large, it was an ethical and a moral solution. Stalin was destroyed; his body could be taken out of the mausoleum (though that was not done for several years to come); his closest aides could be removed; and the new leadership could begin their new policy.

Khrushchev, despite his recent foreign travels, did not understand much about foreign relations. In the USSR the speech, when it reached the population, was either not understood or ignored. But in the Eastern European bloc, where there was already ferment because of the pressure to change economic policies, it created serious problems. Everywhere, but particularly in disaffected Poland and Hungary, there were instant demands for de-Stalinisation. These ended in the Polish and Hungarian revolutions. In other countries, the disorders were suppressed, only to break out later, with a greater intensity.

Outside the bloc the results were even worse. The foreign communist parties were in a quandary. They had for years denied the accusations of Stalin's critics only to have them confirmed straight from the leader of the CPSU. Their position was extremely difficult and many leaders were not at all grateful to Khrushchev for causing the upheaval. There were mass defections from foreign parties and many, otherwise highly intelligent, communists expressed amazement that they had not known of Stalinist horrors. In other words, the speech caused more than revolutions: it caused a total reappraisal of the USSR and communism on a global scale. Hardly any other single speech by any other leader can be said to have done this. Thus Khrushchev goes down in history as the most powerful speech-maker ever: neither Hitler nor Mussolini had ever achieved so much in all of their speeches. The consequences of the 20th Congress will be discussed below.

Notes

1. L. Schapiro, *The Communist party of the Soviet Union*, p. 511.

2. Ibid., p. 559. The date of announcing Beria's arrest is attributed either to June or July 1953, but there is no evidence of his date of death.

3. See O.A. Narkiewicz, *The Making of the Soviet State Apparatus*.

4. See Schapiro, *Communist Party*, Ch. XXIX.

5. Ibid., p. 551.

6. Estimates of the numbers in camps and prisons at the time of Stalin's death vary. Similarly it is difficult to establish the numbers released after his death and various amnesties. R. Conquest, in *The Great Terror*, pp. 687-8, makes an estimate of some 800,000-900,000 inmates left in camps in 1957, basing it on a Soviet source. But he doubts if this is correct.

7. A brief account will be found in A. Nove, *An Economic History of the USSR* (1969 edn), Ch. 12.

8. E. Crankshaw, *Khrushchev*, p. 197.

9. R.F. Rosser, *An Introduction to Soviet Foreign Policy*, pp. 282-3.

10. G.W. Hoffman and F.W. Neal, *Yugoslavia and the New Communism*, pp. 423-4.

11. *Borba*, 28 July 1955, quoted ibid., p. 426.

12. Crankshaw, *Khruschev*, pp. 211-12.

13. *20th Congress*, Vol. I, pp. 34-41 and 111-18: quoted by Schapiro, *Communist Party*, p. 567.

14. Ibid., pp. 302-3 and 322-5, quoted by Schapiro, *Communist Party*, p. 567.

15. The text was never officially printed in the USSR and most writers use the text published by the US State Department on 4 June 1956, though summaries of the speech appeared in communist newspapers in foreign countries. There has been some controversy about the State Department's role in the publication of this speech, which speeded up the events in Eastern Europe in 1956, but its general authenticity seems to be accepted.

16. Schapiro, *Communist Party*, p. 568.

12

Eastern European Communist Parties after 1956

The Polish 'October' and its Aftermath

While Yugoslavia had been following its own 'road' since the late 1940s the Polish leadership was most unwilling to de-Stalinise, and finally did so only under extreme internal pressure. While the logistics of the Polish 'October' are well known and extensively documented, the reasons for the coup (for it was a coup, not a popular uprising) and the aftermath of 1956 are less well understood.

The protest began in the universities and among writers and journalists, who became known as 'revisionists'. In Hungary, the intellectuals protested against Rakosi's regime from October 1955; in Poland the Polish writers' union expelled Stalinist members in April 1956. The revisionists argued as follows: they rejected the concept of the dictatorship of the proletariat, stating that it merely gave power to bureaucracy and monopolistic party leadership. In Poland, Julian Hochfeld resurrected Rosa Luxemburg's views on Lenin's theory. The revisionists also questioned the 'historical mission of the proletariat', maintaining that the intelligentsia always plays the role of the vanguard of progress. Further, they questioned the 'leading role' of the USSR in building socialism and called for relations of 'equals with equals' within the bloc. They have been called 'national' communists, but even though some of the political leaders became just that, the intellectuals merely intended to reject the Soviet model, not necessarily to pursue a narrow nationalist path to socialism. The role of state censorship was attacked strongly; the revisionists called for the ending of party control over intellectual activities in the interests of intellectual truth and the break with the 'socialist realist' tradition. Economic life was to be revised on the basis of the abolition of centralised planning and the introduction of self-management of workers in factories and other enterprises. So far (with the exception of the criticisms of bureaucracy and censorship) the revisionists were very much in the Yugoslav cast; but at this point they went further.

Some of the leading Polish revisionists 'rediscovered the moral roots of socialism under the debris of vulgar materialism'; as Kolakowski summarised it: 'The fact that we regard the advent of Communism as historically inevitable does not make us Communists. We are Communists because we are for the oppressed against the oppressor, for the poor against the masters, for the persecuted against the persecutor. Every practical choice is a choice of values, a moral choice.' His Marxist colleague, Adam Schaff, called philosophical revisionism the product of 'a marriage between Kantian philosophy and existentialism'.[1] New periodicals sprang up, old papers revived under new editors both in Poland and Hungary and new clubs, societies and organisations were set up every day to cater for the intellectual awakening of the two nations. But none of these amounted to more than intellectual protest or intellectual ferment, and, while supported by a great deal of enthusiasm among the educated elite, such events did not produce a national revolution.

It is worth noting that in Poland the revolution (even if shortlived) occurred among industrial workers in Poznan, whose wages were cut artificially as a result of increased production norms. On 28 July 1956, after a peaceful intervention in Warsaw failed to produce any results, the workers in Poznan went out into the streets in a massive demonstration. There were calls for the withdrawal of Soviet troops and the freeing of Cardinal Wyszynski (arrested in 1953) but, above all, calls for more food and better wages. The special forces called out to quell the riots (it is said that the regular army handed its weapons to the rioters and refused to act against the crowds) left an official death-toll of 54 dead as well as three hundred wounded and many arrested. But the revolution had succeeded in its aim: the 'national' leader, Gomulka, was rehabilitated in August, the government obtained a loan of 100 million rubles from the USSR and the repatriation of thousands of Poles who were still in the Soviet Union since the war. The prisons were emptied and a new commander, General Komar, appointed as head of security services. In the meantime, the population began to demand more concessions; religious demonstrations on a massive scale began to take place; the universities were in the hands of 'revisionists'; and finally the Central Committee was forced to ask Gomulka to take over the leadership. He insisted on his appointment as First Secretary, on the resignation of the minister of economics, Hilary Minc (whom he blamed for the state of the economy) and on the recall of the Soviet Commander-in-Chief Marshal Rokossovsky to the USSR. On the day the Eighth Plenum of the Central Committee was to meet (19 October 1956), a highpowered Soviet delegation, consisting of Khrushchev, Mikoyan, Molotov, Kaganovich and Marshal Konev (Commander-in-Chief of the Warsaw Pact Forces) arrived unexpectedly in Warsaw. The intention was clearly to stop the planned changes with a threat of armed intervention. The Polish Central Committee proceeded to appoint Gomulka and his associates, as planned, to the leading posts. The Russians moderated their demands, but it must be pointed out that Gomulka gave very definite assurances — which he kept — that he would not threaten the strategic interests of the USSR, that he would not withdraw from the Warsaw Pact and that he would not break the alliance with the USSR or other socialist countries.[2] The population was not totally reassured, particularly when Gomulka announced on 24 October that Soviet troops would have to stay in Poland, but the economic, political and religious concessions which the new leadership made immediately had a pacifying effect. On 18 November 1956 Gomulka signed an agreement in Moscow which placed the Soviet troops under the control of the Polish government, cancelled Polish debts, granted new credit facilities and made a commitment to supply food to Poland.[3]

In Poland further disorders were stopped by rapid concessions to the population, first, by the rehabilitation of victims of Stalinist purges, an amnesty for political prisoners and the return of Poles in the USSR from April 1956 onwards. These were followed by the reversal of forced collectivisation in September and import of food from the USSR, by the release of Cardinal Wyszynski and many other priests after 21 October, by allowing religious education in schools and by a general liberalisation of intellectual life. The year 1956 gave something to everybody in Poland, and, even if it was not enough, it was sufficient to halt violent revolution.

What happened after 1956 is a story of the decline of economic and political progress.[4] Despite the very real concessions the new leadership had won from the Russians and given to the population, the economy did not take off. The fractionation of collective farms gave prosperity to some farmers while it made more farmers very poor. The industrial scene did not improve drastically, the main reasons being not so much the centralised system of planning and management but the fact that the capital investment in the previous period went into the wrong sector (such as huge and wasteful steel works), whereas the intermediate sector and the consumer sector was neglected. The government after 1956 was unable or unwilling to provide enough capital for the introduction of intermediate industries, and private agriculture, deprived of fertilisers, machinery and technical help, could not produce enough capital to finance industrial investment. Poland began to suffer from a chronic shortage of manufactured goods, while other Eastern European countries (East Germany, Hungary and Czechoslovakia) managed to establish their own industries, providing these goods.

By 1965, the population explosion and the slowing down of industrial expansion began to show on the political front: discontent began to take the form of looking for scapegoats. The Jews fitted into this category easily; not only had many Jews been in the Stalinist apparatus but others had devised the relaxation and were among Gomulka's supporters: besides they could now be blamed, in the overall climate of 'national' communism, for the setting up of the Soviet model. A group of ex-partisans and ex-servicemen led by General Moczar took an extremely sharp anti-Semitic stand. When Adan Schaff protested against this in 1965 his colleague, Professor Chalasinski, commented that Schaff's 'internationalist humanism' was the result of his Jewish origins and 'cosmopolitan' affinities.[5] Too many Jews still held chairs at the universities, posts in economic ministries and in other positions of power to please the 'national' communists. The Arab–Israeli War of 1967 gave rise to a violent anti-Zionist campaign; Gomulka felt forced to buttress his position by stating publicly that 'each citizen of Poland must have one country alone, Poland'.[6] The campaign became stronger not because the Poles became more anti-Semitic but because there was so much sympathy for the anti-Soviet Israel attacked by the pro-Soviet Arab states that an official course of anti-Zionism (which turned into anti-Semitism) had to be instituted for fear of an even further growth of anti-Soviet feelings.

In late 1967 and early 1968 a purge of Jews from the apparatus, universities and other leading posts began in earnest: most Jewish economists and many sociologists left the country, thus depriving it of expertise which was badly needed and allowing foreign observers to claim that Poland was notoriously anti-Semitic. The press, television, film industry, armed services and other areas were cleared next. The student disturbances of February and March 1968 brought about directly by the events in Czechoslovakia were used by the 'partisans' to fan anti-Jewish feelings, the workers' militia was controlled by Moczar and the peasant leadership called the disturbances 'cosmopolitan' and stood aloof from them.

The expulsion of 'cosmopolitan' elements did nothing to help the economy, and the leadership attempted to reform it by raising food prices drastically just before Christmas 1969. Violent riots and large strikes immediately occurred in the coastal cities of Gdansk, Gdynia, Szczecin and Sopot; this time the troops quelled them and the number of deaths was much higher. The USSR reacted quickly by helping Gierek, who had acquired a reputation for efficient administration in Silesia, to isolate Gomulka. On 20 December at a Plenum of the Central Committee at Natolin, Gomulka and all his associates were voted out of the Politbureau, while Gomulka, already ill, was held in confinement in a hospital — the events were almost a replay of Khrushchev's removal in 1964.

The new leadership repealed the price rises and began to discuss economics with the workers. However, Gierek's policy consisted mostly in contracting foreign debts and making ends meet with the help of imports from abroad, a policy which helped at first to mask the real problems of the country but which came to a severe test after 1973, when oil prices trebled, and Poland, which has to import all its oil from the USSR, would have been bankrupt but for Soviet help. At the 7th Congress of the PUWP Gierek stated that meat was in short supply and that the inflation which affected Poland was the result of increased oil, grain, fodder and machinery prices. In June 1976 the government announced that meat would go up by 70 per cent, sugar by 100 per cent and grain by 40 per cent (the 1970 rises only averaged about 30 per cent). On the following day, 25 June, strikes, public protests and riots occurred in many Polish cities, the most violent ones being at a motor car factory in Zeran. This time the government withdrew the price increases within twenty-four hours. Troops were used in a limited way, mostly to restore order, but large numbers of workers were arrested at a later stage and tried on charges of subversion or hooliganism.[7] The brutal way in which the regime handled the arrested workers gave rise to a new wave of dissent among the intellectuals, the first time that the intellectuals had protested since 1968. A Committee for the Defence of the Workers (KOR) was set up, and strong clerical protests were made by leading churchmen.

It is notable that the social conscience of the intellectuals makes them take up the cause of the proletariat, but it is not necessarily a mutual phenomenon. The intellectuals still constitute an elite which appears to the proletariat to be well off, and the proletariat does not appreciate that the intellectuals need freedom of expression as much as the workers need food. The years from 1976 onwards have produced the highest foreign debt of any Eastern European country without a compensatory rise in the standard of living. Though some commentators praise the high industrial investment in Poland in the 1970s,[8] the fact remains that the Polish standard of living has been falling steadily whilst its foreign debt has been rising. The upshot of this was the replacement of the prime minister, Piotr Jaroszewicz, in February 1980, by Gierek's close associate, Edward Babiuch. 'During the closed debates of the Party Congress, the Polish leadership's handling of the economy was severely criticised by delegates, much of the criticism being directed against Mr Jaroszewicz.' The new prime minister assured the country that food prices would rise, though gradually, and that the distortion of cheap food prices (highly subsidised at the moment) must end. 'Austerity ... should become the order of the day,' he added.[9] In the absence of any new leader to replace the already ageing Gierek (he was born in 1913), the continuing economic and political crises in Poland, gave rise to dramatic events in August 1980.

Hungary — a Revolution and a Rebirth

In retrospect the Hungarian revolution of 1956 seems to have been much more successful than the Polish coup. At the time it occurred, however, all that observers could see was that the Polish leadership had managed to avoid bloodshed and had skilfully manoeuvred to placate the Russians, while the Hungarians plunged the country into a violent revolution which cost the lives of many thousands of young people. There are many interpretations of the Hungarian situation: some authors state that its maker was Rakosi:

'The Hungarian tragedy can to a large extent be blamed on Matyas Rakosi — the most hated of all Stalin's lieutenants — who, according to his own close associates, was obsessed with the idea of repression.'[10] Other authorities ascribe it variously to the Hungarians following the Polish example, to the low standard of living of Hungarian workers and to the fact that the Hungarians wanted to 'Finlandise' their country, which would be facilitated by the common border with Austria.

The revolution appears to have been the result of all these factors and to have been kindled by the intervention of the Soviet troops: but the true causes of the violence were almost certainly, in the main, the hatred of the secret police and the low standard of living. As one writer notes, the Hungarians attempted to change the agricultural economy of the country into an 'iron and steel' one, at the expense of farm production and manufactured goods. The standard of living had to be lowered: on the other hand, the agricultural policies were pursued in such a way that Hungary, formerly a net exporter of food, had to import grain in the first Five-Year Plan period (1950–54). Collectivisation was carried out in a harsh manner, with compulsory deliveries, high taxes, fines and penalties, 'ranging from admonition to death',[11] and both the countryside and industrial workers were alienated by these measures. The intellectuals, on the other hand, were alienated by the continuing Stalinist repression of the regime and looked towards Poland, where the revolution had given at least a modicum of intellectual freedom.

The other problems were internal dissensions within the leadership. These were due to the rigidity of Rakosi, the popularity of the liberal Imre Nagy and the fact that he and the centrist Janos Kadar vied with each other for leadership. Some observers maintain that Nagy was not fit for leadership because of his weakness. Gomulka's victory in October was interpreted by the Hungarians as a sign of Soviet relaxation. On 23 October 1956 the Petofi Circle (an intellectual discussion group of the Young Communist League, named after a hero of the 1848 Revolution) called for Rakosi's expulsion from the party, for trials of secret police chiefs and for workers' self-management. On the same day a demonstration was called in front of the statue of General Joseph Bem (a Polish general who had fought in the Hungarian Revolution of 1848) but, instead of an orderly demonstration, angry crowds got out of hand. The radio building was occupied, the giant statue of Stalin was toppled and the secret police were caught and hanged from lamp posts. The government could not call out the troops, as it was uncertain of their support.

Nagy was overtaken by the enthusiasm of the crowds and fell under the influence of Pal Maleter, a young officer who was one of the leaders of the rebellion. On 30 October he announced a return to a system of government based on multi-party democracy. A few days later he condemned the Warsaw Pact and announced that Hungary would from then on be neutral and independent of the Soviet bloc. This was the signal which ended Soviet hesitation: the risk that such revolutions would spread to other Eastern European countries was too great; besides, the Russians were goaded by the Chinese, who had been foretelling this event since de-Stalinisation. Soviet troops entered Budapest on 4 November; by mid-November the revolution was crushed. Large numbers of young Hungarians were killed, imprisoned or escaped to Austria. Nagy, Maleter and other leaders took refuge in the Yugoslav Embassy, from which they were released by a safe-conduct granted by Kadar. They were promptly arrested by Soviet troops and said to have been shot later (June 1958).[12]

After several months, Kadar managed to crush the rebels completely and to stamp out dissent. He used his new power to establish a Gomulka-type regime, but a much more successful one. The regime is liberalised, though not liberal, and the single-party system operates as before. But Kadar has remained politically acceptable to the USSR, has become politically acceptable to the West by the end of the 1950s and has overcome the population's opposition by improving the economy. This was done in the first instance by the granting of massive Soviet and Eastern European aid to repair the damage,[13] and second by profiting from the CMEA's 'division of labour' policies, which had a special appeal to Hungary, a country virtually devoid of raw materials.

Hungarian leadership also adopted economic reforms in the late 1960s: the so-called New Economic Mechanism went into operation in 1968. This system gave much greater flexibility to enterprises, operated a system of bonuses and incorporated both the profit motive and incentive schemes within the economy. The system made Hungary unique in the Eastern European bloc. As one economist says:

As far as its price mechanism goes, Hungary constitutes a case unto itself within Eastern Europe. The Hungarian reforms of 1968 created a mechanism of 'mixed', flexible prices, one of the intended effects of which was to make prices reflect to some extent the relative prices obtained and paid in foreign trade. After five years, the mechanism was put to a severe test by the price explosion in world markets. As a result, in 1973 a new set of measures was initiated. These were designed to mitigate the dislocations stemming from the external development. . . . Drastic measures have also been taken with respect to consumer-goods pricing in an effort to counteract a price-wage spiral.[14]

Hungary has little dissent, and a measure of intellectual freedom is allowed. There is a relatively high standard of living and Kadar has become one of the 'older statesmen' of Eastern Europe, having managed to bridge the gap between East and West, which neither Ceausescu of Romania, nor Gomulka or Gierek of Poland have achieved. To what does one ascribe the Hungarian 'economic miracle' and the consequent political relaxation? Large-scale Soviet aid was helpful: this would not have happened if the Hungarians had not demonstrated their willingness to die for their cause. But perhaps most encouraging was the way in which the Hungarians, instead of looking for scapegoats, have reconstructed their economy and have kept it going along profitable lines. While much of the credit must go to the fact that a small economy is easier to reconstruct and run than a large one, it must be admitted that if the Poles had been half as successful as the Hungarians, the events of 1970, 1976 and 1980 need not have happened.

A Case of Stalinism *Redivivus* — Czechoslovakia

A third Eastern European country whose lack of adjustment to the socialist system had the gravest consequences was Czechoslovakia. It has been said that the Czech leadership refused to de-Stalinise mainly because of fear of consequences. However, at that time, in the mid-1950s the Czech economy was the most thriving one in Eastern Europe, and possibly the leadership felt safe in the knowledge that a prosperous population was not likely to be revolutionary. Besides, the national set-up in Czechoslovakia and the rivalry between the Czechs and Slovaks made it unwise to propose liberalisation. However, pressed by his associates, Novotny was forced to liberalise slightly and partially rehabilitate some victims of earlier purges after the 12th Congress of the party in December 1962. Between 1963 and 1967 the leadership was fighting a rearguard battle to retain centralist control against a background of stagnating economy, technical backwardness and a falling standard of living, at a time when other Eastern European countries were experiencing an economic revival and political liberalisation. An economic reform instituted in 1967 was obstructed by the conservatives in government. The Arab–Israeli War in 1967 gave rise to a crude anti-Zionist campaign, which was reminiscent of the Slansky trials. In June 1967 a number of writers criticised this policy at a congress, and that date proved to be the turning point in the nation's relations with the leadership. While in Poland and Hungary the origins of the revolutions can only partly be traced to intellectual ferment, in Czechoslovakia the revolution had clearly started within intellectual circles, and had spread to party leadership.

On 30 October 1967 the Slovak party leader, Dubcek, took up the cudgels against Novotny, only to be called a 'bourgeois nationalist'. The inner party crisis brewed between then and 4 January 1968, when Novotny resigned (or was forced to resign) the party secretaryship and Dubcek took over the post. Most observers have noted — admittedly after the event — that Dubcek was torn between his wish not to upset the Soviet leadership and his undoubted desire to be a popular new leader and to satisfy both the party liberals and the public. These aims became progressively mutually incompatible. At the end of March Novotny was forced to resign from the post of president of the Republic which he was earlier allowed to retain and General Svoboda was elected to the presidency. The new Action Programme adopted on 6 April 1968 by the Central Committee was totally anti-Stalinist and anti-Novotny.

The programme advocated a separation of powers between the party and the government, accountability of government to parliament and the restoration of the multi-party National Front system. It promised to abolish censorship, to allow foreign travel and to purge the security services. Restoration of relations between the Church and State, decentralisation of the economy and a federal structure for the state were other proposals. Czechoslovakia's liberalisation gave an impetus to the Polish intellectuals to demand more freedom and led to disturbances in Warsaw, which were immediately stigmatised by the Polish leadership as 'Zionist' and which led to the purge of Polish public life of people of Jewish origins. The Czechs retaliated by holding public demonstrations in support of the Poles. The East Germans reacted very strongly. Affected by the Czechs, Ulbricht called the Czech events 'a fit of hysteria', and a counter-revolution.

At the end of May the liberals in the Central Committee managed not only to expel Novotny but also to suspend his party membership and to institute proceedings into his and his associates' role in the purge trials of 1948–54. On 27 June the liberals issued an appeal which came to be known as *2000 Words* to the population to struggle against a revival of the Novotny practices and hinting that, in the event of foreign intervention, the Czechs should oppose the invading troops. Five Warsaw Pact countries meeting in mid-July (Czechoslovakia refused to attend and Romania was excluded) demanded that the Czechs reverse the process of liberalisation and the Central Committee rejected unanimously the demands. The Russians then appeared to desist, and waited anxiously for any sign of weakening on the Czech side, the most important one being an agreement to station Soviet troops on the country's western border. In fact, the USSR was in the meantime mobilising troops and looking for alternative leadership to the popular Dubcek and his main associate, Smrkovsky.

Alternative leadership was found in the persons of Dubcek's fellow-Slovaks Bilak and Husak. The invasion was facilitated by many Czech security officials who cleared the airports to allow the landing of airborne troops. But, most of all, it was facilitated by Dubcek himself, who, while condemning the invasion of Warsaw Pact troops on 21 August 1968, at the same time called on the population and the armed services not to resist the troops.[16] The Soviet gamble paid off: as in 1938 so in 1968 the Czechs would resist peacefully but would not fight. However, even this would not have saved Dubcek's life: he, Smrkovsky, Cernik and Kriegel, the architects of the reform, were arrested and taken to Soviet territory. It was probably the fact that General Svoboda refused to treat with the Russians without first seeing those arrested that saved them from being summarily executed. The whole Czech leadership went to Moscow and signed the protocols of 26 August. These reversed the process of liberalisation, assured the stationing of Soviet troops in Czechoslovakia and gave the leadership to 'loyal' elements. Slowly but surely the Czech experiment of 'socialism with a human face', much more thorough than that which the

Poles or the Hungarians had tried to introduce, was phased out.

The question remains: were the Warsaw Pact states justified in sending troops to Czechoslovakia? Was there any danger of counter-revolution? Was there no danger of armed resistance? And did the Russians not fear military interference from the West, something which the Czechs themselves half-expected? In other words, could Czechoslovakia have become another Yugoslavia, as Hungary had intended to do and as Poland refused to do in 1956? Without looking at the secret agreement between the Western Allies and the USSR, which dated back to the Second World War, one is unable to pass a definitive opinion. However, one thing is certain: the Western military passivity (as opposed to media propaganda) during the Czech crisis, as well as during the Hungarian crisis, points to the existence of a well-defined agreement on 'spheres of influence' going well beyond what we know of the so-called Moscow agreement of 1944 between Churchill and Stalin. If such secret agreement exists it is most likely aimed not so much at giving the USSR a *cordon sanitaire* but much more at keeping the two Germanies divided. A non-socialist or independent government in either Hungary or Czechoslovakia would strengthen Western Germany, and would give the East Germans a greater impetus towards unification. There is little doubt that there is at least one country in Western Europe — France — which would prefer to keep the *status quo*, even at the expense of the smaller European nations. Hence, it is quite possible that the Czechs have overreached themselves: a minor liberalisation or even a Romanian-type economic reform would be allowed; a major breakthrough is not.

Indeed, the further fate of Czechoslovakia may well serve to confirm such a theory. The Czech liberals who chose to emigrate after 1968 had little trouble in finding posts in the West. Those who remained, while discriminated against in most ways and demoted to menial jobs, have not (so far — by 1980) been the subject of real persecution or show trials. The protest movement was almost dead by 1970 and did not revive till a new generation of intellectuals began to find its feet. The resultant 'Charter 77' must be recognised as the work of a new generation of Czechs, post-1968, even if its roots lie in the 'Prague Spring'.

The real losers in the Czech catastrophe were the party members, the intellectuals and the economy. The 1967 reform, which was based on the New Economic Model, never really took off, and was interrupted in 1968. By 1970 the economic reforms were all but stopped, as part of a return to 'normalcy'.[17] The Party and the economic apparatus were purged and a new apparatus grew up. One positive feature of the 'normalisation' was the economic rehabilitation of Slovakia, partly as a result of federalism, partly because the Russians may have wanted to strengthen the Slovaks *vis à vis* the Czechs, as part of their 'divide and rule' policy.[18]

However, the Czech economy did not recover. The oil crisis after 1973 made this improbable, the leadership's hesitation over what route to follow gave the Czechs a lower standard of living than the East Germans and the particularly unpleasant methods of harassing the dissidents after 1977 served to make Husak's regime even more unpopular than it had been.[19]

The Lessons of 'Humanist Socialism'

All the three countries discussed above have attempted to modify their systems and appeared to prefer a socialist model with a 'human face' to a mixed economy model. All failed in some respect and were forced to remain within the bloc by Soviet pressure and an implicit pressure from the West. In each country this attempt to liberalise has produced victims, suffering, bitterness and reactionary policies. Yet none of these attempts were in vain. They forced the USSR to recast its policies in favour of the smaller countries in the CMEA, to rethink its own political system and to hesitate over forcible takeovers in non-Russian countries.

These events also helped to widen the Sino–Soviet split, and made some European countries, like Romania, side with China, if only for a while. The split had a coincidental effect in weakening the Soviet monopoly of Marxist practice and encouraged the Eastern European states to introduce some economic reforms. This meant that Romania and East Germany began to experiment with their planning systems, and in Germany at least, this produced an 'economic miracle' almost matching that of West Germany. Thus the revolutions produced internal and external changes which have long-term implications, both within and outside the bloc.

One other question remains: can one classify these reformist parties into parties which follow a 'national' road and those which follow the 'humanist' road? This is very difficult, but there are certain pointers. Both types of socialism have been called 'revisionist'. They share one common characteristic: they reject the Soviet model. But here the similarity ends. One must agree with Chalasinski (quoted above) when he complained that 'humanist' socialism owed much to the cosmopolitan, international, Western European tradition, whereas 'national' communism was a positive ethnic phenomenon. This is the difference between the theories of the cosmopolitan, internationalist Karl Marx and those of the nationalist Joseph Stalin.

While it is not difficult to understand the drive towards 'national' communism exhibited by various Eastern European governments, in the circumstances in which they find themselves it is almost impossible to equate it with the international brotherhood of the oppressed which Marx had in mind when developing his theories. It may be a utopian aim, but some people never give up. One of them put the aims in this fashion:

> In seeking to achieve these ends, socialist humanism should be guided by a moral ideal — which was that of the early socialists — namely of a community of creative equal and self governing individuals on a world scale..... Our hope must lie in the greater rationality, self-control and sense of responsibility which equal opportunities to participate in the government of society should bring about.[20]

Notes

1. Quoted in F. Fejto, *A History of the People's Democracies*, p. 92.
2. Ibid., p. 106.
3. Ibid., pp. 110-11. On Polish Church—State relations, very important to the subject, there are a number of works. For a brief account, see R.F. Starr, *Communist Regimes in Eastern Europe*, pp. 146-9; for an up-to-date account, see A. Foley *An Analysis of Church and State Relations in Poland, 1945-1979*.
4. Some of these questions, particularly the question of the revival of non-communist political parties and of agricultural and religious developments are dealt with in O.A. Narkievicz; *The Green Flag*, Ch. 11, but the book finishes in 1970, with the phasing out of Gomulka.
5. Quoted by Fejto, *People's Democracies*, p. 297.
6. *Trybuna Ludu*, 19 June 1967: see also Fejto, *People's Democracies*, p. 298.
7. Starr, *Communist Regimes*, pp. 145-6.
8. See, for instance, A Zauberman. 'The East European Economies', *Problems of Communism* March-April (1978).
9. Hella Pick, *Guardian*, 8 April 1980.
10. Fejto, *People's Democracies*, p. 112.
11. Starr, *Communist Regimes*, pp. 118-19.

12. A recent book, V. Micunovic, *Moscow Diary*, mentions this ambiguously. A reviewer comments that 'the mildness of the Yugoslav reaction to the affair . . . seems surprising . . . . . At the time there were strong rumours of Yugoslav complicity in this outrage. Micunovic's account still leaves one question wide open: did the Yugoslavs when they made their deal . . . quietly accept this way of getting rid of their embarrassing protegés?' See L. Schapiro; 'My friend Nikita', *The Sunday Times*, 18 May 1980. Other refugees fared somewhat better; Cardinal Midszenty, released from prison by the Revolution, took refuge in the American Embassy, only to stay prisoner there for many years.

13. Credits reportedly totalled 320 million US dollars in the period 1956-58: see Starr, *Communist Regimes*, p. 122, quoting a Polish source.

14. Zauberman, 'The East European Economies', p. 66.

15. Fejto, *People's Democracies*, p. 229.

16. Ibid., p. 237.

17. For an assessment after the crisis, see E. Taborsky, 'Czechoslovakia: The Return to Normalcy', *Problems of Communism*, November-December (1970).

18. On purges and Slovakia, see ibid.

19. See S. Cotter, *Charter 77 and the Czech Dissidents*.

20. Z. Bauman, *Socialism — the Active Utopia*, p. 120, quoting Tom Bottomore.

13

Western European Communist Parties after 1956

The 'Via Italiana' or Return to Reality?

'Reality revisited' may serve to describe the PCI's dilemma after Stalin's death. While cherishing its myth of independence and of a parliamentary way to power — at least during some periods — the PCI was also intimately tied to the CPSU by more than financial links. The Stalinist purges of the 1930s touched the PCI more lightly than the other European parties, whereas fascist oppression had all but eliminated it. When Italy joined NATO, the PCI would have been totally isolated in a country strongly Catholic, pro-American and devoted to particularist 'family' interests had it not been for its association with the CPSU. Stalin and the USSR were far away and their misdeeds could be anti-communist propaganda; Italian corruption, nepotism and dependence on American finance were close at hand and could be seen at work every day. Italian employers showed a strong bias against employing communists; the Church preached against communism; and elaborate schemes were set up to eliminate the PCI from taking part in public life and virtually made sure that it could not take part in national government. Stalin served as a symbol of communism and the PCI was loath to deprive itself of such a symbol.

'Stalin is dead ... his titanic work, his genius, his life for more than three decades astonished the world and won for his person the gratitude and the infinite care of the peoples... The name of Stalin has been for so many years, for all of us, the beloved name of master, of teacher, and of leader, for so many years an incentive and comfort in the fight, an assurance of victory...', wrote Luigi Longo in a tribute.[1] Togliatti, on his return from the 20th Congress in Moscow, though according to all witnesses aware of Khrushchev's secret speech, was very careful not to condemn Stalin out of hand. He said: 'We know how many Communists suffered and died in our country with that name on their lips. . . . We know that entire armies of our partisans went into battle with that name. We must understand and make others understand that that name means, first of all and above all, faith in our cause, certainty that our cause is just, uncontrollable faith in our victory.'[2]

The Italians have always impressed observers by their ability to combine two apparently directly opposed characteristics: on the one hand, extreme political cynicism, which springs from a long tradition of bad governments; on the other, a faith and belief in symbols, which has been exploited as much by Mussolini as by symbolist film-makers, and which is sometimes ascribed to Catholic upbringing. The PCI has used Stalinism as a symbol of victory for so long that it found it difficult to divest itself of it immediately; but with Italian realism it knew that it had to adjust to the post-Stalinist era as soon and as painlessly as possible.

It was fortunate that Togliatti had always been a pragmatic politician, and that there was a body of Italian communist theory, as expounded by Gramsci, to which he could refer when changing course. This is not to suggest that Togliatti was cynical in exploiting Gramsci's theories to suit the mood of the moment; on the contrary, he had been in favour of applying parts of the theory since 1944. It was on the basis of Gramsci's reasoning that he had involved the PCI in government, had attempted to bring the Italian peasants into the party, had spread the PCI's influence into intellectual circles and had embraced the theory of 'organic' intellectuals which Gramsci had developed. Further, Togliatti had defended the ex-Fascists by equating the Fascist Party with family needs (the initials of *Partito Nazionale Fascista* being the same as *per necessita familiare*, 'for the family's sake'). The Italians became fascists because of the need to keep their jobs and maintain their families — the most sacred code for an Italian. If there was cynicism, then Togliatti saw it on the other side: among the Christian Democrats who, he maintained, accepted the collaboration 'in the government with the communists and with the socialists did so always with the intention to double-cross and with unloyal spirit'.[3] The PCI had suffered from bad publicity because of its Soviet connection: severing this connection would deprive it of Soviet support; keeping it meant dissociating the party from Stalinism. But dissociation from Stalinism would provide fuel for the critics of the PCI in Italy, those who had often accused Stalin of the very things which Khrushchev had now 'secretly' revealed.

Togliatti was too skilful a politician to make a sudden about-turn. He had already shadow-boxed with the Kremlin for several years, refusing to unmask Stalin since July 1953, according to one source,[4] when he had been told to do so during a briefing on the removal of Beria. After the 20th Congress, Togliatti, in his report to the Central Committee of the PCI, developed the theme of 'peaceful co-existence', of national 'roads to socialism' and of what became known in later years as 'polycentrism'. But on 17 March 1956 the Italian press published a report which had appeared in the United States a day earlier, the purported text of Khrushchev's secret speech. The authenticity of the State Department text had never been denied and the question of Togliatti's complicity in the 1930s' purges, while he was a member of the Comintern Secretariat, had to come up. So Togliatti had more to defend than the cult of the dead leader; his own position had to be considered, not least the fact that he was appointed to office after a purged Italian Communist. But the issue became more urgent at a meeting of the parliamentary group of the PCI at the end of March, when Umberto Terracini, who had spent many years in Mussolini's prisons, objected to the lack of discussion within the party. In the local elections, held in May 1956, the Communists lost 1 per cent of the votes to the Socialists but did not suffer greatly. On 4 June the *New York Times* published what was claimed to be the full text of Khrushchev's speech, but the Communist paper *L'Unità* did not comment, apart from a short notice, until 13 June, when it was announced that Togliatti would be making an important statement. Togliatti was by then pressed by dissent from within the party, which could not be contained, on top of accusations from outside the party. The shock of the revelations which Blackmer describes fully[5] is said to have affected the PCI extensively. However, one must take this with a grain of salt. The Italian Party had always consisted of 'workers' and the 'intellectuals'. The workers may have been deceived. The other stratum were the intellectuals. Some of them may have been unaware of the excesses of the 1930s if, like Terracini, they had spent them in fascist prisons. Others accepted the post-war deviations (the 1948 coup in Prague, the trials of communist leaders and the 'doctors' plot') as necessary concomitants of the Cold War. In other words, they saw that the wrongs were not confined to one side only, and they blamed the anti-communists in the West for such events. In a country which had only just been liberated from fascism this was understandable. But there are two facts alone that no-one among the intellectuals could ignore or could have been unaware of: first, that Togliatti had stayed silent while Bela Kun was being accused of disloyalty to Stalin before being executed; and second, that the 'violations of socialist legality' under Stalin had been widely known, even if the motives for them were understandable in communist terms. There was no way in which they could have been ignorant of such basic facts. The only shock which they could have experienced was that of the sudden revelations and, indeed, all the indignant comments point to this.[6]

Togliatti finally answered some of these accusations in an article in *Nuovi Argumenti*[7] and his answer was interpreted as a mild rebuke to Khrushchev. The foreign leaders were much less responsible for the cult of personality than the Russians and less aware of it — hence it would have been up to the Russians either to stop Stalin or to stop exposing him after his death. He suggested that the USSR should introduce some reforms in order to forestall another dictatorship, and the most important change suggested was for the foreign communist movement: it should now be free to develop polycentrism and to follow 'national roads' to socialism. Some authorities suggest that Togliatti's reluctance to de-Stalinise sprang from his contempt for Khrushchev, whom he did not consider to be a serious candidate for power; others suggest that it sprang from confusion about the changes in Soviet leadership. Both hypotheses are possible, but it seems clear, when his attitude is taken in conjunction with that of other communist leaders who refused to de-Stalinise, be they the Chinese or the East Germans, that the old leaders put in by Stalin were, whether by choice or by habit, 'Stalinist'. This is the reason why they had been put in charge in 1929, why they survived the purges and why they were willing to accept post-war purges and abuses of power. It seems hardly worth while to look for other reasons; perhaps the proverb about not being able to teach an old dog new tricks is the aptest summing up of the situation.

However old a dog Togliatti might have been he was also skilled enough to understand that some changes within the PCI were necessary. This explains his new stress on the 'Italian road to socialism' and on polycentrism and his 'turn to the left' in the summer of 1956. All of these were, of course, conditioned not just by internal party troubles but also by the events in Poland and by the reconciliation with Yugoslavia, though the Italian Communist press played down the Polish events for a long time. It was not till the Hungarian events that Togliatti reacted. The crucial dates were as follows: the 8th Plenum of the Polish Central Committee and its encounter with the Soviet leadership occurred on 19 October; the Soviet troops intervened in Hungary for the first time on 23 October and withdrew hastily. On 30 October the Soviet government declared that it was willing to tolerate the national aspirations of the Poles and the Hungarians, and to revise its economic relations with the socialist countries 'on the basis of national sovereignty, mutual interest and equality before the law' and that it would reconsider the question of stationing Soviet troops on their territory.[8] On the same day, 30 October, Togliatti's article in *L'Unitá* appeared, granting that the use of Soviet troops had 'complicated things' and should have been avoided, but implying that it was the fault of the Hungarian leadership that the revolt had started.[9] This, incidentally, was virtually the same line that the new Polish leadership under Gomulka had taken, dismayed at the violence in Hungary. On 4 November Soviet troops re-entered Budapest in large numbers and began to put down the revolt.

The PCI's position became more isolated; in October the pact between it and the PSI was loosened and it was scrapped altogether in November, after the Soviet invasion of Hungary. The Communists themselves staged protests; both the intellectuals and the trade unionists in the CGIL condemned the invasion and the intellectuals' protest called for a 'profound renewal of the leading group of the party'.[10] In response to the crisis Togliatti allied himself wholeheartedly with the CPSU and with the Soviet Union, and forced the dissenters either to retract or to be expelled. In November, Seniga, Raimondi and Fortichiari, three editors of *Azione Comunista*, were expelled from the party.[11] While the spring protest was rather artificial and expressed injured dignity, the autumn protest was much more genuine and struck at the leadership with full force. It came from different circles: the young members, the intellectuals and the workers. Togliatti was for the first time threatened personally, and loyalty to him and to the CPSU was being openly and repeatedly questioned.

Despite the rigid position which Togliatti adopted, and despite the fact that he won in the short run, such protests could not fail to produce a long-term rift in the party. The split was opened at the

Eighth Congress of the PCI held in December 1956, when there was a sharp divergence of opinions between the 'traditionalists' and the 'revisionists'. The revisionist position was well summed up by Giolitti, when he said at the Congress: 'Therefore we can and must proclaim, without reservation or ambiguity, that democratic liberties, even in their institutional forms of separation of powers, formal guarantees, parliamentary representation, are not 'bourgeois' but an indispensable element in building a socialist society in our country .... I believe that this imposes a re-examination in the light of Marxist principles and of historical experience of the Leninist theory of the conquest of power'.[12] Togliatti's attempts to stifle dissent resulted in a large-scale exodus of intellectuals from the party. Eugenio Reale, Fabrizio Onofri and Antonio Giolitti all resigned in the next few months.

Worse was to follow. The PCI was strongly attacked for its 'revisionism' by the PCF. According to Blackmer, the French leadership was put up to it by Moscow, though some authorities suggest that the main element was the personal rivalry between Thorez and Togliatti for the post of the Grand Old Man of European communism. The 'Italian road to socialism' was particularly strongly attacked by the French, who had viewed the whole exercise with dismay. The French criticism may have forced Togliatti to go further towards revisionism than he had intended: on the other hand, he may have felt his position so threatened within the party that he was forced to move towards it in order to save his post. The meeting in Moscow for the fortieth anniversary of the Bolshevik Revolution in November 1957 provided a platform for discussions on revisionism. Unfortunately, a new factor intervened; the opposition of the Chinese to the Soviet formula of peaceful co-existence produced serious problems for all communist leaders. The Conference issued a Declaration which was clearly the result of a compromise, condemning 'revisionism' (Yugoslavia, Poland and Italy) and 'dogmatism' (France and the Stalinist parties), but stating that revisionism was the 'main danger at present'.[13] The Yugoslavs refused to sign the Declaration and Moscow, Beijing and Rome condemned them, though the Italian condemnation was couched in regretful terms.

The PCI henceforth returned to the orthodox camp. It may be unfair to identify its acceptance of the 'Moscow line' as closely with Moscow's political and economic successes in the period as Blackmer does:[14] on the other hand the conclusion must be drawn that, having already lost some ground, the PCI saw no reason to lose more by rejecting the general Communist policy. In any case, the Communists strengthened their electoral position in the election of May 1958, and were ready to join the campaign against the EEC, then led by the USSR, and to oppose the siting of military bases in Italy. They then followed the CPSU's lead in an attempt at the end of 1959 to relax tensions at a conference held in Rome in November. This unity was again threatened by Chinese opposition: by late 1959 to early 1960, the CPC had already developed its own 'Stalinist' line so strongly that it was opposed to any further relaxation of tensions.

The split became apparent at the Moscow meeting of eighty-one communist parties in 1960, when the statement signed by all participants was not even a compromise but an attempt at a compromise. The Italians suggested various formulae to close the rift, and this helped for a time, but not for long. The 22nd Congress of the CPSU was to meet in Moscow, in October 1961. The Congress passed a resolution to remove Stalin's body from Lenin's Mausoleum, and Khrushchev made an attack on Albania, China's European ally. The PCI realised that the relaxation in its ranks had not gone far enough. For the first time, serious threats to Togliatti's leadership began to appear.

The PCI beyond Togliatti

The years between 1961 and 1964 were spent in discussions within the party about the meaning of communist democracy, and a discussion with the CPSU about the validity of the EEC in constructing a 'third bloc' in Europe. The Sino–Soviet quarrel, now out in the open, dominated the inter-party relationships.

In August 1964, while in Yalta waiting for Khrushchev to arrive, Togliatti became very ill. He had just finished writing a memorandum to Khrushchev, which was later published despite Soviet objections and which has become known as 'Togliatti's Testament'. Rather like Lenin before him, Togliatti had become more liberal and more tolerant of change as he got older and weaker. In his last few years, he had watched the Sino–Soviet split, the split in the PCI, where a Maoist wing had arisen in 1962, and an ever-growing debate on the evils of Stalinism and personal rule. He had seen the rise of younger, better-educated, more flexible and more liberal leaders in the PCI. He had also seen that the intransigent line, no longer Stalinist but conformist, had produced more defeats for communism than victories. He was ready to drop the Moscow line and to lead his party towards more independence: the real 'via Italiana'. But it was not to be, and it is only right that a new man, untainted by Stalinism, should have taken up the new cause.

In 1961, summing up the debate after the 22nd Congress, Enrico Berlinguer stated the views of the PCI in this way:

> This [debate] demonstrates that there exists today, more widely than in the past, the realisation that the defeat of imperialism and of capitalism cannot be achieved solely on the basis of the successes that the USSR and the other socialist countries have already attained ... nor on the sole basis of the victories of the liberation movement of the peoples. These factors are of decisive importance, but imperialism and capitalism cannot be vanquished without the intervention of an equally decisive third factor: the struggle of the working class in the West, the advance of a democratic and revolutionary movement which strikes imperialism and capitalism in the heart, in the vital centers of its force and its power.[15]

This began a new stage in the PCI's relationships: instead of looking towards Moscow it began to look towards liberation movements in the Third World, beginning, in the meantime, to shape a European line which later became known as *Eurocommunism*. The working classes of Western Europe were to be wooed and promised a new type of communism which owed something to the Soviet experience but more to 'pure' Marxism and to the experience of industrialised, developed parliamentary democracies. Stripped of jargon, the statement meant that the Soviet experience was unique in that a socialist revolution broke out in an underdeveloped country. This produced deviations, which Marx may have foreseen when he was doubtful about a revolution taking place in agrarian economies. The Western communists, warned by Soviet experience and in possession of a vastly superior economic potential as well as a long democratic tradition, would not make the Soviet mistakes. The working classes could trust them to use proper parliamentary routes to attain power and to retain democracy once power had been attained. It is perhaps to be wondered at why the Western

European workers, who were much better off than their brothers in the socialist bloc, should wish to jettison their positions to try the socialist experiment, but there were various reasons why dissent was growing in Western Europe, and why a modified form of socialism may have been welcomed. These reasons will be discussed later.

In the meantime, to return to Togliatti's Testament, it must be borne in mind that it was written against the background of Moscow's attempts to call a communist conference to condemn Chinese 'revisionism', and the PCI's strong opposition to such condemnation. Togliatti had earlier (in May 1964) published Gramsci's letter about the Soviet condemnation of Trotsky, written in 1926,[16] and made the point that the unity of the 1920s had been bought at too dear a price. He reminded the Soviet Union not to make the same mistakes in the 1960s. The Russians responded by vacillating, but the problems of the Sino–Soviet quarrel led to the deposition of Khrushchev in October 1964. Throughout the summer of 1964, as in the last couple of years of his leadership, Togliatti was paving the way for the line Berlinguer was to take up later: exposing the sterility of the Soviet system, expressing caution on its anti-Chinese policy and stressing the need for independence of the Western parties as well as the need to look towards the Third World rather than towards the USSR.

It must be seriously asked why Togliatti chose to make these statements, and to draft his Testament along those lines at this particular time, when he had for years been one of the more loyal supporters of the CPSU. First, there was a split in the PCI, which led in the first instance to the formation of a pro-Chinese group and, later, to the appearance of extreme left-wing groups. This was the taste of things to come: the revolutions of 1968 were not ripe yet, but their growth could be envisaged in the early 1960s. Second, the Chinese were getting the upper hand in the Sino–Soviet quarrel, not the least because they were successfully developing nuclear weapons. Third, the Vietnam war was a watershed in communist experience: clearly the Vietnamese were developing their own brand of agrarian socialism, while taking aid both from China and the USSR. Fourth, the years of dissent within the socialist bloc had loosened discipline: such discipline could be reinforced by armed intervention, but it was no longer automatic. And last, but not least, the experience of Cuban communism had given the Italians more food for thought: the Castro brand of communism was new and seemed to apply to Latin peoples better than the Soviet brand.

The growing diversification, of which Togliatti, always ready to see which way the wind blew, was increasingly aware, has been summed up well by one writer:

> International communism, Moscow style, has itself become increasingly irrelevant to the new revolutionary processes going on in the world. In a natural life cycle, communist parties have, in more and more societies, become parties of the 'establishment', opposed in turn by the New Left …. The model of a 'world state' and a 'world party' cherished by communists after 1917, vanished long ago. Over time, communists have differed on more and more and agreed on less and less. In the absence of an hierarchical structure in which Moscow can issue orders to subordinates abroad, it has failed to find an adequate formula for dealing with them.[17]

While it is true that, after Togliatti's death, the PCI began to apply his policy of 'unity in diversity' more consistently, it remains certain that under the leadership of Luigi Longo, his main deputy for many years, the changes were not very drastic. As Blackmer put it: 'Longo steered the party onto middle ground.'[18] However, the change in the leadership of the CPSU — when Khrushchev had been removed and Thorez's death in 1964, to be succeeded by the much more flexible Waldeck Rochet — changed the whole concept of communist co-operation. While the PCI developed the theme of co-operation with Socialists and Christian Democrats, by 1965 the PCF began to acquire a distinctly 'Italian' look.

'Since Togliatti's death, relations between the Italian and Soviet parties appear to have entered into a new era. In retrospect, the Yalta memorandum and the March 1965 meeting in Moscow seem to have marked the end of a turbulent and dynamic period during which the Italian party, by challenging traditional Soviet policies and premises, came to be widely regarded as the most consistent and articulate proponent among the non-ruling parties of a new style of international Communist relations.'[19] However, this is to ascribe too much importance to Togliatti alone. The fact is that the whole international relationships have changed as a result of the Vietnam War and the liberalisation within the socialist bloc, and perhaps most importantly in Europe, because of the undoubted economic successes of the EEC. The fact that the PCI as well as the PCF stopped their opposition to the EEC and began, instead, to talk of changing its anti-socialist policies is proof of the changed outlook.

On the other hand, the PCI itself began to lose ground on the domestic scene. Its membership continued to decline, and stood at one and a half million in 1966. In the same year only 300,000 party members were less than thirty years old. Those who called for change in the party line were defeated by a coalition of Longo and Amendola at the 11th Congress in 1966. The new 'positive' attitude towards the Italian problems only began to be exhibited by the PCI in the early 1970s. The positive approach began to appreciate the value of parliamentary democracy: it was left to Enrico Berlinguer, as Vice-Secretary, to voice it in 1970: 'Parliament must function in such a way as to allow the positive contribution of the opposition of the left in the determination of national policy.'[20]

The collapse of the government of the centre-left in 1971 and the election of Enrico Berlinguer as Secretary General in March 1972 hastened the process of legitimation. Finally, the collapse of the Allende government in Chile in 1973 made the Italians wary of aiming for radical changes unless they had the support of all classes in society. The interpretation of Allende's collapse has been twofold: on the one hand, it was assumed that the 'forces of reaction' would bring down any communist government outside the Soviet sphere of influence, hence the Communists had to work within the parliamentary system; on the other, it was tacitly agreed that if the Communists did not have the consensus of at least two or three classes or strata in the population they would be unable to retain power without the use of force.

It is from this formula, as well as from the new personality at the top of the leadership, that the *Historic Compromise* evolved. Unlike Togliatti and Longo, Berlinguer was an intellectual: the son of a landowning family which had been in socialist politics (his father was a socialist senator); married to a practising Catholic; and with good looks and the power of intelligent reasoning which appeals to the young. Berlinguer's thesis was, briefly, that parliamentary approaches to communism were better than revolutionary seizures of power; that a compromise with the Catholic Church was inevitable in a country which is, nominally, at least, 99 per cent Catholic and that a union with the Socialists is not necessary in Italy — where they had been losing ground in any case — but that a union with the Christian Democrats would give the Communists a share in power. Berlinguer's thesis was put to a severe test in the 1976 elections, when the PCI won almost as many votes as the Christian Democrats, but not quite. Not daunted, he arranged for a negative type of alliance; the Communists would not bring the government down by *not voting against it* rather than risk another election or another centre-left coalition with the Socialists.

This typical Berlinguer compromise produced bad results both for Italy and for the PCI. The growth of the radical Left and of terrorist groups followed directly the pact with the government: the PCI began to lose prestige and votes. The result of the growth of terrorism was the kidnapping of Aldo Moro in the spring of 1978 and his subsequent murder. (Moro, a Christian Democratic politician, was well known for his flexible attitude towards the PCI.)

In January 1979 the Communists withdrew their support for the minority government, partly as a result of the losses caused by their negative support. They made it a condition of support that they would be given seats in the cabinet, which the Christian Democrats refused even to consider. Elections, which were held in early June 1979, showed a great deal of damage to the Communists: they lost 4 per cent of the votes and twenty-six seats in the Chamber of Deputies. As one commentator said:

> It seems fairly certain that one explanation for the Communists' setback can be found in the younger electors. In the past it was assumed that many youths voted Communist either out of conviction, or as a generic protest against the Establishment. With the Communists having been, for the last three years, one of the sustaining columns of the Establishment's temple (though not yet allowed into the inner sanctum) the youths' natural options were the Radicals and the Democratic Proletarians.[21]

The leadership of the Christian Democrats took a turn to the right after the murder of Moro: the PCI refused to support a Christian Democrat government unless it was in the cabinet; this the DC could not allow. While on the national front the PCI enjoys the support of ten million voters it is as far from government as before. However, its successes in local government are undoubted. It governs several large regions and most large cities, and it has made inroads into the traditionally anti-Communist south. It is acknowledged to be the party of reform, of cleaning up Italy's pollution and of producing new housing policies. Its successes on the international scene are equally striking. It has objected once again to a Soviet-sponsored meeting of Communist parties in April 1980. As Berlinguer was holding talks with the French Socialist leader, François Mitterand. 'Giancarlo Pajetta ... explained... that the Italians refused to take part in the Moscow-inspired Paris meeting on East–West disarmament because there was no object in holding a meeting at which Afghanistan would not be discussed' while Berlinguer was preparing to leave for Beijing to start official relations with the Chinese for the first time in more than twenty years. 'Although the Italian and Chinese Communist Parties may still be separated ideologically on many important points including the correct future relationship to be maintained with the United States there is a growing convergence of views on the actions of the Soviet Union. There is no doubt that the Peking visit will be the occasion for more sharp words from the Kremlin.'[22]

Is the PCI revisionist? It has certainly become much more interested in improving its image, in becoming the party of moderation and in promoting socialist unity than in supporting the CPSU or in fomenting world revolution. Its balance sheet is one of losses and gains: time alone will tell the final sum.

The PCF — a Mirror Image of the PCI

As the PCI was devising its own road to socialism, whether revisionist or not, its much more powerful sister party the PCF was undergoing a crisis. No sooner had it attempted to adjust itself to the 20th Congress revelations than it was confronted by the creation of the Fifth Republic and de Gaulle's cult of personality. However, unlike the Italian party, the French were used to a much tighter discipline: they had managed many more U-turns than the Italians and survived, and they were supported not only by a stronger and older proletariat than the Italians but they could command the loyalty of a large number of intellectuals.

The success of de Gaulle, first in setting up the Fifth Republic and then in settling the Algerian War, put the PCF on the defensive. If the verdict of the people was in favour of a dictator and if the dictator then proceeded to do what the Communists had been calling for for many years the position of the party is made difficult. Besides, de Gaulle soon proved by his independent foreign policy, aimed at detaching France from the Atlantic Alliance, that his was a 'national road'.

> From the early 1960's onwards the Communists had been finding it increasingly difficult to oppose de Gaulle on foreign policy questions: his disengagement of France from rather complete subordination to American foreign policy and his spectacular gestures (acceptance of independence for Algeria and other French colonies; withdrawal from the unified command structure of NATO; recognition of the People's Republic of China; the blocking of European political integration) were of such a character that the Soviet leadership publicly endorsed French policy.[23]

The death of Thorez on 11 July 1964 and the succession to leadership of the much more flexible Waldeck Rochet completed the primary changes of attitudes. Without exactly supporting the government the PCF found it difficult to oppose it. Apart from that, the new constitution offered something that the Communists coveted: presidential government. It did not escape the PCF's understanding that, if the Fifth Republic was stable and the PCF clever enough, this post was within its reach. In 1965 the PCF supported the candidature of Francois Mitterand, the Socialist candidate for president, and forced de Gaulle into a run-off which was considered to be a victory for the Left. By 1967, the new Secretary-General, Waldeck Rochet, admitted that some aspects of the Gaullist policy were positive in themselves. From 1965 onwards the Communist policy was less concerned with dogma, though it made some cosmetic concessions to the theory of peaceful co-existence, than with the creation, with or without Soviet consent, of a bloc of the Left. The clear aim was a possible left-wing president. It mattered less at this stage that the president should be Communist - though this would come later - than that he should be the candidate of the united Left.

The period between 1965 and 1968 was devoted to joining forces with the French Left, namely the Democratic and Left Federation (FDGS). In December 1966 the PCF signed an electoral agreement with the FDGS, as a result of which in the 1967 general election the PCF increased its share of the vote to 22.5 per cent (from 21.7

per cent in 1962). After agreement on the withdrawal of contending candidates in the second ballot, the PCF increased its number of seats from 41 to 72 and the FDGS from 87 to 118, thus reducing the Gaullist coalition to a very slim majority.[24] As a result of these successes and cooperation in parliament, the PCF and the FDGS signed a common Declaration in February 1968, which Waldeck Rochet described as 'a *minimum platform of action.*'[25]

The events of May–June 1968 took the Communists by surprise and after some hesitation they, together with the FDGS, submitted a motion of censure against the government. However, when Mitterand announced publicly that he would run for president at the next elections and would form a government including the Communists, de Gaulle dissolved the National Assembly and called new elections. The revolts and strikes of May–June had frightened the French electorate sufficiently to produce a defeat for the Left in the elections of summer 1968. There has been some suggestion that the Communists (or more exactly the CGT) negotiated with the government over the results because of a fear of syndicalism produced by the mass strikes: there is also the question of de Gaulle's trip to Baden-Baden before he announced the election,[26] but, by and large, all observers agree that the results of the election showed that the public did not wish for a revolution. They also proved what the Italian electorate has demonstrated since: that as a communist party moves to the right, or closer to the positions of power, so its traditional clientele abandons it, to move far more to the left.

Nevertheless, the defeat of 1968 did not discourage the PCF from a further move towards power, a move possibly facilitated by the illness which deprived Waldeck Rochet of power and by his post being taken over by the Assistant Secretary-General, Georges Marchais. Significantly, Marchais was elected to the post of Secretary-General at the 20th Congress of the PCF in December 1972, and the Common Programme (a document of considerable importance in that it appeared to agree the terms under which the Socialist and Communist parties might co-operate in order to achieve a peaceful transition to socialism in France) was agreed in June 1972. Hence the new approach of the PCF agreeing to a multi-party system was Marchais' own work, and owed more to his efforts than to those of the Socialists. The perennial debate whether the PCF had 'really changed', as Tiersky put it, and was ready to abandon revolutionary Bolshevism, placing parliamentary tactics as the most important way to power, has been put to a severe test since. This debate has not been resolved by 1980.

What is certain is that throughout the 1970s (or to be exact up to the 1978 election) the PCF had expected to reach government: 'In 1975, a respected observer of French Communism remarked that the one thing that could be said with certainty about the evolving French Communist Party [PCF] was that it wanted to be in power.'[27] In the presidential elections of 1974, the Socialists and Communists supported Mitterand, the Common Programme candidate. Though Mitterand lost to Giscard, the public came to regard him 'as the *de facto* leader of the Left, i.e. as the Left's privileged interlocutor with the government and the spokesman of the Left on national issues. Resentful of the public attention thus directed toward the Socialist Party and its head, the PCF went so far as to accuse Mitterand of being too sure of himself and too domineering . . .'[28] The following years were difficult, with the PCF losing ground to the Socialists and the polls forecasting a Socialist victory in the general elections of 1978.

The agreement between the two parties ended with an argument over nationalisation in September 1977, and was not patched up till the first ballot votes were counted and showed losses for the PCF and a much smaller gain than expected for the Socialists. The last-minute agreement did not stop the re-election of a Giscardian–Gaullist majority. The elections led to critical assessments of the party leadership by the intellectuals: on the one hand, the right-wing Jean Elleinstein contended that the party had taken too long to break with the Socialists, that it had not been clear in its rejection of the Soviet model and that it had not carried out internal reforms.[29] The left-wing Louis Althusser complained that the party had reformed too much, had strayed from the basic tenets of Marxism–Leninism and had abandoned its notions of the dictatorship of the proletariat. Marchais, on his part, attacked both his critics and the Socialists for the defeat and ordered a ballot of the membership to eliminate the dissenters. The PCF members ran true to form and supported the leadership over-whelmingly. As Wilson states: 'The dissidents are comparatively few in number and are mostly intellectuals who have little rapport with the ordinary working-class party member.'[30]

However, since 1978, the PCF had moved further away from *Eurocommunism* and nearer to the CPSU, and has even discussed the candidature of Marchais in the presidential elections of 1981.

There have been many analyses of this change of course, among them the most intriguing one being that the change was insisted upon by the USSR, which finds Giscard much easier to deal with than a government and president of the United Left, and the most commonplace one being that it is the result of personal rivalry between Mitterand and Marchais.

In summing up, the PCF has followed the PCI to some extent, but has always retreated at the last moment. It may not be exactly the opposite in its policies, as the theory of 'mirror image' suggests, but it has certainly seldom taken the initiative in relaxation of tensions except where it hoped to gain power — power on its own conditions, not those of the United Left. An observer is presented with the image of a party which is much more petrified, much less intellectually alive and much more easily led than the PCI.

The British Communist Party

The PCF and the PCI are the largest non-ruling parties in Europe and their position is of the most importance. However, as they developed their new tactics, so did the smaller parties. The Spanish and Portuguese Communist Parties were built anew in the era of *Eurocommunism* and hence deserve a separate mention. The other parties shed their Stalinism as the old leaders retired or died and developed differing degrees of independence. The most interesting one is the Communist Party of Great Britain, which suffered from various disadvantages such as extreme Stalinism, small membership and no parliamentary representation, and which after 1968 was further subjected to pressure from the extreme Left, from the Eurocommunists and from splinter Communist parties in Britain. It finally decided to reform completely and in 1978 issued its own 'road' programme,[31] which was one of the most decisive documents — apart from the PCE's statements — rejecting Soviet interference. It also opened its discussions, allowed a television company to televise meetings of the Central Committee and began to insist on party democracy.

The CPGB's efforts were not crowned with great successes. Despite some politicians' insistence that it has far-reaching contacts within the Labour Party and the trade union movement, such influence is not easily detected by the general public. When the Communist shop steward Derek Robinson was sacked by British

Leyland in 1979 the party did not even muster a strike on his behalf. Neither has the TUC Day of Action on 14 May 1980 provided any proof of large-scale infiltration of trade unions. Cynics might say that the CPGB can afford to be liberal for it has no chances of gaining power in Britain. Others will doubt that it had 'really' changed. An independent observer will note that the USSR has always preferred Conservative politics in Britain: hence the conclusion may well be that the CPSU has little incentive in either influencing the CPGB or in encouraging it to develop. Few will doubt, however, that the appearance at least of the CPGB has changed dramatically and that its programme is Eurocommunist in that it envisages a parliamentary democracy, a pluralist state and a peaceful transition to socialism. Thus far, at least, the Italian and the French Communist parties have influenced British communism.

Notes

1. 'Gloria a Stalin', *Rinascita*, **X**.2, 1953, pp. 65-8: quoted by D. Blackmer, *Unity in Diversity*, p. 29.

2. Togliatti, on the 20th Congress of the CPSU, quoted by Blackmer, ibid., p. 26.

3. *Momenti della storia d'Italia*, p. 160, quoted in A. Morawski, *The PCI and the Italian Road to Socialism*, Unpublished Dissertation (Department of European Studies, UMIST 1978), p. 21, n. 16. For a well-considered and succinct account of Togliatti's case, see A. Morawski, *Gramsci and Togliatti — from Theory to Pragmatism*, Ch. 2, pp. 15-19.

4. G. Seniga, *Togliatti e Stalin*, quoted by Blackmer, *Unity*, p. 30.

5. Ibid., Ch. 2, Section 3: 'The Internal Crisis of the PCI'.

6. On Togliatti's role, see R. Conquest, *The Great Terror*, pp. 579-80.

7. *Nuovi Argumenti*, No. 20, May-June, 1956, quoted in Blackmer, *Unity*, pp. 51-8.

8. F. Fejto, *A History of the People's Democracies*, p. 109.

9. See Blackmer, *Unity*, p. 83.

10. Ibid., p. 89.

11. Morawski, *Gramsci and Togliatti*, p. 40.

12. VIII Congress, p. 231, quoted by Blackmer, *Unity*, p. 108.

13. D. Floyd, *Mao against Khrushchev*, quotes the text of the 1957 Declaration on pp. 296-307.

14. Blackmer, *Unity*, pp. 149-50.

15. *L'Unità*, 21 December 1961, quoted by Blackmer, ibid., p. 356.

16. See Chapter 4.

17. A. Dallin, 'The USSR and World Communism', in J.W. Strong (ed.), *The Soviet Union under Brezhnev and Kosygin*, pp. 222-3.

18. Ibid., p. 398.

19. Ibid., p. 403.

20. *L'Unità*, 12 July 1970, quoted by Blackmer, 'Italian Communism: Strategy for the 1970's, in *Problems of Communism*, May-June (1972), p. 45.

21. G. Armstrong, *Guardian*, 6 June 1979.

22. D. Willey, *Observer*, 6 April 1980.

23. Tiersky, *French Communism 1920-1972*, p. 232.

24. Ibid., p. 246.

25. *L'Humanité*, 26 February 1968: also Tiersky, *French Communism*, p. 250.

26. Tiersky, ibid., p. 252, calls this a 'puzzling trip' but does not suggest with whom de Gaulle may have been consulting. On the other hand, he suggests that the PCF did not really want to win the elections in any case.

27. F.L. Wilson, 'The French CP's Dilemma', *Problems of Communism* July-August (1978), p. 1, quoting Georges Lavau.

28. Ibid., p. 3.

29. Articles of 13, 14 and 15 April 1978 in *Le Monde*: see also Wilson, 'French CP's Dilemma', p. 8.

30. Wilson, ibid., p. 11.

31. The Communist Party of Great Britain, *The British Road to Socialism — Programme of the Communist Party* (London, 1978).

14

The Sino-Soviet Split in Global Perspective

The Origins of the Schism

A new chapter in Sino–Soviet relations opened when the CPC came to power in 1949. Mao Zedong went to Moscow in December 1949 for the celebrations of Stalin's 70th birthday. Stalin had been distrustful of Mao since the late 1920s and did little to help him against the Kuomintang. After the CPC's victory in the summer of 1949 the Russians retained their diplomatic relations with the KMT, rather than acknowledge the Communist government. Hence, negotiations were difficult and Mao stayed in Moscow for nine weeks, finally signing a Treaty of Friendship, Alliance and Mutual Assistance on 14 February 1950. This assured China of Soviet support against attack by Japan or any other state co-operating directly or indirectly with Japan. A separate agreement provided for Soviet credits to China of 60 million US dollars annually for five years, a very modest amount compared with US aid to Kuomintang or Soviet aid to Eastern European countries. In exchange for the credits, Mao was forced to accept the continued presence of Soviet troops in Port Arthur and Dairen until 1952 — a promise which Stalin failed to honour, and the troops were only withdrawn after his death. He also recognised the independence of the Mongolian People's Republic, implying by this that it was in the Soviet sphere of influence. This went right against Mao's long-asserted belief that Outer Mongolia was part of China and would join it voluntarily as part of a communist federation.[1] There is little doubt that Mao was bitterly disappointed and resentful of the imperialist behaviour exhibited by the Russians.

Mao was a realist in those days, however, and on leaving Moscow on 17 February 1950 he issued a statement declaring that Sino–Soviet friendship was 'eternal and indestructible', and asserted that Soviet achievements would serve as a model for the construction of communist China. This friendship was to be severely tested on the outbreak of the Korean War, which seems to have been started on the presumption that the US would not intervene and the North Koreans would overcome South Korea on their own. At the time the war broke out, in late June 1950, Mao was engaged in the Land Reform programme and he envisaged an invasion of Taiwan to defeat the remnants of Chiang's forces. Hence the American intervention in Korea and its declaration of intent to defend Taiwan met with Chinese indignation.

Instead of consolidating his hold on China and defeating Chiang, Mao was forced to send troops to Korea, and was directly involved in conflict with the USA, in what he considered to be a Soviet war. In 1963, after the split, the *Peking Review* published a bitter article concerning the war:

> The leaders of the CPSU . . . accuse us of hoping for a 'head-on clash' between the Soviet Union and the United States and trying to push them into a nuclear war. Our answer is: No, friends. You had better cut out your sensation-mongering calumny. The Chinese Communist Party is firmly opposed to a 'head-on clash' between the Soviet Union and the United States, and not in words only. In deeds too it has worked hard to avert armed conflict between them. Examples of this are the Korean War against U.S. aggression, in which we fought side by side with Korean comrades. . . . We ourselves preferred to shoulder the heavy sacrifices necessary and stood in the first line of defence of the socialist camp so that the Soviet Union might stay in the second line.[2]

Mao had every right to be bitter; on the other hand, it must be assumed that he had an element of choice in the matter, and that he sent Chinese troops in either to stop American progress in Korea, or to stop any threats to Chinese borders, which MacArthur's march to the river Yalu appeared to pose. It was too late to complain about the involvement after three years of war, and a return to *status quo*. Had China and North Korea been victors then no doubt Mao would have claimed a famous Chinese victory.

In other words, China joined the war in the hope — justified by the American policy so far — that the war would be short and victorious. It only began to complain about the war openly after its break with the Soviet Union. The clear inference must be that the war was a joint Soviet–Chinese venture in which each side hoped to gain the most benefit. When neither gained, the alliance was strained almost to breaking point.

But it did not break yet. After Stalin's death in March 1953, Mao called him 'the greatest genius of the present age' and a man who loved the Chinese ardently. Simultaneously, the Chinese and Soviet governments began making arrangements for ending the Korean War. In September 1953, probably by way of recognising Chinese losses in the war, the Russians stepped up their economic aid to China. And in September and October 1954 Khrushchev visited Beijing and made further gestures, including increased economic aid, the return of Port Arthur and Dairen to China and the abandonment of the Soviet share in the joint-stock companies formed in 1950.[3] It was clear that the Chinese were being offered the same treatment as other communist countries: more independence, more equality and more esteem. They took the Russians at their word and began to expect full equality. That is why the break finally occurred.

Khrushchev's 20th Congress speech in 1956 was the starting point of the quarrel. While the Chinese approved of many facets of de-Stalinisation they resented the fact that they had not been consulted about the speech beforehand, while European communist parties had been told in advance, and they were fearful that the speech would produce a ferment in the communist world. It is not clear why the Chinese were not told but it may have been connected with Soviet fear that they would reject such uncompromising denunciation of the former leader. On the second count, Mao was right — the speech did produce unwanted repercussions and created more trouble than it solved for the USSR. The third possible reason, that Mao was counting on gaining the position of the top communist leader in the world after Stalin's death, and that he resented remarks about the cult of personality, which he had built up around himself, one can only conjecture about. But there is little doubt that Mao did come to believe in his own infallibility and that the demolition of the Stalinist cult did not come at a convenient point in his own leadership.

China and the Bomb

By coincidence, the period dating from Stalin's death and through Khrushchev's 1956 speech was also one during which another important debate developed in China: this was the debate on the use and usefulness of nuclear weapons. China had at first made little of America's nuclear potential, though after the USSR announced it had the Bomb (an announcement was made in *Pravda* on 6 October 1951), it reassured the citizens that the American monopoly had been broken. By 1953 the Soviet hydrogen bomb tests were acknowledged by the Chinese, and in December of that year the Chinese press began to take note of peaceful uses for atomic energy. The Chinese suppressed the Bikini incident in March 1954, which provoked a strong reaction in Japan, and it was only in October of that year, when the USSR proposed talks on renouncing atomic weapons, that the press began to support the Soviet initiative, suggesting that China would participate with other powers in such talks. The Americans rejected Chinese participation and the Chinese accused them of wanting to conduct a nuclear war against China. Finally, in 1955, the Chinese leadership admitted that nuclear power was of importance, that a nuclear war could happen and that China could be involved, though the position that in such a war communism rather than capitalism would win was adopted.[4]

China's position began to clarify in late 1954, under the impact of its campaign to liberate the offshore islands and Taiwan. It appears that the fear of American nuclear strikes in the event of a Chinese invasion made the Russians advise the Chinese to desist. The Sino–Soviet agreement of October 1954 provided for scientific and technical co-operation and for the transfer of the Soviet share in the Non-ferrous Rare Metals Company in Xinjiang, an interesting development in view of the fact that there is a strong belief that uranium was discovered in Xinjiang in 1949. In January 1955 the USSR announced that in return for contributions of raw materials, China, Poland, Romania and East Germany would be helped to develop peaceful atomic energy projects. Apart from aid given to all these countries, China was to receive a research reactor which would be fuelled by uranium rods containing $_u235$ to a 2 per cent enrichment and would use heavy water. It has been generally assumed that China, unlike the Eastern European states, would be helped to develop her own nuclear weapons.[5] A reorganisation of the Chinese armed services line of command followed, which represented a change from a 'citizen' army approach to that of a professional army. It appeared that the Chinese were departing from the theory of guerrilla warfare to that of a professional war.

In March 1955 the American Secretary of State, John Foster Dulles, announced that Chinese aggression against Taiwan would be countered by the USA and the use of nuclear weapons would not be excluded. In the same month in response to a Japanese remark that nuclear weapons may be stockpiled in Japan by the Americans, the Chinese issued a statement threatening Japan with destruction by nuclear weapons in such a case.[6] However, by April 1955 the Chinese dropped their plans for invading Taiwan and called for negotiations with the USA; a clear sign that they had no independent nuclear deterrent and that the Russians had refused to become involved in a nuclear war on their behalf. In July 1955 the Five-Year Plan gave priority to the development of peaceful atomic energy research. In the autumn of 1955 the USSR carried out large-scale hydrogen bomb tests, and the Chinese debate followed the line that the Soviet Union's deterrent capacity was sufficient for the Socialist bloc, and that China's resources could be used to develop her economic potential — though the implication was that nuclear weapons would and could be developed within this economic reconstruction.

The military strategy of old campaigners continued to prevail, and as defence budgets were being cut, the Minister of Defence, Peng Dehuai, told Japanese officers in 1956 that the Chinese were not afraid of nuclear warfare:

> Because China has 600 million people. Even if 200 million people were killed by atomic weapons, 400 million people would still survive. Even if 400 million people were killed, 200 million would still survive. Even if 200 million survived, China would still constitute a big country of the world. Furthermore, these 200 million people will absolutely not surrender. Therefore, at the end America will lose the war.[7]

In August 1957 the Soviet Union tested its first Intercontinental Ballistic Missile, and in October she launched her first earth satellite. In November 1957, at the celebrations of the October Revolution, Mao spoke openly to the Congress of the Soviets about the Third World War, saying: 'If the imperialist warriors are determined to start a third world war, they will bring about no other result than the end of the world capitalist system.'[8] And in private conference, Mao is said to have stated that he debated nuclear war with a foreign statesman (believed to have been Nehru): 'He believed that if an atomic war was fought, the whole of mankind would be annihilated. I said that if the worst came to the worst and half of mankind died, the other half would remain while imperialism would be razed to the ground and the whole world would become socialist.'[9] In 1963 the Chinese also asserted that under an agreement signed in October 1957 the Russians agreed to provide China with a sample atomic bomb and technical data on its manufacture. Hence, Mao's statements on the possibility of a nuclear war made the Soviet leaders wary of providing China with Soviet weapons.

At this stage the nature of relations between China and the Soviet Union begins to be less clear. Schram ascribes it to a break in personal relations between Khrushchev and Mao at a secret meeting in July/August 1958, when apparently Mao vetoed Khrushchev's idea of talks with the US about the Middle Eastern crisis.[10] Lagley Hsieh, who provides a far more reasoned analysis, suggests that the idea that the Chinese could make another attempt at offshore islands, shielded by the now superior Soviet weaponry, was Zhou Enlai's, and was taken up by Mao, because he had little understanding of what a nuclear war would mean.[11] Schram, despite his obvious bias in favour of Mao, also suggests that the 'romantic' streak was winning over his rational thought. In 1958 Mao was already 65 years old, an age which is deemed to be too old for other men to work. Hence, the 'romanticism' may simply have been the onset of senility, of which Mao gave many examples at a later stage. At any rate, it is agreed that the relations between the two leaders foundered in 1958 on one specific point: 'It is likely that Khrushchev ... informed Mao of the Soviet Union's unwillingness ... to make use of its nuclear power *vis-à-vis* the United States in support of overt Chinese military moves. That the Chinese were not prepared to take on undue risks without Russian aid, but did not necessarily concur in the Soviet estimate leading to this policy, was suggested by their subsequent behaviour.[12]

Sino–Soviet relations were complicated by the fact that the Great Leap Forward, which was started in May 1958, was coming to grief, and that Khrushchev made fun of Mao's communes to the Americans on the one hand, and on the other, attempted to put economic pressure on China. The CPC was breaking up into a pro-Soviet section, which was eager to get rid of Mao, and into a section with Mao and his supporters. The failure of the Great Leap Forward and retreat from this policy in August 1959 began to strengthen Mao in his resolve to purge the party of Soviet supporters, to stand apart from the USSR and to test Chinese power in a small conflict. The first was easy: Peng Dehuai, who made a pro-Soviet speech in August 1959, was dismissed in disgrace. The second was happening as the Russians began to withdraw their technical aid to China. The third was being enacted simultaneously, as China was at the height of its conflict with Taiwan and was in the middle of a border conflict with India.

On 30 September 1959 Khrushchev arrived in Beijing, straight from a visit to the US, and at a banquet in his honour he sharply attacked those 'who wanted to test by force the stability of the capitalist system'.[13] Khrushchev further emphasised that China must recognise Taiwan's separation from the mainland. This completed the break between the two men. In April 1960 the theoretical organ of the CPC published an editorial which is said to have been partly written by Mao. This propounded Mao's views on a nuclear war: 'Should the imperialists impose such sacrifices on the peoples of various countries, we believe that, just as the experience of the Russian revolution and the Chinese revolution shows, those sacrifices would be rewarded. On the debris of imperialism, the victorious people would create very swiftly a civilization thousands of times higher than the capitalist system and a truly beautiful future for themselves.'[14] It was a re-statement of Mao's belief that China could survive a nuclear war, and that such a war should be desired by true socialists.

Khrushchev made a vehement attack on the Chinese at the Romanian Party Congress in June 1960, when he brought up the Sino–Indian dispute, the Great Leap Forward and the dismissal of Peng Dehuai. He called the Chinese 'madmen', who wanted to unleash a nuclear war and who were nationalists in their relations with India. He also declared that the future of international relations would depend on Soviet–American co-operation, rather than on Sino–Soviet co-operation. All the communist parties present in Bucharest, with the exception of Albania, condemned China. In July 1960 the Russians unilaterally withdrew all the remaining Soviet experts in China within one month, thus ending abruptly all the existing agreements and contracts.[15]

The Moscow Conference of communist parties in November 1960 brought the differences out into the open. Mao's representatives insisted that all communist parties were equal, and had the right to determine their own policy. The Chinese delegation also insisted that a mention of aid from experienced democratic countries (i.e. the USSR) to underdeveloped socialist countries would not be included in a clause in the joint statement at the end of the Conference. Obviously, Mao had come to believe that each country had to proceed on its own path of development and the withdrawal of Soviet aid to China helped him to formulate the need for self-sufficiency. Though the winter of 1960/1961 was a hard one in China and she was forced to buy grain from Canada and Australia, it was not a hopeless one. China had already found one ally in Eastern Europe, Albania, and she was beginning to get sympathetic responses from several Asian countries, who considered her the champion of non-European socialism.

Two more incidents were of the utmost importance in confirming and strengthening the split between the two countries. At the 22nd Congress of the CPSU in October 1961, when Khrushchev made vicious attacks on Stalin, Zhou Enlai, the leader of the Chinese delegation, ostentatiously laid a wreath at Stalin's tomb. Second, there was a Soviet announcement that Russia would supply MIG planes to India in the new Sino–Indian border war in the autumn of 1962. The Cuban crisis brought Chinese accusations of Soviet adventurism and appeasement of imperialists. On 7 January 1963 *Pravda* attacked the Chinese openly and explicitly for the first time and Mao replied in one of his poems, comparing the Russians to ants climbing up a locust tree.[16] The two communist states have taken different roads, which have not converged since.

Two more points are of importance in this context: first, that in the period up to the break with the Soviet Union Zhou Enlai's moderating influence played a large part in playing down the differences;[17] and second, that the break with the Soviet Union coincided with the rise in the influence of Mao's wife, Jiang Qing, and was connected with very radical policies. The culmination of these policies was the death of Lin Biao in 1971 — possibly as a result of a Soviet-inspired military coup which failed. The 1960s were a period of violent radicalism in China, and the 1970s continued to be so until the death of Mao. The influence of Jiang Qing on this radicalism is well known and has since been acknowledged.

Sino–Soviet Relations after Khrushchev

In October 1964 Khrushchev was deposed in what has been termed as a 'palace revolution'. It had very little in common with such revolutions as they were practised in Russia. Khrushchev was not strangled like Emperor Paul, nor shot like Beria; he was simply removed from power and asked to live in his country villa, from which he periodically issued various statements, culminating with his famous memoirs. It is a measure of the revolution Khrushchev himself had effected in the USSR — a change as radical as that which had occurred in 1917.

Some authors attribute Khrushchev's downfall directly to the Chinese situation:

> The downfall of Nikita Khrushchev and the almost simultaneous explosion of the first Chinese atom bomb are stupendous triumphs for Mao Tse-tung and communist China. Khrushchev is, metaphorically speaking, the first victim of the Chinese bomb. ....
> The initiators of the conspiracy were above all anxious to mend the breach between Moscow and Peking. They probably knew about the forthcoming nuclear explosion, and the foreknowledge induced them to speed up their action.[18]

Khrushchev's fall is attributed to the Chinese quarrel, to the brutal methods which Khrushchev used to combat the Chinese and to the 'utter disarray into which Khrushchev has thrown the whole international communist movement'[19] as a result of the split with the Chinese. It is also maintained that Togliatti's famous 'testament', which was written as an anti-Khrushchevian polemic and published in *Pravda*, partly because Togliatti opposed Khrushchev's policies on China and partly because he had been personally offended by him, was intended as a *coup de grâce* and served the anti-Khrushchevite faction very well.

Whatever the wishes of the new Soviet leadership may have been in relation to China, the split remained after Khrushchev was deposed. This was due partly to the gap on nuclear weapons, with the USSR standing by the Nuclear Test Ban Treaty; to the stand towards America, where Russia insisted on peaceful co-existence; and to ideological grounds, with Russia remaining 'revisionist' and China 'left-wing'. It was also partly due to the internal Chinese struggle for power, where Zhou Enlai was in favour of a compromise with Russia, and Liu Shaoqi was in favour of a struggle against the Russians.[20] By 1965 the situation was also complicated by the Vietnam War, with the Chinese accusing the Russians of meanness in allocating aid to the Communists and the Russians accusing the Chinese of making a common front against imperialism impossible. Chinese support for Sukarno, the Indonesian leader, and for Boumedienne in Algeria as well as the Chinese Cultural Revolution all alienated many friends in Africa, Asia and Eastern and Western Europe. China and her supporters were isolated after 1965–6, and although the Chinese had demonstratively refused to attend the 23rd Congress of the CPSU in the spring of 1966, the Russians kept a diplomatic silence on the Chinese question, beyond Brezhnev assuring the Congress that there would be a resolution of the crisis. Writing after the Congress, Deutscher noted that:

> The resolutions of the congress and the reticence of the leaders *vis-à-vis* China conceal at least two conflicting attitudes. There are ... those among the leaders who have in fact no desire for a reconciliation with China and are determined to continue the feud to the 'bitter end', but hold that it is good tactics for them to go on refraining from public polemics, to counter Chinese criticisms with insubstantial verbal concessions, and so to place the odium of the breach on the Chinese. Others ... are genuinely anxious to come to terms with the Chinese, to co-ordinate policies and action, and to intervene more decisively in defence of North Vietnam. American escalation works to strengthen this latter group; and both groups fear that if the Russo–Chinese conflict is acted out in the open, the Americans may feel encouraged to attack China; and in that case the Soviet Union might find itself drawn into global conflict.[21]

In the event, partly as a result of the upheaval of the Cultural Revolution, the North Vietnamese followed Soviet advice, and opened negotiations with the Americans in the spring of 1968. As one observer wrote at the end of the 1960s: 'The Vietnamese position in the intra-communist disputes is indicative of the present fragmentation. While Peking has forfeited much of its support abroad, Moscow has not been able to capture it.'[22] This was right insofar as one point was concerned; the opening up of American–Chinese relations in the early 1970s led directly to the ending of the Vietnam War, as the Russians decided not to leave a vulnerable flank open and the Americans felt safe enough to withdraw from South-east Asia. Both Beijing and Moscow lost much credibility, while South-east Asian communists gained a considerable victory.

In the 1970s Chinese policy must be divided into the period up to Mao's death in 1976, during which pro-American policy was pursued externally, while internally radical policies were still, if only partially, adhered to: and after 1976, when the Chinese made a series of U-turns, some liberalising, others tightening up policies. The Maoist leaders became the 'gang of four': in 1979 English spelling of Chinese names was changed to the *Pinyin* system, making, for example, Chiang Ching to be spelt *Jiang Qing*. Vice-Premier Teng (now Deng) visited the US in January 1979, and in November of that year, the *Guangming Daily* criticised the cults of Mao and Stalin.[23] On the other hand, the CIA reported that 'China's weapons technology lags 15 to 20 years behind the Soviet Union'[24] and Jonathan Mirsky, visiting China after seven years in 1979, called it the 'land of little red lies', saying: 'When a faultlessly uniformed and barbered professor says, "Peasants are peasants, and teachers are teachers . . ." enthusiasts should count to ten before they applaud. Tomorrow, or next month, or next year, egalitarianism may be back in fashion.'[25] The history of China in the 1970s may belong to the history of communism, but to an impartial observer it seems to support the theory Wittfogel developed about 'oriental despotism'. A change of despots brings about a radical change of policies; the only thing which remains is the despotism.

This gives the Russians reason to treat China with sadness rather than anger: as an article on collective security in Asia claimed, the Russians would be only too glad to have China participate in such a system. 'The Soviet Union would welcome the participation of the People's Republic of China in steps aiming at strengthening Asian security.'[26] It is left to other communists to expose Beijing's opportunism: in the same issue of *Far Eastern Affairs*, an East German commentator stated that

For many years the Maoist policy and ideology have been one of the main suppliers of themes for imperialist and opportunist propaganda. From this murky source the latter eagerly draw themes and arguments for anti-Soviet pronouncements which attempt, above all, to split or to paralyse the anti-imperialist movement. This in line with the recommendations given by

Zbigniew Brzezinski, that well-known ideologist of anti-communism, in one of his writings, which suggests that Sovietology should be regarded through the prism of 'Sinology' if it is to develop properly.[27]

On the other hand, the Americans make the most of their cordial relations with China. In a special issue of *Problems of Communism*, entitled 'Beijing Looks Ahead' a commentator noted that the Chinese have realised in the 1970s that 'the USSR posed a broad-gauged geopolitical threat to Chinese interests', that it expanded Cuban–Soviet influence in Africa; and above all, that 'Soviet accomplishments in Indochina are without question the most disturbing recent development for Beijing'.[28] As a result of its anti-Soviet policy, the Chinese leadership has been promised new technology (possibly including nuclear potential) by the Americans.

The split between communist parties which resulted from the Sino–Soviet quarrel is of importance. This is less significant in 1980 than it was in 1970: at that time one commentator noted that, in Europe, Albania was the only communist country to give complete support to China, whereas there were splinter communist parties in about twenty-four countries, including Australia, Belgium, Italy, France, Austria, Switzerland, India, Japan and Brazil. In most instances, the numbers involved were insignificant.[29]

The Maoist parties lost ground when China began to court reactionary regimes, like Pinochet's Chile, in order to annoy the USSR. But the global communist split fed on itself when, after the 1968 revolutions, the Soviet Union's monopoly on communist theory and practice ended and radicals throughout the world began to look for new solutions. This gave rise to increased independence of Eastern European countries, to the loosening of ties between the CPSU and non-ruling communist parties, and culminated in the short-lived, but very important, phenomenon of *Eurocommunism*.

Notes

1. S. Schram, *Mao Tse Tung*. pp. 253-7.
2. 'Two Different Lines on the Question of War and Peace', *Peking Review*, No. 47, 1963: quoted by Schram, ibid., pp. 264-5.
3. Schram, ibid., pp. 283-4.
4. For the CPC's position till 1954 see A. Langley Hsieh, *Communist China's*

Strategy in the Nuclear Era, pp. 1-8.
5. Ibid., pp. 20-1.
6. Ibid., p. 29.
7. Akio Doi, *Tête à tête with Mao Tse-Tung* (Tokyo, 1957), pp. 65-6: quoted by Langley Hsieh, ibid., p. 52.
8. Mao's speech of 6 November 1957, quoted by Langley Hsieh, ibid., p. 83.
9. Quoted by Schram, *Mao Tse Tung*, p. 291. This text was only released by the Chinese in September 1963.
10. Schram, ibid., p. 295.
11. Langley Hsieh, *Communist China's Stragegy*, pp. 91-4.
12. Ibid., p. 96.
13. Schram, *Mao Tse Tung*, p. 301.
14. 'Long Live Leninism', *The Red Flag*, quoted by Schram, ibid., p. 302.
15. Schram, ibid., p. 303, see also J. Gittings, *Survey of the Sino-Soviet Dispute*, p. 123.
16. Schram, *Mao Tse Tung*, pp. 306-7.
17. See J. Van Ginneken, *The Rise and Fall of Lin Piao*.
18. I. Deutscher, *Russia, China and the West 1953-1966*, p. 291.
19. Ibid., p. 294.
20. Ibid., pp. 298-9.
21. Ibid., p. 330.
22. A. Dallin 'The USSR and World Communism', in J.W. Strong (ed.), *The Soviet Union under Brezhnev and Kosygin*, p. 204.
23. *Guardian*, 27 Nov. 1979.
24. *The Times*, 17 Aug. 1977.
25. *Observer*, 28 Oct. 1979.
26. V. Vorontsov and D. Kapustin, 'Collective Security in Asia', in *Far Eastern Affairs*, No. 1, 1976, p. 49.
27. W. Neubert, 'Maoist and Imperialist Ideological Alliance on an Anti-Communist Platform', in *Far Eastern Affairs*, No. 1. 1976, p. 82.
28. H. Gelman, 'Outlook for Sino-Soviet Relations', *Problems of Communism* September-December (1979), pp. 50-66.
29. Dallin, *The USSR and World Communism*, p. 226, n. 21.

Part four:

Nationalism, Regionalism and Neo-Marxism

15

The Growth of Neo-Marxist Movements

The Campus War

Come Mothers and Fathers
Throughout the land
And don't criticise
What you don't understand;
Your sons and your daughters
Are beyond your command ...   (Bob Dylan)

By the 1960s the USSR had become an institutionalised post-revolutionary state, while China was undergoing the Cultural Revolution. The Soviet Union had become 'respectable' in international relations, and China was well on the way to becoming so in the near future. The socialist bloc was a fact of life, and in Latin America a new socialist state, Cuba, was taking its first faltering steps towards communism. The big powers had agreed to retain the *status quo*, to ban nuclear proliferation and to refrain from interfering in their respective spheres of influence. All was relatively quiet, stable and orderly, almost as it had been in 1848, under the rule of the Holy Alliance in Europe. As in 1848, so in 1968, the world was roughly shaken by a series of student revolutions. As after 1848, so after 1968, things were never to be the same again.

Most contemporary student revolts consist in challenges to and attacks on university authorities ... In what follows, we shall see these three factors — the search for the sacred, the creation of adversary relationships, and the rejection of all authority — at work again and again.[1]

We socialists are not fanatics or timeservers. We are socialists because we see the prospect which life holds out for all working people. We want the commitment of workers who laugh and love and want to end the wretchedness and despair which shuts love and laughter out of so many lives. We do not have to spend the rest of our lives, and leave our children to spend the rest of their lives, wrestling in struggle against a mean and despotic ruling class. Society *can* be changed, but only if masses of working people abandon the rotten shipwreck of the 'leave it to us' reformers, and commit themselves to change from below.[2]

What precisely has gone wrong in Western civilisation, that at the very height of technical progress we see the negation of human progress: dehumanisation, brutalisation, revival of torture as a 'normal' means of interrogation, the destructive development of nuclear energy, the poisoning of the bioshpere, and so on? How has this happened?[3]

These three quotations, as well as Bob Dylan's lyric, summarise well the disillusionment which proceeded from (1) the failure of the USSR to produce a satisfactory alternative to the capitalist system, as acknowledged by Khrushchev in 1956; (2) the events of the Cultural Revolution, in which the young revolutionary guards could rampage with impunity through the country; (3) the real but naive wonder that high technology did not equal high civilisation; and (4) from the age-old generation gap. Despite statements that 'youth culture' is a new phenomenon which owes its existence to mass media, this is not so. The generation gap, the rejection of the authority of the elders and the development of one's own 'culture' are normal stages in the process of growing up. It is the *means* of protest, not the *need* to protest that change.

In 1968 Herbert Marcuse became the prophet of protest. Marcuse was born in Germany in 1898 and was influenced by Luxemburgism, founding the 'Frankfurt School' of sociology, which developed Marxist sociology of knowledge. Forced to leave Germany by the Nazis, Marcuse went eventually to the US, where he developed a theory that Stalinism was a peverted form of socialism, and that socialism could be equated with the 'dictatorship of the proletariat'. He argued that the Soviet state exercised its functions against the proletariat, that the centralised authoritarian organisation had a class character and that the bureaucracy had a vital interest in maintaining and enhancing its privileged position. Hence the theory that the 'Socialist state is the proletariat constituted as the ruling class' was wrong.[4]

Some authorities trace the beginnings of the student revolutions to Marcuse's works, but they had a much wider and more long-lasting impact. They gave rise not only to the student revolutions (which were, in the US, as much the product of the Vietnam War as of theoretical writings) but to a whole series of new radical groups — one can scarcely call them parties, because of the anarchistic and fluid character of their membership and pro-grammes. In Britain the theories of the New Left were developed by Tony Cliff, the founder of the International Socialist Party. Cliff argued that, because the Bolshevik Revolution was not followed by a world revolution, the Russian working classes lost ground to the bourgeoisie. Soviet bureaucracy became the ruling class and moulded all political life in a totalitarian pattern. The result was 'state capitalism', which was not only the exact opposite of socialism but the extreme political limit which capitalism can reach.[5] According to Cliff, state capitalism is based on class conflict and class exploitation, and the social institutions (i.e. the family and the educational system) operate exactly as under capitalism.

Cliff's theories have been criticised as essentially Menshevik ones, because the Mensheviks used to claim that the Bolshevik Revolution could not be a Marxist one as the Russian society was not sufficiently developed.[6] However, Cliff's theories were not unique: they follow the precedent of Marcuse (who himself followed Rosa Luxemburg) and were taken up by various Marxist schools of thought. Perhaps the most popular view in the late 1960s (a view furthered by the events of the Cultural Revolution) was that expressed by George Thomson, who maintained that Maoism as then practised in China was a true Marxist movement, whereas the post-Stalinist developments in the USSR were 'revisionist' and a backsliding towards capitalism.[7]

The arguments about dictatorship of the proletariat and the role of the Soviet Union in retarding or bringing about socialism were confused further by an injection of economic theories, based on Trotsky's ideas about a workers' state. These were in essence that the Soviet Union is not a state capitalist system, because the bureaucracy is not a capitalist class and cannot transmit its privileges to its heirs. On the other hand, the bureaucracy's privilege consisted in its abuse of its powers. Ernest Mandel, a

Western European Marxist, developed this theory further in 1968 and 1969. It was his view that the Soviet-model systems are not state capitalist and the International Socialist movement must support them in any conflict with capitalist systems. He maintained that the Soviet-model systems are transitional; halfway between capitalism and socialism. The USSR was not a classless (therefore a socialist) society because there existed a parasitic class, the bureaucracy, whose interests were the opposite of the interests of the workers; but this was merely the result of Russian backwardness, the product of the country's capitalist past and capitalist environment. Socialism was impossible in one country. The implications of this philosophy were that a workers' revolution was essential in advanced capitalist countries; that there must be revolution on a global scale for socialism to be successful; and that, given the above, classical Marxism would be possible and a genuine workers' state could be constructed.[8]

The Soviet ideologues, on the other hand, have always argued that these movements are revisionist, leftist or anarchistic. All such movements have been condemned by Lenin at various times, therefore it is safe to assume that such labels would deal a death-blow to the 'splinter' groups. In fact, the radical socialists, to use a term they would themselves reject, have, for one reason or another, continued to thrive during the late 1960s and in the 1970s. Therefore it is worth analysing their theories briefly, which can be summed up under six headings:

(1) The Bolshevik Revolution created conditions for the development of the capitalist mode of production;
(2) Socialist relations of production do not follow directly from state ownership of the means of production;
(3) State ownership of the means of production may give rise to a ruling class deriving its power from the *control* of the means of production;
(4) Working classes can only be liberated by a revolution embracing all economic, political and cultural institutions;
(5) The Maoist wing, in addition, relied on the dictatorship of the proletariat to continue during the socialist stages of development, till a full development of communism;
(6) The International Socialist wing stressed the importance of the global character of a socialist revolution; a revolution which occurred in the Western capitalist states must be

accompanied by change in the Soviet-type states and in China.

The International Socialists became known in Britain as the Workers' Revolutionary Party, later re-named the Socialist Workers' Party. Paul Foot, one of the leaders of the party, published a brief book in 1977 entitled: *Why You should be a Socialist*:

Socialism, is about human beings, and human beings make mistakes. There will be plenty of mistakes made by a workers' democracy, plenty of wrong decisions taken.... Socialism provides only the structure in which men and women can cooperate to put their mistakes right.... By the same token, the precise details of a socialist society cannot be laid down in advance. The case for socialism is not built on precise guidelines, all clearly marked out — with the guarantees against mistakes and bureaucracy written into a constitution. We're describing a society to be brought about by the efforts of the common people, so we cannot be exact at a time when those efforts have not been made.... But we *can* describe the broad outlines, the necessity for public ownership, for equality, for a workers' democracy. And we can say with absolute certainty that the alternative is barbarism.[9]

This ideology, based more on faith than on scientific analysis, appeals to the young: the generation gap and opposition to the *status quo* have ensured that such philosophy found a ready response in one class: the students. The International Socialist ideology did not lead to a workers' revolution; it did lead to a series of student revolutions, which have been extremely important in their effects. In the late 1960s and in the 1970s the people in whose name this ideology was preached, the workers, were — with very few exceptions — only interested in what had always interested them: a higher standard of living. Perhaps the most striking example of the workers' indifference to the intellectuals' aspirations was the 1968 student revolution in Poland, which culminated in a rout of the intellectuals, without a single working-class voice being raised in their defence. Given such response, why did the students make revolutions? There are many theories, and obviously one cannot analyse every movement. One can only look briefly at the 'campus revolutions' and make an overall assessment.

The New Culture

The analysis of campus revolutions suffers from one main problem: that it was left to political scientists and sociologists, rather than to historians and psychologists. Thus, instead of perceiving them as part of a traditional conflict between generations we are told, on the one hand, that they were a search for a new dimension in socialism; on the other, that they were a sinister anarcho-communist plot against the established order. Thus one sociologist stated:

> Daring or timorous, far-flung or cautious, all these attempts have one thing in common: they all start from the assumption that the guiding ideas of the new culture can no longer be found within the commonplace and the ordinary. Something much more far-reaching than just a reshuffling or rearrangement of the bits and pieces of reality is necessary. Neither the objective of making everybody as well-to-do as the rich of today, nor that of elevating inner-factory planning to the societal level, raises high expectations about the degree of human happiness and human emancipation that it may bring. So the utopia-seekers of today look beyond the boundaries at which their predecessors used to stop. The advanced socialist thought of today is breaking new horizons, reaching beyond the historical limits fixed by the industrial epoch for both bourgeois culture and its traditional socialist counter-culture.[10]

On the other hand, a liberal political scientist commented:

> The most striking tactical device of this generation of student activists is the conversion of student anxieties and aspirations on national and international moral questions into hostility against universities and university authorities. A student is worried about the war in Vietnam or the continuation of racial discrimination. What can he do about it? Not much, or so it would first appear. But suppose you can convince him that the enemy is here at home on the campus, that the president of Columbia is the local repository of racism, or that the Harvard administration is actively supporting the napalming of Vietnamese peasants. And suppose ... that as 'proof' of this you can offer the fact ... that it is expelling from the university the most effective fighters against racism and militarism. Then the indignation is not only

further aroused but it is particularised against a visible and vulnerable enemy.[11]

In the welter of contradictory comments, one may feel lost. Were campus revolutions a spontaneous or a conspiratorial phenomenon? Were the students sinister manipulators of innocent universities or noble exponents of a new culture? Many hypotheses were advanced by both sides. The original student revolts occurred in the US as a result of student opposition to the call-up for the Vietnam war. The opposition was strengthened by the feeling that this was not a 'just' war.

Thus, in protesting against the universities, the students in reality protected their own lives: expulsion from university almost certainly meant draft, which could result in death, mutilation or a long period spent as a prisoner — not an attractive prospect. The protest began in 1964, and was met with incredulity by the US universities and the authorities, which had not been used to such protests. The universities were part of the 'Establishment' in any case. In the United States all universities depend on industrialists for goodwill and at least part of their income. In Britain, a study of one university shows that a large part of its income comes from industrial gifts, even though the university is not a technological one. Thus the myth of an 'independent' university is largely disposed of.[12]

The American universities, after an interlude of sympathising with the radical students, stiffened their position for fear of being (literally) ground between the right and the left.

By the late 1960's this rhetoric had grown a little tired ... there was much less willingness to destroy the authority of the administration for the sake of a particularized sacred issue .... In general this shift in attitude occurred on campuses which had actually had substantial experience of student unrest. The Berkeley faculty, for example, responded quite differently to the People's Park crisis of 1969 than to the Free Speech Movement of 1964. The dramatic categories had slowly but perceptibly shifted in favour of authority.[13]

At this stage the protest shifted to Europe. The French students centred their initial protest on the Fouchet Plan, which intended to cut down on the growth of universities. The German students were disappointed in the lack of contact with East Germany and wanted to be able to travel in the socialist bloc. The British students had to look for much more specialised issues. But it was possible to mobilise the students at the London School of Economics, with its large number of American students, in a fight against the appointment of Dr Walter Adams, who came from Rhodesia, as Director — this despite the fact that his anti-apartheid record was not bad in the context of the African situation.

In March-April 1968 there were riots both in France and Germany: bombs exploded on various 'imperialist' targets and many students were arrested, among them the future terrorist leaders, Andreas Baader and Gudrun Ensslin, and the German Trotskyite leader, Rudi Dutschke, was shot. In May there were large-scale student demonstrations, first in Nanterre, then in Paris, and a boycott of lectures in West German universities. By mid-May the French trade union organisations called for a general strike: de Gaulle dissolved the National Assembly by the end of the month and called for general elections. The elections in June gave de Gaulle a landslide victory, and a partial reform of the university system was undertaken. In October a trial of Baader and Ensslin was held in Germany against the background of protest from other radicals such as Daniel Cohn-Bendit. Very soon, Baader and Ensslin escaped from German prisons and hid in Paris, staying in a flat owned by Régis Debray. Thus, the wheel had come almost full circle: the anarchistic German students found refuge with someone who was to make his name in a Latin American revolutionary situation.

It is certain that the bungling attitude of educators and politicians in all Western countries contributed handsomely to the growth of the neo-Marxist myth and, indirectly, to the growth of terrorist movements. Had the universities managed to absorb the protest and channel student activities towards peaceful activities: had they enjoyed student confidence; and had they reacted reasonably instead of calling in the National Guard and riot police, closing down universities and installing iron gates, the tide might have been stemmed by reason instead of by force.

The terrorist campaign which followed the suppression of student revolts in Europe had little to do with the New Left: it had even less to do with the idealistic aims of nineteenth-century anarchists. It was an expression of thwarted power-drives and hurt vanity rather than a quest for a new socialist Utopia. Before condemning it completely, however, the educators in the Western world would have to ask themselves if they were not to blame for educating a materialistic, selfish and unanaytical generation of students, who not only could not tell right from wrong but, even worse, maintained that right was wrong and vice versa.

A New Culture in Eastern Europe?

While student revolutions were breaking out in America and Western Europe, in Eastern Europe another drama was being played out. Here, too, there was protest against the established authorities. In Czechoslovakia, which had suffered under a particularly oppressive regime while other socialist countries were liberalising, a new liberal faction came to power in the spring of 1968. In Poland, where the intellectuals were disappointed with the growth of the right-wing 'national' communist faction (led by Moczar) and with the weakness and ineptitude exhibited by Gomulka, there was strong ferment from early 1968. The banning of a play by Mickiewicz at a Warsaw theatre, on the pretext that it might give rise to anti-Soviet feelings, led to violent student demonstrations.

Polish intellectuals watched as the Czechoslovak Reform Movement grew in strength, ovbiously hoping that the same reforms might be introduced in Poland. Instead, Warsaw University was occupied by armed forces in March 1968, and the 'Partisan' group led by Moczar attributed the disturbances to the action of 'a group of conspirators affiliated to the Zionist Centre . . . and which was plotting a *coup d'état'.*[14] A purge of the party machine, the press, radio, cinema and the universities was ordered, and the victims were mainly communists of Jewish origin, accused of Zionism. This helped the Partisans to arouse anti-Semitic feelings in Poland, and the anti-Zionist purge turned into a purge of all liberal and 'cosmopolitan' elements, many of whom were close to Gomulka.

The nationalistic elements were almost sure of winning in 1968, and of eradicating Gomulka and his entourage. But they had overreached themselves. Their patriotic propaganda required that they show a hostility — be it only covert — towards the Soviet Union in order to find favour with the masses. The USSR tolerated anti-Zionist propaganda: anti-Soviet propaganda was different.

Moczar's group was silenced, though by that time thousands of Poles of Jewish origin were deprived of posts, and Gomulka was allowed to stay on in power till he was finally roughly unseated to make way for Gierek.

The attempt at a New Culture in Eastern Europe was squashed even more roughly than the student revolutions in the West. But the effects were politically disastrous. In Poland a technocratic government was installed which was unable to bridge the chasm between itself and the population. In Czechoslovakia, the whole Reform Movement was eradicated and a new government installed, giving rise to the growth of a large dissident movement. In France, the revolution brought down de Gaulle, a dictatorial but charismatic leader, in favour of petty rulers. In Germany, the Social-Democrats felt obliged to make a sharp right-turn. And in the US a reactionary president was elected. Richard Nixon was elected on the platform of 'law and order', a programme which resulted directly from the student disturbances.

An Assessment of the Results of the Neo-Marxist Movement

The Neo-marxist movement sprang up directly as a result of de-Stalinisation in Russia and the Sino–Soviet split, followed by the Cultural Revolution. It had begun as a straightforward political split from the mainstream of communist thought as incorporated in the pro-Soviet communist parties all over the world. It continued as an attempt at independence by various communist parties, both ruling and non-ruling. It was then taken up by fringe groups, students who called themselves Marxist, but who exalted either Trotsky or Mao — anti-heroes in official Soviet ideology. Those fringe groups later influenced large sections of the student population, both in the West and in the East, to produce vehement uprisings and upheavals in many countries. When the revolutions were suppressed, there remained the hard core of revolutionaries without a revolution. These then took up the next best thing — terrorism, whose apparent aim was to break down the system of government and little else. These were anarchist, even nihilist, aims. Again, there is little new in such progression and it could be claimed that it is a straight replay of the second half of the nineteenth century.

Yet there are differences. First of all, the split was not all among the young. Many communist parties split up into pro-Soviet and pro-Chinese factions. Many communists deserted their parties, or were expelled for 'factionalism'. The split grew into a bitter war between the factions, with both the CPSU and the CPC claiming moral and political victories. Each ruling communist party was keen to obtain converts. But perhaps the most important reason for the quarrel was a genuine loss of faith. We have already seen that the New Left in Britain called for faith rather than reason. Similar calls were made in other countries, and one neo-Marxist, Bauman, stated that one must look 'beyond the old boundaries' in search of socialism.

The split was reflected among communist intellectuals. This was especially notable when Roger Garaudy, one of the foremost French communist philosophers, was expelled from the PCF in 1970. He had begun to doubt the party from the moment of the 20th Congress: Khrushchev, he later said, had 'fundamentally challenged, in the eyes of the whole world, an image and method that have led a socialist regime' to commit crimes against socialism. He later welcomed with enthusiasm the Czechoslovak reforms in 1968 and called for such reforms to be carried out in other socialist states.[15]

It is strange that Garaudy should have baulked at an exposure of Stalinism when he was able to support Stalinism as long as it was not exposed. But this is not all. The second strange thing in Garaudy's revised Marxism is his conviction (as expounded by Cranston) that the 'common humanistic concern of both Christianity and Marxism' provides a basis for cooperation between the two.[16] What is basic to Marxism, Garaudy argued, is the belief that knowledge is active, that man creates his own history through work, and that the role of philosophy is the transformation of the world. As for Christianity, he suggested that basically it is a 'religion of action', seeking the salvation of man not just in eternity but also in the present world. 'Hence', he continued, 'Christianity does not rule out, but actually implies, militant effort turned towards the future and its construction. In these terms, Marxism and Christianity are brought into common ground'.[17]

The dates of Garaudy's conversion (the mid-1960s) and his expulsion (in 1970) are significant. Not only do they fall within the period of a surge of neo-Marxism but they are also parallel with developments in Latin America, where the Catholic Church had begun its painful progress to support the disinherited against dictatorial governments, simultaneously as the first hesitant steps were taken towards a Latin American brand of Marxism. His expulsion also came only slightly earlier than the Italian Communist 'historic compromise' and the growth of Eurocommunism.

A dialogue between Christians and Marxists had begun in Poland much earlier, but was distrusted both in clerical and communist circles. This was something new: a communist philosopher actually striking out on his own in saying that Marxism had more in common with Christianity than with Stalinism. It was at one and the same time an admission that Marxism did not have all the answers, and was an invitation to Christians, most particularly clergy, to strive for the improvement of the human condition in 'this world' rather than the 'next'.

Garaudy's expulsion from the PCF signifies little except that that party is, and always has been, very unimaginative. What is more significant is that from 1970 onwards the dialogue has developed. It is difficult to say at this point in time whether the Marxists have ventured into the region of faith, or the Christians into the region of dialectic materialism (though an observer might be inclined to believe the latter), but the most important effects of such a stance can be seen not in Italy, or in Eurocommunism (however important they are), but in Latin America.

Notes

1. J. Searle, *The Campus War*, p. 16.
2. From a Socialist Workers' Party recruitment leaflet, 1977.
3. Herbert Marcuse, in a BBC interview with Brian Magee, published in *The Guardian*, 31 July 1979.
4. H. Marcuse, *Soviet Marxism: A Critical Analysis*, pp. 103-5.
5. T. Cliff, *Russia: A Marxist Analysis*, 1964: and *State Capitalism in Russia*, 1974: a brief note in D. Lane, *The Socialist Industrial State*, pp. 30-1.
6. Lane, ibid., p. 30
7. G. Thomson, *From Marx to Mao Tse Tung: A Study in Revolutionary Dialectics:* brief note in Lane, *The Socialist Industrial State*, pp. 33-4.
8. E. Mandel, *Marxist Economic Theory*, 1968: and *The Inconsistencies of State Capitalism*, 1969: a brief note in Lane, *The Socialist Industrial State*, pp. 36-9.
9. P. Foot, *Why You should be a Socialist*, p. 46
10. Z. Bauman, *Socialism — The Active Utopia*, p. 111.
11. Searle, *The Campus War*, p. 21.
12. E.P. Thompson (ed.), *Warwick University Ltd*, 1970.
13. Searle, *The Campus War*, pp. 117-18.
14. K. Kakol, in *Prawo i Zycie*, 24 March 1968: quoted by F. Fejto, *A History of*

the People's Democracies, p. 228.

15. See M. Cranston 'The Thought of Roger Garaudy', in *Problems of Communism* September-October (1970), pp. 11-18.

16. Ibid., p. 16.

17. Ibid., p. 16.

16
Marxism in Latin America

The Origins of Latin American Marxism

Without some understanding of how European and Chinese communism influenced Marxism in Latin America and was itself, in turn, influenced by it, it would be difficult to recognise the basic changes in ideology and practice of Marxism in the 1960s and, even more, in the 1970s. Latin American Marxism developed out of anti-American feelings, which grew after the European colonial powers left the continent.

As colonial powers became weaker, the United States gained influence in Latin America. The formulation of the Monroe Doctrine in 1823, aimed at the Holy Alliance and its designs on Latin America, stated that the extension of such a system to the continent was 'dangerous to our peace and safety', and that the independence of Latin American states should be respected, while any attempt to interfere would be considered unfriendly to the United States.[1] The Monroe Doctrine was further modified and extended throughout the nineteenth and twentieth centuries, and was generally resented by the Latin American governments as 'imperialist'. The presidency of Franklin D. Roosevelt and his new 'Good Neighbour Policy' helped to heal the wounds somewhat, and during the Second World War many Latin American governments co-operated with the United States. The disappointments began in 1945, when the United States turned its attention and most of its material help towards Europe, to the great bitterness of Latin America: the fact that Roosevelt was dead by that time may have been pure coincidence. This anti-American feeling grew and 'was particularly noticeable during the goodwill visit of the United States Vice-President Richard Nixon to Argentina and seven other nations of South America, in April–May, 1958. In Peru and Venezuela, Mr Nixon was the victim of various indignities from enraged mobs which broke police controls.'[2] The 'Progressive Alliance' began by President Kennedy in 1960 was hopeful, but was undermined by his assassination and by President Johnson's declaration in 1965 that any attempt to establish a communist regime in Latin America would call for armed intervention.[13] Relations between the United States and Latin American countries had always bordered on the two uneasy compromises: the United States now trying out a colonial role, now rejecting it; the Latin American governments sometimes welcoming the interference, sometimes rejecting it.

Latin American politics are very complex, which adds to the difficulties. As a book which attempts to synthesize Latin American politics[4] stresses, the very word 'party' has a different meaning from that in Europe, being primarily a faction gathered round a charismatic leader. 'As a result, contemporary party politics, the product of a troubled history, are themselves still troubled.'[5] The author divides the political parties into 'historic parties' of the first generation, like conservatives and liberals; 'modern parties' of the second generation, like socialist or social-reformist parties; and finally 'contemporary parties' of the third generation, which came into being in the 1950s and 1960s mainly under the influence of the Chinese and Cuban revolutions.

The last have emerged from the belief that the Chinese and Cuban revolutions have demonstrated that the peasants have a massive, though dormant, political strength in a revolutionary cause. Moreover, they were helped by certain clerical elements, particularly after the Second Vatican Council, and military elements, who have been described as 'Nasserite'.[6] The 'third generation' parties were generally far more revolutionary than the 'official' communist parties, still tied to the CPSU, and a feeling grew that the communist parties were unable to promote real change, which was expressed in 1952 in the following manner: 'The Communists are the post-revolutionary vanguard of the non-revolutionary rear-guard'.[7] Fortunately for Latin American communist leaders, Khrushchev's 20th Congress speech gave them some ideological backing by promoting the theory of peaceful co-existence, thus making them appear as the leaders of a peaceful progressive force against the 'wild' new revolutionary parties.

However, the split between the far-left Marxists, with their theory of an immediate revolution and armed struggle of the masses, and the communists widened under the impact of the Sino–

Soviet dispute in the 1960s. Mao's emphasis on the leading revolutionary role of the peasants, as against the Soviet doctrine of revolutionary proletariat, found keen followers in a continent where the majority of the population was still agrarian. There was also disillusionment with the orthodox communist parties, which were felt not only to follow Moscow too closely but also to have become 'soft' and opportunistic. The whole emotional climate of politics in Latin America was geared to the heroic and spontaneous, and against the careful and organised. As a result, traditional left-wing politics underwent a complete change at the beginning of the 1960s under the combined effect of the Cuban Revolution and the Sino–Soviet split.

Castroism, Cuba and the Revolution

Cuba is a microcosm of Latin America, but with all the features accentuated. It had been liberated from Spanish rule very late and did not achieve independence till 1899, though there were several independence wars since the mid-nineteenth century. Independence was only achieved with American help, and the USA took over the protection, both political and economic, of the island. This was for obvious reasons, as Cuba is the USA's nearest southern offshore neighbour, and much of Cuba's production was tied up with US business interests. The habit of US governments of regulating the 'sugar quota' system according to Cuba's obedience or disobedience was highly irritating to Cuban rulers, even those installed by the Americans themselves. This applied to the Batista regime, whose power lasted, with some interruptions, from 1936 to 1959. The constitution which Batista introduced in 1940 provided for 'a semi-parliamentary regime, the president to appoint a sort of prime minister who can be removed when he fails to obtain a vote of confidence in the chamber. The president was to be elected for a four-year term, by direct popular vote.'[8] Batista's opponents described the regime as a crude form of semi-military dictatorship, and he often annoyed the Americans by the shortcomings of his rule.

Any Cuban government had to govern a highly difficult nation. The Cubans were a mixture of descendants of African slaves, Indians and Spaniards. There was only one main crop, sugar, and an additional crop, tobacco, which used to account for 6 per cent of Cuban exports. The largely agricultural population was uneducated; in the 1950s 43 per cent of the adult rural population were illiterate. There was a large bureaucratic class (20 per cent of the whole workforce) employed by the government. Between 3 and 8 per cent of private landlords owned 60–80 per cent of the land. Sixty per cent of rural families lived in dwellings with earth floors and roofs made of palm leaves; nearly two-thirds of rural houses had no water closets or latrines; and only one out of fourteen houses was wired for electricity. Rice provided 24 per cent of the average diet, kidney beans 23 per cent and root crops 22 per cent. There was widespread tuberculosis and bowel disease.

The Cuban middle classes were mostly employed by American companies, and were alienated from the rural population. Cuba's dependence on American economy (American imports averaged 80 per cent of total imports) was matched by the American dilemma: how to protect American investment — over one billion dollars — and keep Cuba dependent economically. These problems kept the Cuban economy underdeveloped and contributed to its backwardness. Corruption was inbuilt into the system (there was an anecdote that parking meter revenues provided an allowance for Batista's wife). It is said that Batista himself amassed a fortune from stolen public funds. In the years preceding the revolution, the average amount of bribes in public works alone is said to have cost as much as the works themselves.

Fidel Castro was a genuine product of the Cuban conditions. He was the son of a Spanish immigrant, who, after working as a land labourer, had acquired some land in the Oriente province, his mother being the house servant at the time of his birth (though his parents were married later). There were two children of a first wife and seven by Castro's mother. At his mother's insistence — she was very devout — Castro was sent to a Jesuit school and later to a fashionable Jesuit college in Havana. He graduated from there in 1945 and entered the Faculty of Law at Havana University, graduating in 1950, and he practised law between 1950 and 1952.

What led the young lawyer to abandon his law practice and attack the Moncada Barracks in Santiago de Cuba on 26 July 1953 as a leader of 165 men and two women, all university graduates and all under thirty years old, is not entirely clear. The attack was a complete failure, the majority of the revolutionaries were captured (including Raul, Fidel's brother) and many were killed after being tortured. Fidel's life was apparently saved by the intervention of the Archbishop of Santiago; he was imprisoned and released after eleven months, under a general amnesty decreed by Batista. The main outcome of the attack seems to have been the name of the Castro movement, which took the name of the Moncada Movement, or 26th July Movement, from then on.

After his release, Castro took refuge in Mexico to prepare for a more successful revolution. Finance proved difficult to raise, but he was joined by other Cuban refugees and by a young Argentinian, Ernesto Guevara Lynch. In December 1956 82 men went on board a leaking old boat, the *Granma*, and landed in Castro's home ground: the Oriente province in Cuba. From then on, till the collapse of Batista's regime in early 1959, Castro led guerrilla warfare in the mountains, getting help in the form of volunteers, arms and food from local peasants. At no time did Castro hint that he had communist or Marxist sympathies. The Manifesto of the 26th July Movement, issued in November 1956, before the invasion of Cuba, refers constantly to the liberal reformer Jose Marti and calls for an end to colonialism, American domination and the sugar quota. Some vague proposals about distribution of land to the peasants and nationalisation of public services are made, but the general tone is that of a democratic patriot, keen to be friendly with the USA, and interested in setting up a liberal democracy, in keeping with Western political thought.[9]

Castro and his followers won almost by default: the regime collapsed on 1 January 1959, Batista and his family fled to the Dominican Republic and on 8 January Fidel Castro and his bearded companions made a triumphant entry into Havana, greeted by almost all the population as liberators. Cubans and all other Latin Americans were certain that a form of parliamentary democracy would be introduced by Castro, not only because of the Manifesto but because of the mutual hostility between the Communist Party of Cuba and the 26th July Movement. In fact, Castro moved away quickly from the idea of introducing a democratic regime and kept postponing the date of elections. He began to rule by acclamation: addressing the excited crowds in Plaza Jose Marti, he would ask whether a certain measure was right, and if the crowd yelled 'Yes', would announce that he had popular support for such measure. His second step was to outlaw political opposition, an opposition which would have supported him fully if he had allowed at least a formal democracy. The main onus of persecution, after a purge of Batista's followers, fell on the intellectual elite: anti-Castroism became counter-revolutionary.

In late 1959 Castro finally turned to Marxism, though many consider that he did so regretfully. Some historians maintain that he wanted to keep Cuba independent and non-Marxist had the USA been willing to support him, instead of blockading the island. Others consider that he had been a crypto-communist all along, and merely revealed his true colours in 1959. While anti-Americanism was popular with the intellectuals, the Marxist measures and the censorship which accompanied them was not. Thus Castro lost a large number of educated supporters, whom he could ill afford to lose if he intended to push the country into the twentieth century and produce an economic miracle. On the other hand, the masses adored him, and he was the epitome of a Latin American charismatic leader in the first decade of his rule. In general, in the first phase, there was little inclination to follow the Soviet model. Much more likely is the theory that Castro outlawed opposition because he feared for his role as the 'maximum dictator'. In many ways, Castro was much more like Trotsky, had he come to power, with his accent on dictatorship and 'permanent revolution', than leaders like Tito and Nasser with whom he had been compared.[10]

The process of introducing political Marxism in Cuba was slow, partly because of Castro's own reluctance to become a satellite leader and partly out of fear of Cuba's Catholic hierarchy and the American naval power. On the other hand, the USSR was unhappy about Castro's independence and slow to receive him into the socialist fold, while the Americans did not want to intervene in Cuba's internal affairs. Thus while Castro formed an open alliance with the old Communist Party (*Partido Socialista Popular*) in 1959, he did not proclaim his government to be Marxist–Leninist till 1961. In July 1961 the 26th July Movement was united with the PSP, and it was not till 1965 that the Community Party (*Partido Communista de Cuba*) was created. Some observers have called it 'no more Leninist than Nasser's Arab Socialist Union'. In the 1960s Castro purged a large number of old Communists, who were either jailed for long terms, or went into exile, leaving the leading posts to Castro's men. Castro is said to have leaned towards the 'Jacobin Left' in Cuba and in Latin America during this period though he changed this attitude in the late 1960s under the impact of failures on the Latin American continent.[11]

The Bay of Pigs incident in April 1961 destroyed the credibility of the US government, which had assured Castro, only a few weeks earlier, that no armed intervention would be contemplated and virtually invited Soviet intervention. When this occurred, in the form of missiles and the following crisis in September/October 1962, the break was complete. It has not yet been established what really caused the crisis: the US had always firmly denied that it intended to invade Cuba; Khrushchev maintained that Castro had asked him to instal the missiles; and Castro had since hinted that the installation was a condition of Soviet economic help.[12]

Soviet–Cuban relations were seldom stable, and Castro never made a comfortable ally for the Russians. At a conference in 1966 the Cuban delegate said bitterly that 'We Cubans . . . don't need to receive lessons on anti-imperialism from anyone' — hardly calculated to make relations with the USSR smoother.[13] Castro often proved to be more of a liability than an asset to Moscow. Cuba was an expensive luxury (in the early 1970s it cost the Soviet Union a million dollars a day), and Castro's enthusiasm for revolution, whether in Latin America, in the Far East or in Africa, has often forced Russia's hand and made it committed to causes for which it had little desire or stomach. At times, the Soviet–Cuban tension grew worse: only a third-rate official represented Cuba at the 50th anniversary celebrations in Moscow in 1967, and Cuba sent an observer to the 1969 meeting of communist parties, instead of a participant — both supreme insults. The Soviet Union finds it difficult to support Castro, even at his most pro-Soviet, yet cannot abandon him. He is the only surviving communist ruler in the Latin American area and, as such, has to be nursed through his friendly and less friendly phases. No doubt the USSR wishes it could apply the sanctions of the sugar quota, as the USA used to do, but this would be too dangerous. Castro has indicated often enough that he is ready to listen to the USA if pressed too hard.

Castro in Power

Castro's policy has been called 'communism — Cuban style'. It is based on local conditions: backwardness, a large rural population, lack of trade with most Latin American countries and lack of US economic trade and imports. All these have produced 'economics of scarcity'. In 1962 drastic food rationing was introduced in Cuba, partly as a result of the peasants' violent opposition to nationalisation of land. The land reform introduced in May 1959 stipulated the division not only of large estates but of small ones as well. Its progress was slow and uneven, partly because the farmers opposed the new co-operatives, and partly because it was supervised by army officers drafted in the INRA (National Agrarian Reform Institute), rather than by elected farmers' representatives. A second law was necessary in 1963, which resulted in the following division of land: the state sector had 60.1 per cent, the private sector 39.9 per cent. More than 60 per cent of sugarcane fields and 60 per cent of cattle went into the state sector. Various lesser measures were introduced between 1963 and 1967, including the return of some farms to their owners and the confiscation of abandoned holdings by the state.[14]

Various organisational forms were tried in agriculture, and finally in 1963 all state farms (hitherto called 'people's farms') were re-named 'state farms' and grouped into large organisations, called *agrupaciones*, under the direction of the General Administration of State Farms. The state owned all means of production and land, and workers were paid wages by the management. Though the apparent reasons for this change were political it may have been the need to improve the technology and provide larger machinery and sugar refineries which made this move necessary. In 1966 there were 575 state farms which were grouped into 58 *agrupaciones* each with an area of from 13,000 to 100,000 hectares.

The small farmers were organised into an Association of Small Agriculturalists (ANAP), which was to ensure that farmers kept to production targets consistent with the national plan. Later ANAP became a channel for credit, machinery and scarce materials for smaller farmers. Similar measures were introduced for cattle-breeders, but it has often been admitted that Cuban agriculture is over-centralised and over-administered, and this applies both to the state and private sectors.

Industrial development has been rather less emphasised in Cuba than in other socialist countries, which may have been a mistake. Castro always laid stress on agriculture, but the real problem was that industrialisation has been difficult because of lack of capital, skilled labour and technologists. In the first three years of Castro's rule some 300,000 refugees left Cuba, most of them doctors, teachers, engineers, scientists and lawyers. Most industries, large and small, have been nationalised and the economy is run by a Central Planning Board (JUCEPLAN). The plan had always been to create light industries producing consumer and intermediate goods from national resources, but for various reasons this has failed and the Cuban standard of living has been falling progressively as far as non-essential goods are concerned. There have always been shortages of consumer goods such as toothpaste, electric bulbs and detergents; the shortage of cars is well known and widely publicised. The population is most hard-hit by the rationing of coffee and meat, which has been the one consistent feature of the regime.

What keeps Cuba Marxist? Or neo-Marxist? And what keeps Cuba going? First of all, there is the contrast of a country where housing, education, the health service and basic foodstuffs are supplied to the population on a mass basis, whereas in other Latin American countries poverty is appalling. Every visitor to Cuba comments on the difference between this island and the countries in the Caribbean and on the Latin American mainland. Compared with the plain but sufficient diet of Cuba, other Latin Americans starve to death. The Cuban houses may not be luxurious but they are in a different class from the 'bidonvilles' in other Latin American countries. The Cuban health service is an example to other Latin American countries.[15]

Cuba is not a free society as it is understood in the West. But most Latin American countries are not free or democratic either. As to political prisoners and their treatment, Cuba is more civilised than Chile, Paraguay, Brazil and Argentina. Cuban political prisoners survive many years of imprisonment instead of dying under torture. In 1979 Huber Matos was released after twenty years in prison. Though he complained that he was held 'incommunicado, often naked, beaten, and for years kept in concrete boxes, where the windows were covered with metal and even the guards were forbidden to look at him', he had actually come out alive at the age of sixty, whereas the same cannot be said for political prisoners in other Latin American countries. Brutality is common in Cuban prisons but institutionalised torture, on the Chilean model, is not suggested even by the most anti-Cuban sources.

Throughout the 1960s and 1970s every Cuban had work if he wanted to work. In the last years of the 1970s the situation deteriorated but not to the extent of the general Latin American situation. Unemployment is still rare in 1980, and those who are surplus to the economy have been allowed to leave for the United States. It is not certain how many refugees left Cuba at the beginning of 1980, but it is certain that everybody who wanted to go was allowed to do so. In a very astute way Castro demonstrated his liberalism and the US had to react by forbidding the entry of the Cubans, thus appearing to be less liberal than Cuba. The demonstrations in Miami against the Cubans (who may take other people's jobs) show that the Cuban system, however harsh, may not be the worst choice.

Cuba's economy was helped by the booming sugar prices in the mid-1970s. In 1974 and 1975 it obtained large credits from France, Spain, Britain and Canada because of the sugar boom. It became recognised internationally, particularly after the American defeat in Vietnam, and stopped being ostracised, particularly in Latin America.[16]

Most spectacularly of all, Cuba began to export revolution successfully, to African countries. Cuba's large standing army, which was beginning to be a burden on the small island and possibly something of a threat to Castro, was exported to Africa, to fight in Angola, Mozambique and Ethiopia. Most impartial observers agree that while the USSR is not unwilling to see the Cubans succeed, it is a Cuban initiative and a Cuban effort which keeps the neo-Marxist governments in power in Africa, and it is Cuban technology which helps them to develop. The number of Cuban troops and technical personnel in Africa may not be as large as has been assumed: it is the fact that they are there and are helping the revolution which matters.

Not content with helping the revolution along, Castro also set himself the aim of leading the Third World. The visit of Brezhnev to Cuba in January 1974 signalled the start of a new, firmer and friendlier relationship. The successful Cuban intervention in Angola has, according to some sources, given Cuba new leverage in the Third World, and also with the Soviet Union. In 1976 a five-year economic and technical agreement was signed which is highly beneficial to Cuba, particularly in that it indexes sugar prices to oil prices. In 1977 Cuba signed an agreement with the USA on fishing rights and began to encourage American tourism.[17]

In September 1979 Cuba hosted the conference of 'non-aligned' nations in Havana. This was notable for the strongly anti-Israeli and pro-PLO line taken by Castro, which produced protests from the more 'moderate' leaders like Tito and Nyerere.[18] The 'non-aligned' bloc has become closer to Cuba and this is clearly not unconnected with Cuba's help to Caribbean nations. In a report from Havana it has been claimed that Cuba has been helping Jamaica, Guyana and Grenada, both with advice and some arms, to consolidate their socialist regimes. It has also sent doctors and nurses to those and other underdeveloped countries as part of help in return for aid it has received from the Soviet Union. 'Overseas duties also mop up some of the big surplus of doctors, teachers and agronomists produced by Cuba's much-praised education system which has not been accompanied by equally successful industrialisation and agricultural diversification . . . .' The report continues: 'None of the new breed of progressive Caribbean leaders is ideologically committed to imposing the full Marxist system, and all are willing to seek foreign aid wherever they can get it. Whether any of them is driven into the Marxist camp depends as much on the West's policies as on Castro.'[19]

This is, of course, the crux of the matter. Cuba, like the Soviet Union before it, can offer full employment (or 'over-employment'), full stomachs, education for the people and health and housing services. The West, under the aegis of the International Monetary Fund, can only offer deflation, even greater unemployment and 'tightening up of belts'. As Michael Manley of Jamaica complained, this policy may work in developed countries, where the people may actually have some fat to lose: the Caribbean peoples have always had their belts on the last hole anyway; if they tighten them any more they will surely die.

Just as Castro came to power by default and proved that he could overcome the US boycott, the same phenomenon could work in other Caribbean and Latin American countries. Castro has one more ace in his hands: as massacres and kidnappings continue daily even in those Latin American countries which had a history of stable government, he can show twenty-one years of uninterrupted rule, a history of stability, despite the economic and political crises, and an impressive cultural, technical and military expansion for a small and poor country. It can hardly matter to other Latin American countries that this could not be achieved without Soviet aid: what matters must surely be that, uniquely in Latin America, it works.

Notes

1. A. Curtis Wilgus and R. d'Eca, *Latin American History*, p. 400. The first statement incidentally, and the more important one, was concerned with the prevention of further Russian expansion on the north-west Pacific coast, and declared that no further colonisation was to take place on the American continents.

2. Ibid., p. 407.

3. Ibid., p. 412.

4. J. P. Bernard *et al*: *Guide to the Political Parties of South America*.

5. L.F. Manigat, Introduction, ibid., p. 13.

6. Ibid., p. 19.

7. Luis E. Aguilar, 'Fragmentation of the Marxist Left', in *Problems of Communism*, July-August (1970), p. 3.

8. Wilgus and d'Eca, *Latin American History*, p. 371

9. See 'Program Manifesto of the 26th of July Movement', in R.E. Bonachea and N.P. Valdes (eds.), *Cuba in Revolution*, p. 113-40.

10. See T. Szulc, *The Winds of the Revolution*, ch. 4.

11. R.J. Alexander, 'The Communist Parties of Latin America', in *Problems of Communism*, July-August (1970), pp. 42-4.

12. See H.L. Matthews, *Castro — A Political Biography*, ch. 7.

13. R.J. Barnet, *Intervention and Revolution*, p. 81.

14. For details, see Bonachea and Valdes, *Cuba*, particularly ch. 12.

15. For the impressive growth of Cuba's social services, see Bonachea and Valdes, ibid.

16. E. Gonzalez, 'Complexities of Cuban Foreign Policy', in *Problems of Communism*, November-December (1977), p. 5.

17. Ibid. pp. 12 and 21.

18. *Sunday Telegraph*, 9 Sept. 1979.

19. *Observer*, 16 Sept. 1979.

17

Hispanism and Neo-Marxism

The Theory of Revolution and Guerrilla Warfare

In May 1976 newspapers carried the following notice: 'A group calling itself the Che Guevara International Brigade has claimed responsibility for today's assassination of the Bolivian Ambassador here [in Paris], General Joachim Zenteno. General Zenteno, aged 55, who commanded the Bolivian forces, which killed Guevara in 1967, was shot dead outside his embassy.' And further: 'The statement accused General Zenteno of having justified to the French Government the liberation in Bolivia of the Nazi leader, Klaus Barbie, head of the Lyons Gestapo and butcher of Jean Moulin and a hundred other resistance men.'[1]

This was a fitting end to one of Latin America's more dramatic revolutionary episodes, a continent which specialises in revolutionary drama. Che Guevara, the young Argentinian who accompanied Castro on his successful venture to Cuba, was born in 1928, the son of middle-class parents with liberal leanings. He qualified as a doctor and spent some time travelling through various Latin American countries (including Bolivia), becoming convinced that the poverty and misery of the peasants was such that there was no time to wait for the Marxist 'objective conditions' to make a revolution. His apprenticeship with Castro, among the Cuban peasants, convinced him that Marxist revolutionaries could count on support from all oppressed peasants in Latin America. Finding Castro's Cuba uncongenial, for reasons which have not been made very clear but which seem to have been connected with his disillusionment about Castro's personality cult and dictatorship, he spent some time on foreign missions for Cuba, and finally arrived at a chosen base in Bolivia on 7 November 1966.[2]

Che (a nickname he acquired in his student days) developed the doctrine of guerrilla warfare and of peasant revolution. Some sources describe him as a Marxist philosopher, others contend that his philosophy is a blend of Latin American *machismo* and of Utopian idealism. It is quite true that only Latin American conditions could have created Che: and it is also true that, despite his personal gentleness, his philosophy had given rise to savage terrorist campaigns in all parts of the world carried out in the name of his principles.

Lamberg maintains that Che's philosophy evolved and could be divided into three distinct phases:

> In the first, theoretical notions were formulated *ex post facto* to explain and glorify Castro's successful revolution in Cuba; the classic expression of these theories was Guevara's famous volume, *Guerra de Guerrillas*, published in Havana in 1960. In the second phase, Castroism was elaborated and infused with doctrinal concepts that placed it unmistakably in the ideological orbit of communism ..... See Guevara's *Guerra de Guerrillas: Un Metodo* .... 1962 .... The third phase witnessed the amendment of Guevara's theories of guerrilla warfare to emphasise the need for armed struggle by guerrillas operating independently from political control (reflecting Havana's impatience with peaceful politics and tactics of the pro-Soviet communist parties on the continent). The chief articulator of this last phase of ideology was the Frenchman Jules Régis Debray. See in particular his *Revolution in the Revolution* ... 1967.[3]

Further, the author continues:

> To understand Guevara's course of action, it is necessary to know something about the revolutionary theory on which it was based. First formulated by Guevara in his book *Guerra de Guerrillas* — and elaborated over the years in the statements and writings of Castro, Guevara, and finally the Frenchman Jules Régis Debray — this theory departed from the traditional Marxist and Leninist views of the conditions necessary for revolution to propound the notion that a guerrilla force could serve as the 'nucleus of armed insurrection' — or *foco insurreccional* — creating a revolutionary situation by its own momentum. According to Guevara, a small band of armed revolutionaries, by gaining popular support, could grow in numbers and strength

to the point where it could defeat a national army. On the Latin American continent, the best locale for such an armed struggle was the countryside, where the guerrillas would have more mobility against enemy forces and would be less liable to exposure than in densely populated areas. More important, Guevara believed that the peasants ... would join with the guerrillas in fighting the 'oppressors', thus he assigned the peasantry a key role in the revolutionary warfare that he envisioned would 'liberate' the Latin American continent.[4]

While Lamberg attributes this theory to the Cuban experience and maintains that it was faulty because Castro was not initially a Marxist and he had the support of the intellectual classes, an observer of Marxism can see the reflection of the Chinese experience much more clearly. Half a century before Castro began his struggle, Mao, forced to the hinterland by the KMT forces, developed the theory of a peasant Marxist revolution, and devised what has been called the 'war of the flea'. This is defined in the following terms: 'The guerrilla fights the war of the flea, and his military enemy suffers the dog's disadvantages: too much to defend; too small, ubiquitous and agile an enemy to come to grips with'.[5]

Much has been made of Che's apparently unheeding slide into a revolutionary situation particularly in view of the catastrophe of his Bolivian mission. Yet he himself had said that a revolution may not be easy to start: 'Where a government has come into power through some form of popular vote, fraudulent or not, and maintains at least an appearance of constitutional legality, the guerrilla outbreak cannot be promoted, since the possibilities of peaceful struggle have not yet been exhausted.'[6] It is also notable that Debray, Guevara's chief apologist and commentator, stated (admittedly after the 1967 debacle) that: 'The future of the revolution, or rather perhaps the question of whether or not there can *be* a revolution, depends on the union of the urban petty bourgeoisie with the popular forces, the poor peasants, the proletariat, and revolutionary intellectuals'.[7]

Yet when Guevara began his revolutionary guerrilla war in Bolivia after careful preparation by his assistant, Tamara Bunke ('Tania', who was killed by the Bolivian forces), he had, according to all sources, thirteen men, mostly Cubans, and expected some twenty Bolivians to join them. At no time, apparently, had the force exceeded fifty men, and during the last fight with government forces there were sixteen men, including Guevara himself.[8] Yet this handful managed to keep going for nearly a year, and the stories which were circulated referred to hundreds of guerrillas, and a serious revolutionary threat in Latin America.

Until the very last moment Guevara never gave up hope and expected help to arrive, despite the fact that the Communist Party of Bolivia (pro-Soviet), the Bolivian Communist Party (pro-Chinese), the reformist MNR and PRIN and the Trotskyite POR either refused to help or paid lip-service to the movement and did nothing else. It is true that two Bolivian Communists actually fought with Che, but this was a private decision, not approved by the party. There are various theories about the campaign of the guerrillas, two of which deserve attention.

The first theory, suggested by Lamberg, is that not a single one of the guerrillas responsible for the launching of the movement made a study of the changing conditions in Bolivia since 1952, that they misjudged the attitude of the peasants, who had become much more prosperous, and that they underestimated the strength of the Barrientos government and the popularity of the Bolivian army.[9] This explains why the peasants gave the army directions on how to find the guerrillas, which they undoubtedly did. It hardly explains the fact that, after Che was killed, large queues of peasants started to form outside the mortuary where his body lay[10] and he was given a saint's status by the people immediately after his death. Also, while Debray was kept alive, in order apparently to be interrogated by the CIA, Che was killed immediately, even though he would have been a much better source of information.

The second theory is that Che was so disappointed with Castro's revolution that he engineered a kind of spectacular suicide, as a protest against the Cuban dictator. What we know of Che militates against this theory. The third theory, that Castro sent Che to his death because he feared him as a rival, can be dismissed out of hand. Disposing of Che could have been done much more simply. And, despite his growing popularity, Che was not Castro's rival for the leadership of Cuba, as Castro must have known all along.

There remain other possibilities. The whole affair was a gigantic error, produced for propaganda reasons, and carried to a point from which it was impossible to retreat. This is possible, but does not seem very likely. Whatever Castro and Guevara can be accused of, they had always been pretty successful in their undertakings. It is likely that the whole truth about Guevara's expedition will one day emerge. In the meantime, one can only recount the known facts.

Guevara's debacle in Bolivia proved that even in Latin America revolution was not that easy. Marxism had to be introduced gradually and with caution. This gave rise to the next episode in Latin American history: that of Allende's government in Chile.

Parliamentary Marxism in Latin America

The defeat of the Bolivian revolution after Che Guevara's death may have proved to be the touchstone of a new policy: that of a peaceful acquisition of power through the ballot box. It may have been instigated either by the USSR, unable to finance revolutionary wars, or by Castro eager to have Marxist allies on the continent but without the problems Che had created in Bolivia. Or it may merely have been a natural development in Chile, sparked off by years of unpopular governments and the need to modernise.

Despite the fact that Chile has always been described as an example of a stable, democratic and prosperous Latin American state, a closer look at its history proves that, while stabler than other states on the continent, it was about as democratic and stable as Spain and Portugal in the nineteenth and twentieth centuries.[11] The main point made is the fact that Chile is a country inhabited by a homogeneous population, mostly of European origin. On the other hand, it has been pointed out that the ties between Germany and Chile are very strong and that there was a strong Nazi movement in Chile, which was only suppressed by the US, which accused Chile in 1942 of harbouring Nazi agents, inducing it to break diplomatic relations with Germany, Italy and Japan in 1943. Despite this, Chile never declared war on the Axis, and only declared war on Japan in April 1945. Hence, there were strong reasons to believe that the Nazi influence on Chilean life and politics continued to exercise some pull after the Second World War, while democracy was a relatively weak plant, requiring cultivation.

Despite its rich mineral resources, Chile depended on foreign capital, partly because of natural disasters (like the earthquake of 1940) and partly because the mining industry was American-owned and the wealth of the country was exported to the States. Much has been made of foreign exploitation of Chile, and while this is undeniable, it remains to be explained why the Chileans themselves, not ignorant or destitute, allowed this state of affairs to continue. The explanation, or part of it, must be that they acquiesced in the situation either because it suited them or because they were not sufficiently interested to change it.

Chile had a large number of political parties of the 'European' type, and a relatively stable political system. But the right wing was splintered into the extreme right (some of it Nazi or neo-Nazi) and the conservative right of landowning and industrial interests, while the left was splintered into so many groups that most authors prefer not to enumerate them. The Workers' Socialist Party joined the Third International in 1922; this was opposed by one socialist, Manuel Hidalgo, who later formed a Trotskyite Communist Party.

> By the end of 1931 there were many socialist and revolutionary parties . . . . The division of Chilean socialism did the movement a great deal of harm . . . on 19 April 1933, the socialist forces regrouped themselves into a single party, the Socialist Party, which the Trotskyists later joined . . . . It rejected the Third International and the USSR's predominance over the international labour movement, and thereby assumed a fairly anti-Communist position, matched by bitter opposition to it from the Communist Party.[12]

In 1957, after a series of splits, the Socialists established a new united Socialist Party, one of whose leading members was Salvador Allende. The Communist Party suffered from being made illegal during various periods, but in 1961, after legalisation, obtained 11.5 per cent of the votes in the congressional elections, a record which it improved slightly by 1965. Its minimum programme called for the eradication of imperialism and large estates and the nationalisation of banks, insurance companies and mines. It was a very 'gradualist' party, which argued that a peaceful acquisition of power through the ballot box was possible, and it desired co-operation between the Socialists and the Communists with this aim in view.[13]

In this it differed from the ultra-left MIR (Movement of the Revolutionary Left), formed in 1965, which seceded from the Socialist Party. When the front of Popular Unity was formed in 1969, out of the Communist and Socialist Parties and several smaller centre-left parties, MIR did not join the group but voted for its candidate, Allende, in 1970.[14] The Communists in particular were strongly attacked by the MIR as 'bourgeois', 'reformist' and 'sybaritic'.

In other words, the Chilean left was very divided and was made weaker by the gradualist position of the Communist Party on the one hand, and the uncompromising stand of the extreme left on the other. There is little doubt that at this stage the CPSU supported the caution of the Chilean Communist Party, for reasons which had much to do with difficulties created by Castro and with Guevara's debacle in Bolivia. 'Such considerations lead one to speculate that the continuation of the Christian Democrats in power would probably have been quite acceptable to the Russians,' stated one commentator.[15]

If the Chilean left was no different from other Latin American movements, Allende himself was typical of Latin American left-wing leaders. The son of a well-to-do liberal family, he had trained as a doctor, was a Marxist, but was also a freemason with a liking for a comfortable life. He had been a senator for many years, and had been described as a 'pragmatic and crafty politician'.[16] Allende counted Ho Chi Minh and Fidel Castro among his personal friends, and he helped to found OLAS (Latin American Solidarity Organisation) in 1966, a Castro creation to counteract US influence in Latin America. He had always expressed a wish to introduce social and economic reforms by gradual change. In other words, though a friend of revolutionaries, he was no revolutionary himself, and though he held anti-imperialist sentiments, he was keen to get American investment in Chile.

These points may have been working in Allende's favour, but he had much to contend with. His nomination was controversial in 1970, with the MIR refusing to endorse it and his own party, the Socialists, only agreeing to it after bitter opposition. The Radical Party delayed his endorsement, and the Communist Party hesitated to support him and tentatively advanced the Communist poet, Pablo Neruda.[17] However, the Popular Unity candidate had a lot of factors in his favour.

First of all, the country was tired of the ruling Christian Democrats, under President Frei, who had been in power since 1964. The government had promised to carry out major reforms, but when in power its agrarian reform was feeble, and its attempt to break the US hold on the copper industry, which accounted for 70 per cent

of the country's foreign exchange earnings, fell below the expectations of the population. Its slum-clearing programme was not
very successful, and its policies in general helped to alarm the
conservative circles without satisfying the radical and left-wing
circles. Above all, Frei failed to control inflation, which had
reached 30 per cent by 1969. In his place, the Christian Democrats
nominated Radomiro Tomic, a former ambassador to Washington,
who tried to appeal to radical elements, and they lost convervative
following as a result.

The third candidate was a conservative, Allessandri, put up by
the National Party and the Democratic Radical Party. He was a
former president, aged 74, and appeared to be old and sick. The
lack of overwhelming support for any party was demonstrated in
the election results on 4 September 1970. Allende received 36.3
per cent of the votes, Allessandri 34.9 per cent and Tomic 27.8 per
cent. Because none of the candidates had a clear majority the
Congress had to select one of them and it chose Allende as the
front-runner. In a round of hard bargaining, the Christian Democrats
decided to support him, provided he upheld a specially drafted
Statute of Democratic Guarantees: these were (1) to preserve the
political system, the constitutional guarantees of individual freedom
and the legal system; (2) not to interfere in the neutrality of the
armed forces; and (3) to preserve the independence of the
educational system and the trade unions.

Allende's government carried out many of its pledges of social
and economic reform, such as the breaking-up of large estates and
the nationalisation of the copper mines (this last was carried out
with compensation but by a process of fixing excess profits, and
two major American companies, Anaconda and Kennecott, ended
up by owing money to Chile), followed by nationalisation of other
industrial and mining enterprises.[18]

The land reform itself, though well intentioned, was followed by
chaos, as seizures of estates reduced agricultural production and
made the country even more dependent on imports of food.

Yet, after two years of Allende's regime, there were signs of US
approval: 'Allende seems to have confounded his critics on both
sides. He has made important changes in the direction of state
control of the Chilean economy and a more egalitarian distribution
of income — and he has also preserved a basically free Chilean
society.'[19] Despite this, in Allende's last year in office, the country
was suffering from a high rate of inflation, partly produced by

increased consumption and partly by lack of foreign credits; the middle classes were in open revolt; and the armed services were planning a new coup every day. Finally, Allende was overthrown, in mysterious circumstances, and died.

Writing soon after his death — which is claimed by his opponents to have been a suicide and by his supporters to have been murder — the same American commentator ascribed his fall and death to Chilean action.[20] At the same time, pro-Allende sources maintained that his fall was engineered by the CIA, in league with American business interests.

There is little doubt that there were very many Chilean forces which had had enough of Allende by 1972. Already by 1971 Allende found it difficult to raise loans from various international but American-dominated banks, because of the failure of his measures to compensate the copper companies for nationalisation of the mines. This meant that it was necessary to print more money and to devalue the currency. It also meant that there was a shortage of goods which had to be imported. This in turn led to accusations and counter-accusations, the middle classes being accused of hoarding, the proletariat being accused of ruining the economy with forced seizures of enterprises. The armed services were not as neutral as had been claimed. The navy had always been anti-Allende, but the air force and the army tended to support the government. However, a series of strikes (said to have been organised by the CIA) by middle-class interests gradually pushed the armed services into opposing Allende.

On 11 September 1973 Allende broadcast his last message from the presidential palace, saying, perhaps prophetically: 'My voice will no longer come to you, but it does not matter. You will continue to hear it: it will always be among you. At the least, you will remember me as an honourable man who was loyal to the revolution.'[21] Seton-Watson, not, by his own testimony, an admirer of Marxism, has this to say about Allende: 'Allende himself seems to have been genuinely devoted to freedom of opinion, and at least the leading newspapers of the opposition had been permitted to attack his administration in savage terms.' However, he argues that the many illegalities committed by the MIR committees, the economic problems and Allende's own violations of the constitution, told against him, so at the end only his own personal guard were prepared to defend him.[22]

When inquests were held on the demise of the first Marxist

regime among various communist parties it was admitted that the main problem of the government was that it had alienated the middle classes and the armed services without a compensating growth of power among the proletariat and rural population. This gave rise to various theories, among them the theory of Euro-communism developed originally by the Italians, which insisted that the ruling classes will never allow the working classes to come to absolute power, and hence the communists should try to ally themselves with centre and even right-wing parties in order to come to power. This theory will be discussed below, but at this stage it is worth looking at the Chilean situation in its own context. For the purposes of this analysis, one can ignore the assertions that the coup was engineered by the Americans, although one does not dismiss them. The fact remains that revolts by the armed services can only be successful where there is already a large amount of dissatisfaction among the population in general; otherwise they would not stand a chance. Foreign aid, or direction, may help such revolts, but it is not the decisive factor in their success or the subsequent retention of power.

One has to look for other explanations. One of these is obvious, that is, the comparison of the Chilean Marxist government with the the ill-fated Bavarian government. In Bavaria, as indeed elsewhere in Germany, the country was developed with a strong middle class, a unionised and disciplined proletariat and a relatively successful farming class. In Marxist interpretation there existed 'objective conditions' for a revolution. Leninist interpretations would disagree, maintaining that a successful revolution required a large degree of poverty, an upheaval such as a war and a weak and liberal middle class. Indeed, one look at the Bolshevik Revolution or the Cuban revolution would show that this was the case. A further theory developed by Mao maintains that only a dissatisfied peasant class is a successful vehicle for a Marxist revolution. This, again, is true of the Bolshevik, Cuban and Chinese revolutions.

In Chile the conditions were much nearer to those of Bavaria in 1918 than those of Cuba in 1960, i.e. it was a developed country by Latin-American standards, with a well-organised proletariat which was, by and large, highly successful, a strong middle class well organised into political parties and a small, localised rural proletariat, either on the large estates or in the south of the country. In those conditions it was safe for the middle and upper classes to allow a

Marxist government, even a very mild one like Allende's, to come to power not so much in order to carry out social and economic reforms, as to 'de-Americanise' the economy and allow the indigenous interests a larger share of the profits. This is clear from the way in which Frei's government became unpopular because it failed to reduce the American influence.

However, it proved impossible for Allende to carry out this policy successfully while at the same time maintaining discipline among the radical left and the poorest classes of the population. This is similar to the situation in Bavaria, where the Communist government failed to free Bavaria from Prussian hegemony (the main aim of the Bavarians) while it unleashed the radical left, much to the horror of the middle and upper classes. Like the Bavarian Communists, Allende paid the price for being an unsuccessful tool of national interests, not only a price in his own life but in the lives of thousands of Chileans after a draconian regime had been imposed on the country.

From a Marxist point of view the Pinochet regime is a much better starting point for a communist revolution than the Frei regime had been, and it will be interesting to see whether such a revolution will occur.

This will be difficult in view of the fact that the left is not united. Besides the split between the official communist parties there is the wider and much more damaging split between the Communists and the far left. It has been shown that the official communist parties in Latin America were unhappy about Bolivia, and not very happy about Allende's government, though in the end the Chilean Communist Party supported him loyally. It has been demonstrated that the USSR prefers to deal with established governments, of whatever hue, rather than to embark on 'adventurism', if not for ideological reasons then for simple financial ones: Cuba has proved an expensive proposition and the thought of having to support much larger countries must fill the Soviet leaders with dismay.

Hence the Carter Administration's analysis, which wanted the US to support the liberal, elected governments in Latin America, was probably the correct one. Latin America is still the hinterland of the USA, whether the nationalistic leaders like it or not.

One more factor has changed in Latin America in the 1970s: this is the position of the Catholic Church. From being a staunch supporter of the establishments it has become an ally of the revolutionary forces. This change has been brought about partly by genuine outrage at the excesses of the pseudo-fascist regimes and partly by the changing face of the Church itself. The Society of Jesus has been in the forefront of the revolutionary forces and it has always been acknowledged that, where the Jesuits start, the rest of the Church follows. In a continent which is still very much under the influence of clerical forces, particularly of clerical education, such a change is bound to result in far-reaching repercussions.

Latin American Marxism: Neo-Marxism or Hispanism?

Latin America still suffers from its colonial heritage, and it is a matter of course that outside forces are always being blamed for disasters and that aid is being sought from the outside rather than generated from within. Thus an ultra-left-wing commentator said that Chile was unable to help itself and needed 'a whole period of time in which external aid could be provided so that the country could be reorganised from within . . . . The USSR alone, for example, is in a position to solve this problem. But it is questionable whether the prospect of victory for "socialism" in Chile is compatible with the USSR's current relations with the United States, which involve far-reaching political and economic issues. This may well be the decisive factor in the gradualist "stages" policy of the Chilean communist party, and its hope of stabilising the situation by means of an "advanced democratic" regime in which the reformist wing of christian democracy will participate'.[23]

Such demands must be put down to Latin American 'Hispanism' rather than to revolutionary or Marxist ideology. While no-one denies that it helps to be helped, the Russians and the Chinese pulled themselves up by their own boot-straps, though admittedly at a very high cost to themselves. The Latin Americans are always ready to blame outside interests; they are seldom ready to work out solutions for themselves in a continent which is far richer in many ways than any other area of the world.

While the Latin American revolutionaries demand help from the outside on economic and social issues, they are always ready to carry out feats of *machismo* such as the Che Guevara expedition appears to have been. This has been particularly obvious in the development of urban guerrilla tactics. The growth of the Tupamaros in Uruguay is better documented than most other guerrilla groups because it is the oldest. It is typical of Latin America that the nihilist tactics of destruction which Lenin condemned in Russian anarchists are thought to be the height of revolutionary effort. Having suffered defeat in the countryside, the revolutionists moved to the cities in the 1970s. This was also partly caused by a typical Latin American phenomenon: the enormous growth of Latin American cities since 1945, which

> has led to the rise of enormous slums that provide an easy refuge for both criminals and revolutionaries... In many countries, the peasants are now in a minority. Nearly 75 per cent of Uruguay's population are townsmen; the comparable figures for Argentina, Chile and Brazil are respectively 72, 68, and 50 per cent. Mao Tse-tung's vision of the countryside surrounding the cities is hardly applicable under these conditions. And ... the great attraction of the city for a small revolutionary group is that it offers enormous scope for self-dramatization.[24]

Nowhere in the world has the growth of urban slums reached such a stage as in Latin American countries. The urban guerrilla thrives in a huge urban slum, populated by a despairing and illiterate peasant population. From countless reports in the British press, one is picked at random to illustrate the case:

> Day by day, death by death, the tiny Central American nation of El Salvador is slipping toward the abyss of a civil war which could surpass in savagery anything this bloodstained region has endured for many years. ... The extreme Left, sustained by a campaign of indiscriminate terrorism, which has netted them an estimated £30 million in kidnap ransoms, is now far more organised and infinitely better armed .... Almost two hundred people died in January: kidnapped from their homes, tortured, shot to pieces or slashed with machetes .... The Union of White Warriors, a frankly fascist group which specialises in torturing alleged left-wing leaders, confronts the murder squads of the three main Marxist–Leninist parties, who recently demonstrated their hatred of all things American by killing the manager of a ... hamburger house.[25]

The violence and terrorism is a Hispanic phenomenon. When urban guerrilla tactics were tried out in Europe the revulsion of public opinion gave the governments the necessary mandate to virtually wipe them out. In Latin America, this has been a long-drawn-out phenomenon which shows no signs of abating.

Hence the Latin American Marxist or Neo-Marxist movements are definitely of an 'Hispanic' type: their devotion to violence, which stems partly from traditional *machismo* and partly from political illiteracy and which is fed on the population explosion and the urban slum sprawl, has much more in common with the nihilism of the nineteenth century than with twentieth-century Marxist movements, even though it owes part of its debt to Mao's Cultural Revolution. Even Cuba, where the model is nearer to the Marxist one than in Allende's Chile, depends much more on Castro's charisma and his *machismo* than on Marxist dogma.

This is not to say that one belittles the successes. The Chilean experiment might have lasted and become successful if Allende had not alienated so many powerful interests. But Chile is a special case. The Cuban experiment has not been unsuccessful: it is customary for visitors to Latin America to quote the contrast between living standards of the people in Cuba and Brazil; but again, Cuba is a special case, partly because of its small size and partly because it could rely on sustained Soviet aid throughout Castro's rule. Bolivia, Argentina, Brazil and the Central American republics are all in the grip of a constant crisis. While this is said to be the classical 'pre-revolutionary' situation, the revolutions — if they occur — are more likely to be 'Hispanic' national revolutions than Marxist ones.

Notes

1. *Guardian*, 12 May 1976.
2. A full account of Che's life and his last months was given on BBC2 Television on 12 October 1977, the tenth anniversary of his death. This account was sympathetic, an indication of the fact that after ten years Guevara had acquired the status of a martyr. A much more hostile essay by R.E. Lamberg 'Che in Bolivia: The "Revolution" that Failed', in *Problems of Communism*, July-August (1970) provides a useful contrast.
3. Lamberg, ibid., note 1 p. 25.
4. Ibid., p. 27
5. R. Taber, *The War of the Flea*, p. 29.
6. Che Guevara, *Guerilla Warfare*, p. 16.
7. Régis Debray, 'Notes on the Political Situation in Bolivia', in *Prison Writings*, p. 22.
8. See Lamberg, 'Che in Bolivia', quoting various sources.

9. Ibid., p. 35.

10. BBC 2 broadcast: see note 2.

11. See Wilgus and d'Eca, *Latin American History*, pp. 264-77.

12. J.P. Bernard *et al.*, *Guide to the Political Parties*, pp.246-7.

13. Ibid., pp. 251-3.

14. H. Seton-Watson, *The Imperialist Revolutionaries*, p. 17.

15. L. Goure and J. Suchlicki, 'Whither Chile?' in *Problems of Communism*, May-June (1971), p. 55.

16. Ibid., p. 52.

17. Ibid., p. 52.

18. P.E. Sigmund 'Chile: Two Years of "Popular Unity"', in *Problems of Communism*, November-December (1972), p. 41.

19. Ibid., p. 38.

20. P.E. Sigmund, 'Allende in Retrospect', in *Problems of Communism*, May-June (1974), p. 61.

21. 'El Ultimo Dia de Allende', from a tape recording, quoted by Sigmund, 'Allende in Retrospect', p. 61.

22. Seton-Watson, *The Imperialist Revolutionaries*, pp. 19-20.

23. M. Raptis, *Revolution and Counter Revolution in Chile*, pp. 75-6.

24. R. Moss 'Urban Guerrillas in Uruguay', in *Problems of Communism*, September-October (1971), p. 14.

25. Philip Jacobson *Sunday Times*, 2 March 1980.

18

Neo-Marxism and Africa

The New Scramble for Africa

A new Scramble for Africa is threatening the continent less than two decades after most of its 49 States became independent. ... The last Scramble, in the middle of the nineteenth century, was ended by the Treaty of Berlin in 1884, which allocated spheres of interests to the competing imperialist nations. Needless to say, no Africans were present in Berlin. The new Scramble is different in three aspects. Now it is the Russians who are playing the role of the leading imperialist Power, skilfully using smaller Powers as their surrogates. The present mood of the Western powers, except for France, is that they don't again want to become involved in Third World imbroglios ... unless there is an actual threat to the world balance of power. And, this time, Africans are themselves active participants in the Scramble.[1]

This piece of, perhaps unconscious, irony was produced by a serious journalist on African affairs at the height of the *detente* in 1978. The problem about Africa is that any attempt to divide it into 'spheres of influence' or, as Legum put it 'into three distinct groups: those who work with the Soviet bloc; those who work closely with the West; and those who still cling to non-alignment'[2] has always been bound to fail, because Africa had already been divided into various spheres by natural, demographic and historical factors. These have made her northern areas Arab and Moslem-dominated, her central areas colonised by the Europeans and her southern extremity settled by a particularly tenacious European community. Nor is there any question that Africa is totally

267

heterogeneous as far as climate, population, religions and economic matters are concerned. The additional problems of the continent having massive natural resources (be they timber and game, or oil, diamonds, copper, uranium and cobalt), many of which are unobtainable anywhere else, has made it a rich prize for any imperialist.

European colonialisation de-tribalised the Africans and brought about urbanisation and a population explosion. This was noted all over Africa, but one example can be seen in Algeria, where the population had tripled between 1830 and 1950 but the production of cereals in 1950 remained at the same level as in 1880. Islamic fundamentalism has made a mockery of 'socialist revolutions'. As one sympathetic observer wrote to Libya under Gadafi: 'All this makes Libya's an inarticulate and even a nervous revolution . . . an intellectual whom I tried to engage in a general discussion about pre-coup Libya and the causes behind the change advised: "When you see Gadafi you can ask him about the causes of the revolution".'[3] And in areas where Marxism is unhampered by the teachings of the Koran (and shaped by the missionary brand of Christianity which has been preached for a century) it has had to adapt to the local conditions to an extent which makes Chinese Marxism positively orthodox by comparison.

It is not safe to say either that the African brand of Marxism is 'local'; a close enquiry will show that most of the socialist leaders of today or yesterday have close connections with European Marxist parties, and their experience does not stand them in good stead in African conditions. Neither is it true to say that Marxism stands a better chance in badly ruled ex-colonial territories than in the ones which have been ruled relatively well. The best proof of that is that the first socialist regime was established in an ex-British colony, Ghana, and that it was established by a nationalist 'graduate' from a British prison, Kwame Nkrumah. Part of the Gold Coast colonies, Ghana received a limited autonomy in 1950, when Nkrumah's Convention People's Party won a decisive victory in elections. Guided by the precedent of India, the British government transferred power gradually and full independence was conceded in 1957. The popularity of the CPP government among the masses did not spread to the important chiefs in the country, who saw an erosion of their privileges. Nkrumah attempted to stifle opposition by violent methods and this brought about his downfall.

The relatively high standard of living in Ghana (where the

income per capita had been above that of Portugal) was maintained under independence, and in some instances, as those of cocoa farmers, it rose. But wages stagnated, the balance of payments situation worsened and there was the problem of a new high-school-educated generation without job prospects. In 1962, in order to remedy some of these problems the government promulgated a seven-year development plan, which provided for an expansion of the state sector of the economy, raising of agricultural productivity and diversifying production from a one-crop economy (cocoa) into a diversified one.

'Socialism . . . is the only pattern that can within the shortest possible time bring the good life to the people,' said Nkrumah in April 1961[4] and this expressed the desires of most of Africa's socialist leaders. Such pragmatism may be very popular in non-Marxist circles (though it did not prove so in Ghana) but it ignores the essential factor of ideology. It was an ideological commitment to 'creating' socialism which enabled the successful revolutionaries to gain and hold on to power. A modest commitment to improving life fits into a moderate parliamentary type of regime, and hardly makes the people ready for a need to change their life-styles drastically.

Nkrumah's government nationalised mining companies, set up 'people's shops', introduced state farms (against Soviet advice), set up various industrial projects, including the huge Volta Dam project, and encouraged the setting up of large factories by foreign capital in the country. All these were financed by large USSR, Eastern European and US loans. While the economy of the country was improving these gains were not reflected in popularity. A very sympathetic observer noted that: 'This political weakness . . . was greatly increased, after 1961, by a persistent failure to enlarge or even maintain the democratic structure of the CPP.'[5] The introduction of preventive detention hardly helped matters. To make the position worse, the price of cocoa, which was going down since 1961, collapsed in 1965.

The end came swiftly. In February 1966, when Nkrumah was in Beijing, an army coup overthrew the government, and after some stormy periods of military dictatorship, civilian government was restored in 1969. A multi-party system was restored and a 'middle-class' solution was sought by the new government. It was only many years later that an ex-CIA officer claimed that the CIA played a major role in the overthrow of Nkrumah. He further stated that the Agency acted without prior approval of the high-level committee which is supposed to monitor its activities. This committee apparently rejected the Agency's request that Nkrumah be overthrown, and the CIA proceeded to do so with a generous budget and 'maintained intimate contact with the plotters as a coup was hatched. So close was the station's involvement that it was able to coordinate the recovery of some classified Soviet military equipment by the United States as the coup took place'.[6]

Even without American involvement, the fact remains that Nkrumah's government was unable to satisfy the majority of the people or, at least, that majority which was politically articulate. Had it done so, the coup would not have been successful. What elements were missing in Ghana's revolution? It has been pointed out above that Nkrumah lacked revolutionary fervour and opted for a pragmatic solution. But Ghana's socialism failed for many other reasons. It is worth analysing them because they apply in most African states.

Tribalism still plays a very large role in Ghana; not only the chiefs but also the different tribes tend to mistrust each other. Africa is largely an agricultural continent, with industrial development provided by non-Africans, though the unskilled labour may be African. Large-scale nationalisation measures always upset foreign capital and skilled staff is withdrawn. Hence industrial development is stopped. This situation may be remedied in time, as more Africans are trained as technologists and more capital is raised by local resources; but it is almost certain to continue for at least another generation. While at a later period some recourse has been had to Cuban technologists, there is evidence that the Cubans are regarded as imperialists in much the same way as the Russians, Europeans and Americans, even though African governments may be forced to use them. The situation is complicated by increased urbanisation in independent states, as colonial controls to stop the flow of the peasant population to the cities are removed (the opposite attempt by the South African government to decant the urban population into the countryside has been highly unsuccessful right from the start), and by increased literacy in general and higher educational standards of the young people in particular. In other words, the revolution of expectations has arrived in independent Africa; it has not been successfully fulfilled in any independent state, possibly not even in the most prosperous and 'bourgeois' ones, such as Kenya. And the position is bound to get worse, as the population increases and the continent cannot feed its multitudes. The massive famine in East Africa in 1980, which was caused mainly by drought but also by over-population and de-tribalisation, is proof of this.

Such conditions may make even the most moderate leaders look at introducing 'full socialism' in an effort to pre-empt disaster. There are two states in Africa where a form of socialism with a Marxist background has been attempted.

Angola and Mozambique — Neo-Marxism in Operation

If the Convention People's Party in Ghana started off as a nationalist party and only adopted a modified form of Marxism later, the parties in Angola and Mozambique had a different beginning, which was based on historical factors. There are many reasons why Portugal held on to her African colonies for so long and they are analysed by various authors.[7] The economic reasons which are often advanced are inadequate, particularly as Portugal became more Eurocentred in the 1960s; the emotional reasons — the smallest country in Europe with the largest empire — are not very satisfactory. The main reason seems to have been the fact that as the dictatorship of Salazar increased its oppressiveness and became ever more petrified, it was impossible to change anything. De-colonialising Portugal would have been more than a change, it would have been a revolution.

The additional reason was that Portugal was a vital (if small) link in the NATO security system and provided American bases in the Azores; therefore she could count on American support in her colonial stand, particularly because of the anti-communist position Salazar's regime maintained. This very dependence on military factors made Portuguese colonies vulnerable. The long dictatorship was oppressive, but never penetrated the armed services with a secret police network. On the other hand, the armed services became revolutionised as the dictatorship became harsher. After Caetano succeeded Salazar in 1968 the regime relaxed its vigilance and the armed services became more left-oriented than before.[8] Hence the colonial wars were doomed to be lost long before they actually happened, as the Portuguese could not rely on any indigenous politicians and were relying only on the armed services to defeat the insurgents.

On the other hand, the colonial peoples had everything to gain and nothing to lose from a war. There was a long history of anti-colonial struggle in Portuguese territories, dating back from the nineteenth century, but it was so savagely repressed by the Portugese that in 1956 a writer could not observe any signs of a nationalist movement in those colonies. The repression of all dissent and particularly of left-wing dissent merely helped to drive it underground and to make it much more violent than would have been the case otherwise. For the violent way in which nationalism was repressed there is plenty of testimony,[9] and one is hardly surprised by it in any case. The Portuguese dictator was harsh with his opponents in Portugal: one would expect more harshness for black nationalists in far-off colonies.

In fact by the early 1960s there were three separate nationalist movements in Mozambique (the Angolan ones were founded even earlier): UDENAMO (National Democratic Union of Mozambique), founded in Rhodesia in 1960; MANU (Mozambique African Union), founded in East Africa on the models of the Tanganyikan and Kenyan parties TANU and KANU; and UNAMI (African Union of Independent Mozambique), founded in Malawi. In 1962 the three movements merged and became FRELIMO (*Frente de Lebertacao de Mocambique*), electing Edward Mondlane as the first president. FRELIMO suffered badly from lack of educated personnel: the Portuguese had not developed schools and the only education provided was that in Protestant missionary schools, which were not numerous in Mozambique. Educational programmes were started in Tanzania, where FRELIMO had its headquarters, and a large number of young people were sent abroad to be trained. It is not surprising that many of them went to the USSR or other Eastern European countries, where the educational facilities were offered free.

By 1964, the guerrilla war began, and a British correspondent was sufficiently impressed to call the FRELIMO a 'miniature' Viet Cong. In 1967 FRELIMO had about 8,000 troops trained and equipped, and controlled large areas of Mozambique. Portugal increased its military budget from 25 per cent in 1960 to 42.4 per cent in 1968 and increased the number of its troops from 60,000 to 200,000.[10] Of these, some 60,000 were sent to Mozambique in 1967.[11] Yet the guerrillas moved on. In the period of 1967 to 1970 they began large-scale attacks on Portuguese military posts and air bases, made possible by the availability of new heavy weapons.

In the areas under FRELIMO control food production was increased, while cotton production, compulsory under Portugal, was phased out. Clinics and primary schools were set up, and the people were encouraged to participate in production. In 1968 a new front was opened, adjacent to Zambia, which was of crucial importance because of the joint South African Portuguese Cabora-Bassa hydroelectric project. In 1969, a postal parcel bomb killed Mondlane, and he was succeeded by Samora Machel, a much 'stronger' Marxist. (He is the present president of Mozambique.) The Portuguese response to the war was partly to employ American tactics used in Vietnam and partly to introduce reforms. The former proved to be inadequate, the latter too late and too little. By 1970 the total number of Portuguese troops in Africa was estimated at about 160,000: Portugal's defence budget soared and her foreign debt mounted.

The April 1974 coup which deposed Caetano was carried out by the armed forces, which were totally demoralised by the war in Africa. The new Portuguese government granted Mozambique complete independence in June 1975. Samora Machel introduced a brand of government which he calls Marxist–Leninist. There are no opposition parties: political agitators are institutionalised and the government controls (or tries to control) the economy and models itself on the most restrictive patterns, like those of East Germany. Since there was a mass exodus of whites, skilled jobs were difficult to fill. Housing, church schools and hospitals were nationalised. Services deteriorated and urban life became uncomfortable. But, by contrast, many communes were set up, plantations collectivised and co-operatives established. All land was nationalised and 'people's shops' were set up to combat speculation and rising prices. Private medical and legal practices were abolished and health and educational services were reorganised to serve all the people, not just the whites, as previously.

A correspondent who went to inspect Mozambique more than a year after FRELIMO came to power said: 'President Machel's background provides a key to understanding Mozambique's present policies. He was brought up in an impoverished rural community which is why he sees socialism and agrarian reform as the twin pillars on which the country's future will be based.'[12] Mozambique's economic aid used to come from the USSR and Cuba, and the 3rd Congress of FRELIMO held in February 1977 opted for a course of 'scientific socialism'. This included re-education for the unsocialised. A report from a re-education camp in the same year has more praise than blame to apportion. A young vegetable salesman, in the camp because he could not produce an identity card in 1975, said that the policeman who arrested him had been a member of the colonial force and was now a FRELIMO policeman. 'It was the same policeman, following the same regulations which existed in colonial times. I thought, "FRELIMO has come but nothing has changed." But it had. At the centre I was not beaten. I was treated like a human being and I went to school for the first time. Now I am in standard three.'[13]

By March 1978 another correspondent reported on Mozambique's agricultural revolution. The system of the state farms which was formed out of abandoned Portuguese estates had a mixed success. 'The Matama state farm ... has received 39 new tractors, one French agronomist, a team of 17 Chinese agricultural technicians and a modern irrigation system.'[14] But the villages nearby had no irrigation and even Matama did not receive the motor pumps necessary for the system. A system designed by the Chinese technicians, without the pumps, was being used. Unemployment was still very high and work mostly seasonal, but the wages of labourers had gone up almost four times. Much of the country's wheat, the staple food, was still being imported, despite the attempts to restore agriculture. This depressing story was amplified a year later: 'The combination of near-bankruptcy and stalled development had led to bitter disenchantment ...' reported another correspondent.[15]

The problems Mozambique faced were aggravated because, for ideological reasons, it had closed its border with Rhodesia in 1976 and had cut off its vital economic links with the rest of the world. 'Two years later, the border remains closed, the war has worsened, and ... Smith is still there.'[16] The Mozambique government gave help and refuge to the Mugabe forces for many years. In place of a swift victory or Western pressure to depose Ian Smith, they saw the white Rhodesians resisting nationalist guerrillas and the Muzorewa government installed — yet another miscalculation, which made the regime bitter. 'The president's May Day speech matched the mood of suspicion ... with intemperate attacks on the Catholic Church, trade unions, long hair, and women who wore tight jeans or figure-hugging blouses.'[17] More than a year later Samora Machel had, at last, got his reward: in August 1980 he visited Salisbury, as the guest of his friend, Robert Mugabe, and the main street of the city was named in his honour. But will this reception help him to improve the economy? And will Mugabe go Marxist with Machel, or rather advise him to become more right-wing? Much will depend on the help the West is prepared to give. The Soviet bloc is not at the moment as involved as it had been, for other reasons. Thus Mozambique's troubles are far from over, and the independence of Zimbabwe may make them worse rather than better.

While Mozambique reached independence in this fashion the other major Portuguese colony, Angola, had a different history. Angola's problems were similar to those of Mozambique: lack of education, lack of skilled Africans and poor economy, but it had the advantage (or disadvantage) of great natural riches and bordered directly on South-west Africa (Namibia), where South African interest predominated. Despite the fact that in 1958 out of a population of four and a half million just over a thousand had secondary education and forty-seven were in Portuguese universities, the Angolan leadership was well educated and sophisticated. The Marxist leader of the country till his death in 1979 was Aghostino Neto, an intellectual and a poet, who was under the strong influence of the Portuguese Communist leader, Alvaro Cunhal, himself very pro-Soviet.

It may have been because of these differences that the three Angolan liberation movements, the MPLA (Movement for the Liberation of Angola) founded in 1956 by Neto, the FLNA (National Front of Angolan Liberation) founded by nationalist leader Holden Roberto in 1961, and UNITA (Union for Total Independence of Angola) founded in 1966 by an ex-Roberto aide, Jonas Savimbi, did not unite. Instead, when the Portuguese troops were withdrawn rapidly after the revolution the three main parties began to fight against each other, supported by external interests. By the time Angola became independent on 11 November 1975 there were said to be 15,000 Cuban troops fighting for the MPLA.

The Cuban involvement has been questioned then, as it is now. It has been said that the MPLA, knowing that the other parties had stronger forces and were supported by foreign interests, asked the USSR for Soviet volunteers, and that the Russians refused but the Cubans obliged. There is no doubt that the Angolans relied heavily on Cuban troops and still rely on Cuban personnel to stay in power. The Marxist government of Neto survived many de-stabilisation attempts variously ascribed to South Africa[18] like the coup of 27 May 1977, or to France and Portugal.[19] In March 1978 the *Observer* reported that 'a secret fund of almost £10 million has been raised by a coalition of Arab, Iranian and French interest to combat Russian and Cuban influence in Angola.'[20] And in May 1978 came the startling revelation by William Colby, the director of the CIA, 1974-5, in the following testimony to a Congressional committee: 'If the CIA had not been involved in this latest operation in Angola, would the Cubans have gone in? . . . No, they wouldn't have had to because the MPLA would have won.'[21] In 1978 the Russians were said to be building up forces in Angola[22] and in December of the same year Angola's prime minister was dismissed for 'petty bourgeois tendencies'.[23]

In September 1979 Neto died, and his successor as the leader of the MPLA was elected. His is a man of thirty-seven, who has completed a civil engineering degree in Moscow, and his name is Jose Eduardo Dos Santos. He also became the President of the country, a function which he filled after Dr Neto's death. 'Known as a supporter of Dr Neto's "non-aligned" foreign policies, he specialised in dealing with the country's oil interests. He is said to have supported Dr Neto's recent moves towards more open relations with the West.'[24]

It is clear that neither Mozambique nor Angola have a clearcut road ahead of them. While Mozambique became much more Marxist than Angola it will be seen whether the independent Zimbabwe next door will induce it to relax Marxism, or whether they will join in a Marxist bloc. On the other hand, Angola has little chance of peace unless and until South Africa has become a black country, like Rhodesia. Until such time it is in the same position as Mozambique, in danger of being attacked from the outside, with the additional danger of an existing large indigenous anti-Marxist movement, which is still at war. Angola also has large mineral deposits, which make it doubly desirable.

The two countries are typical of highly neglected ex-colonial territories which adopt the creed that happens to suit the needs of the moment. It is the support they get — or do not get — from the outside, which will determine their political future. The Neo-Marxist phraseology does not hide the fact that neither Angola nor Mozambique have the necessary base for socialism, agrarian or otherwise: in Lenin's phrase, they are still feudal, and before socialism could be introduced they would have to produce a proletarian base.

Which Way Africa?

The ex-Portuguese colonies are not the only African countries which have attempted a form of Marxism to help their problems. Some other colonies — Tanzania, Zambia and Mali — have introduced a form of control which has variously been called 'Christian Socialism' or the 'African Road to Socialism'. Others, like Zimbabwe, are on the brink of a decision before they are pushed by circumstances one way or another.

Does this mean that Africa is going Marxist, Soviet or Socialist? Much depends on the interpretation. After the 1979 Commonwealth Conference, Peregrine Worsthorne wrote the following words in defence of Bishop Muzorewa's government, which was already doomed:

> His political needs coincide with those of the white minority. He needs them and they need him. Either they hang together or they hang separately. So far as Britain and the Western world are concerned, this hard fact is of crucial importance. It could mean that multi-racial Zimbabwe–Rhodesia remained a rich and stable country firmly in the Western camp . . . and influencing its black neighbours in that direction.[25]

It is against this type of argument that most African independent states react. White domination, coming after white colonialism is not welcome.

On the other hand, it has been demonstrated that the imperialist interests of several states, including the two super-powers, played a very important role in Angola. A similar struggle has been going on in the Horn of Africa. There, three states claim to be Marxist: Ethiopia, Eritrea and Somalia. A recent report stated:

> The Horn of Africa is today one of the most potentially explosive areas in the world. The United States, in the aftermath of Afghanistan, is anxious to acquire military 'facilities' at Somalia's Red Sea port of Berbera. The Somali Democratic Republic is likely to hold out for a high price for such facilities in terms of re-equipment of the SDR's armed forces, which are now very weak, having been heavily defeated by Ethiopia, with Soviet and Cuban support, in the Ogaden War of 1977/78.[26]

Asked about the Soviet and Cuban aid in this context, the leader of the Ethiopian military junta, Colonel Menghistu, said that 'The Soviet and Cuban military and other aid ... is not only exaggerated, but also fully distorted.' This aid, the colonel maintained, stemmed purely from the belief in internationalist proletarian and socialist solidarity: 'It is an obvious fact that both the Soviet Union and Cuba are now giving us considerable help ... with our effort to develop our country socially, and economically....' And his message to the West was that:

> We know the state of material and spiritual development in the West, but what we see as paradoxical is the growing cooperation of the West with precisely those countries which promote outmoded policies of racism and apartheid and other social evils.

The correspondent concludes:

> It is probable that some people are now considering ideas for 'destabilising' Ethiopia's revolutionary regime, both internally and externally. The chasm between ... the leaders of Somalia and Ethiopia ... may seem to such people to offer a promising opening for such moves ... Mengistu's history shows him to be no Allende. But efforts of this kind ... could have tragic consequences in pushing the Ethiopian revolution out of its present relatively mild — and often humanly constructive — phase ... and at the same time bringing about ... a much greater degree of Russian involvement in the Horn of Africa.[27]

Africa does not know which way she is going. As a continent she had been 'de-stabilised' in the nineteenth century. Her previous nationalism turned often either to Marxism or a crude military dictatorship. But Marxism is adapted to African conditions, and the longer it is in operation the more chance of it becoming a new kind of socialism, not a simple 'Neo-' or 'Pseudo-Marxism'. It is the power struggle between extra-African blocs which provides fuel for further de-stabilisation.

African states, like African politicians, seldom have the experience, power base or the backing to remain independent. What is more, they face catastrophic famines in the wake of natural disasters. It would be easy to push Africa, separately or jointly, into some form of dictatorship, operated by an extra-European power. It would be more difficult to maintain such a dictatorship for long, and it would be even more difficult to live with the consequences of such a move. South Africa apart (and this is a special case), the indigenous nations have, for the first time since the eighteenth century, native governments. While these governments may not be very good, interfering with their processes can only further the harm to Africa.

It has probably been Africa's biggest misfortune that she has been discovered, and that she is so wealthy. If she is allowed to recover from the after-effects of that discovery she may yet develop her own forms of government, possibly more satisfactory than the imposed ones. But this outcome is unlikely in the present political climate. All in all, one cannot consider that any European ideology, whether Marxism or capitalism, has much chance of satisfactory development in the continent. The new forms should be allowed to take shape in the historical context of development.

Notes

1. Colin Legum, *Observer*, 28 May 1978.
2. Ibid.
3. R. First, *Libya: The Elusive Revolution*, p. 26.
4. Quoted by B. Davidson, *Which Way Africa?*, p. 90.
5. Ibid., p. 193.
6. J. Stockwell, *In Search of Enemies: a CIA Story*, quoted in *The Times*, 10 May 1978.
7. Two of the most recent analyses will be found in D. Porch, *The Portuguese Armed Forces and the Revolution*, and D. Minter, *Portuguese Africa and the West*.
8. Strong indications that the penetration was simply a form of reaction against Salazar and Caetano rather than organised Communist infiltration will be found in Porch, *Portuguese Armed Forces*, and A. Hottinger, 'The Rise of Portugal's Communists', in *Problems of Communism*, July-August, 1975.
9. See B. Davidson, *In the Eye of a Storm* and *Which Way Africa?*: Minter, *Portuguese Africa*.
10. Porch, *Portuguese Armed Forces*, p. 38.
11. Minter, *Portuguese Africa*, p. 68.
12. N. Ashford, *The Times*, 17 Nov. 1976.
13. D. Martin, *Observer*, 14 Aug. 1977.
14. M. Honey, *Guardian*, 30 March 1978.
15. J. MacManus, *Guardian*, 15 May 1979.
16. Ibid.
17. Ibid.
18. See *The Times*, 4 Feb. 1977, on Pretoria's admission of joint operations with nationalist forces.
19. See *Sunday Times*, 3 July 1977.

20. *Observer*, 26 March 1978.
21. Quoted in the *Sunday Times*, 28 May 1978.
22. *Sunday Times*, 18 June 1978.
23. *Guardian*, 11 Dec. 1978.
24. *Guardian*, 21 Sept. 1979.
25. *Sunday Telegraph*, 5 Aug. 1979.
26. *Observer*, 9 March 1980.
27. Ibid.

Part five:

*Competitive or
National Communism?*

19
Pseudo-Marxism in Asia

Competitive Communism

Writing in the early 1970s a political scientist pointed out that, in sharp contrast to the majority of established communist regimes in Europe, those in Asia retained a continuing commitment to violence. 'Externally, it manifests itself in the strenuous resistance of these regimes to the whole concept of peaceful coexistence between socialist and capitalist states and in their active encouragement and support of "wars of national liberation".'[1]

In an attempt to understand the tendency to violence, even before the competing communist governments began to indulge in wars among themselves, this writer points to the fact that Asian communism is 'different', i.e. it owed its beginnings to the work of European Marxists in Asia, or to Westernised Asians, who became Marxist. 'It is not surprising, therefore, that the Asian communism of this period was both *avante-garde* and wholly derivative.'[2] Further analysis leads the author to isolate some special elements of Asian Marxism in contemporary conditions: the leaders of Marxist parties in the second half of the twentieth century tend to come from lower socio-economic classes than their predecessors, they tend to be less educated, their background is often rural rather than urban, and their following is predominantly rural. He further stresses the fact that such a following is not 'nationalist' in the European sense of the word, but tends to be 'localist', and hence, 'Communist movements seeking revolutionary victory have found that their most effective appeal is one that is based on a mixture of economic, social and political issues and strongly oriented toward *immediate* and *local* grievances.'[3] When one adds to the above features, the lack of tradition of 'majoritarianism' in Asia and the weakness of political institutions, particularly where the power of a personal ruler has been undermined, it is understandable that political parties take on a violent struggle against a real or supposed enemy, and are unable to drop it even after the enemy has been defeated.

While this explanation is partially sufficient, particularly to understand the persecution of ethnic minorities (as in Vietnam), it tends to leave out the historical traditions of domination in Asia in general and in South-east Asia in particular. Unlike Africa, Asia has a long history of non-European colonialism, though some parts of Asia had also been subjected to European colonial rule. A brief look at the territories which had been colonialised by the Europeans, by the Asians or which had remained independent does not prove to be fruitful, insofar as it can be demonstrated that in every one of those regions a semi-authoritarian government has been installed, with many of them exhibiting a tendency to violence. This applies both to regimes which call themselves Marxist and to those which are violently anti-communist. The one exception to this pattern, India, merely confirms the rule, and has a specific background both of non-violent Buddism and of a long, relatively orderly, British colonial past.

Having accepted the fact that governments in Asia tend to be committed to violence for various historical reasons one has to look for further explanation of this and the allied phenomena. Traditions of violent government are not enough for the continuation of sustained violence. Part of the blame must be attached to the low state of the concept of 'nationhood' throughout Asia. 'Localism' is not a rare phenomenon in Asia: it is ubiquitous. This reflects not only the size of the continent and its subcontinents, and the poor state of communications; it is based on a long history of conquest, on large migrations of national or racial groups and a low level of central government power. The concept of a modern European state, with its regulating policies towards all its citizens, may appear oppressive, but it is at the other end of the spectrum from Wittfogel's description of Chinese bandit-kings: because, uniquely, the modern state establishes connections between its own minorities and insists that they live under the rule of law. When this concept breaks down, or is broken down, as in Hitler's Germany, the result comes much nearer to the Asian situation than any European would wish to imagine.

Another difference in Asia as a whole is the phenomenon of population explosion and the accompanying lack of proper infra-structures for such an increase in numbers. Hence it is not simply the African or Latin American phenomenon of urbanisation but all three phenomena linked together: overpopulation on a massive scale; lack of services for such overpopulation both in the urban and rural areas; and, finally, the inevitable natural disasters which do not always serve to wipe out surplus population but which do diminish seriously the resources which serve the population. Added to this must be the lack of modern technology to cope with most of the difficulties, and, even worse, the misapplication of modern technology to Asian conditions. One example of this last was the much-hailed 'Green Revolution' in the post-war period, when improved strains of rice wiped out famines in many Asian regions and served to fuel a large rise in the birth-rate and a drop in infant mortality, the only factors which kept the population within permissible levels.

Viewed in this light, the problems of Asia do not appear to lend themselves to the application of Marxist theory, which pre-supposes a high degree of development, urbanisation and industrialisation, as well as exploitation of class by class. While both Lenin and Mao have attempted to modify the theory — Lenin in the abstract, and Mao from the viewpoint of a successful rural revolution — its application is bound to create more difficulties than it solves. This is proven by the way in which the post-Maoist Chinese leadership has been jettisoning Marxism in favour of capitalism in order to further quicker development. This does not prove that Marxism cannot be made to work successfully, which is a completely different question; it does prove that it is very difficult to make it work in Asian conditions, because it was not designed to do so, and has not been adapted to such conditions even by the most revisionist Marxists. On the other hand, Asian conditions do prove to be fertile ground for Marxist experiments, because here, literally, the rural proletariat have nothing to lose but their hunger and misery. Hence we have the paradox of trying to apply a sophisticated theory intended for developed countries to the world's least advantaged populations; and the subsequent disasters which are variously ascribed to poverty of Marxist thought or to 'imperialist' intervention.

If Marxism has yet to find its feet in Asia, it need not worry about the size of its following. By 1980 several major areas in Asia have become, by their own definition 'Marxist', even though most of them practise different kinds of Marxism. This variety of Marxist ideologies has been called 'competitive communism' by one writer. Writing in the early 1970s he suggested that India was a unique case study of competitive communism, and defined it in the following way: 'The author has put forward the concept of "competitive communism" as a special field of study because the Soviet and Chinese models of revolution and development are now competitive models that not only operate, respectively, in the two largest Communist states, but also compete against each other in the world Communist movement and in individual developing countries.'[4]

In the early 1970s there were three separate communist parties in India: the Moscow-oriented Communist Party of India (CPI), the independent Communist Party of India (Marxist) or CPI (M), and the Beijing-oriented Communist Party of India (Marxist–Leninist), or CPI (M–L), apart from a number of minor Maoist groups, which split off the last one. Each of the three communist parties had its own ideology and its own, conflicting, model of development. The CPI had also the unique experience of having been elected to power in one Indian state, Kerala, in 1957, and after the split the CPI was included in the 1967 coalition governments in Bihar and Punjab, while the CPI (M) served in coalition governments in Kerala and West Bengal.[5] While the electoral strength of all the communist parties is obscured by the Indian electoral system, studies have shown that they are second only to the nationalist Congress Party (before it split), and that they draw their support from the working classes and poor peasants as well as from the middle classes and the young. The Marxist and Maoist groups have also gained considerable following in the countryside through their agressive policies on land ownership.

It is interesting to note the different policies of those parties. While the pro-Moscow CPI was in favour of retaining the national-bourgeois state, before feudalism could be eradicated and a socialist state set up, the CPI(M) was in favour of immediate replacement of the current government by a 'people's democracy'. While the CPI, on the whole, approved of parliamentarism, the CPI(M) rejected it, claiming, in Marxist tradition, that they would never be allowed to carry out fundamental reforms in such a system. Nevertheless even the CPI(M) accepted that the parliamentary system would have to stay and flexibility would be needed in order to adapt it to its aims. Similar views were adopted on revolutionary struggle, with the CPI claiming that it was not necessary while the CPI(M) accepted that armed struggle, while not desirable, may be necessary to attain its objectives.

Although the views of these parties were obviously coloured

both by the traditional Indian preference for non-violence and by the fact that they played an important part in the state, the author stresses the revisionist character of both parties' ideologies: 'For the present, both Communist groups evidently remain convinced that parliamentary institutions can effectively be used to advance their goals, and though there is a growing emphasis on extra-parliamentary tactics of mass mobilization, these tactics are primarily intended to radicalize the parliamentary process rather than to replace it with a proletarian dictatorship.'[6] The defeat of the Gandhi Congress Party in the 1977 national elections gave a new boost to the CPI (M), partly because repression against it ceased and partly because the CPI had been electorally connected with the Congress Party and was defeated with it. The result was that the CPI (M) allied itself with the right-wing Janata Party then in power and lost much of its political standing. While not dropping its final objective of a radical solution, the CPI(M) approved of parliamentary democracy as a way of stopping the Gandhi authoritarianism. 'What distinguishes the CPI(M) from most, if not all, other Communist groups in the Third World is that although it strongly favors expanding friendship between the developing countries and the two Communist powers, it just as strongly opposes Moscow's or Peking's involvement in their domestic affairs, especially links on the part of either with indigenous revolutionary movements in the Third World.'[7]

This transformation of a radical party into a parliamentary one with close connections with the right is by no means unique. It follows closely the Chinese attempts to switch to the right, while retaining a revolutionary left-wing ideology, the victory of the communists in Vietnam and parallel developments in South-east Asia and Western Europe. Nor was Indian communism the only example of competitiveness. It could not be unknown to the Indians that a very similar situation existed further east, in Japan.

The Japanese Communist Party, like the Chinese and Indian Communist Parties, dated back to the early 1920s when it became the domain of left-wing intellectuals and was dominated by the politics of the Comintern. The post-war situation changed in the late 1950s as a result of the Sino–Soviet dispute, and by 1962 the party adopted a pro-Chinese stance which persisted till 1965. This led to a split into three parties: a new pro-Moscow group 'Voice of Japan' competes with the pro-Chinese Communist Party of Japan (Left) and with the mainstream Communist Party of Japan, which is independent of both influences.

> The Japanese Communists see the root of Communist disunity
> in Soviet and Chinese 'great-power chauvinism'. . . [and] the
> effort of the two big Communist powers to establish their
> hegemony over other Communist parties. . . . Differences
> between fraternal parties, it is pointed out, cannot and ought not
> to be resolved forcibly but only through patient discussion.
> [And] the Japanese further point out that the two major
> Communist powers have departed from Leninist norms to the
> point where they have actually engaged in military conflict . . . .
> the Sino–Soviet confrontation diverts the resources of the
> Communist camp from the struggle against the principal enemy,
> U.S. imperialism.[8]

Though these words were written well before the Communist
victory in Vietnam, the rapprochement between China and the
USA, and long before the Sino–Vietnamese War, not to speak of
other intra-Communist wars in South-east Asia, they point to the
essential change in the policy both of the two major communist
powers, and of the consequent necessity for change among the
non-ruling communist parties. While these Japanese statements
have some relation to the phenomenon of 'Eurocommunism', they
are shaped by different circumstances. The most important of
these is the fact that the Japanese Communists are as close to
Chinese pressure as Western European Communists are to Soviet
pressure. Hence their viewpoint bears the marks of a new pluralism
rather than of a concerted and unified change of direction.
Nevertheless, it is a significant point in the switch of policies.
Moreover, the Japanese attitude was bound to be influenced by
the changing position in the Indo-Chinese Peninsula.

Indo-China

Nowhere has communist ideology had to stand such a severe test
as in the Indo-Chinese Peninsula. Since the victory of Marxism in
several countries on the Peninsula has been hailed as a major
breakthrough, and as a major victory over American imperialism,
it is well worth looking at the facts.

The myth is so well established that it is almost forgotten now how the war began. It started as a result of the Japanese invasion of China and Indo-China. In 1941, the National Front (*Vietminh*) organised by Ho Chi Minh in Chinese Nationalist territory, operated against the Japanese in the mountains between China and Vietnam. It received sufficient material from the Allies to equip a small but cohesive and disciplined partisan force. Looking for a group capable of obstructing Europeans, and well acquainted with Ho's Marxist views, the Japanese transferred to him the governing powers in Tongking (North Vietnam) after their defeat in August 1945. The Kuomintang forces were to occupy Vietnam north of the 16th Parallel till the French colonial forces could return. Since the Chinese were unable to do so, on 2 September 1945 Ho Chi Minh proclaimed an independent Democratic Republic of Vietnam in the territories he controlled. Not daunted, the French colonial troops arrived back in Vietnam in March 1946 and proceeded to occupy North Vietnamese cities.

The determination of a small communist group, the nationalist passion of many educated Vietnamese, and the legitimate hatred of peasants against landlords and their supporters enabled Vietminh partisans to attack the French in December 1946 and to continue the struggle until victory. The Soviet Union and China recognized Ho's regime in January 1950. Between North and South Vietnam the French expeditionary forces numbered over 200,000 men. By the end of 1952, French losses amounted to 50,000 men killed or missing, and the war had cost over $5 billion.[9]

'In Vietnam south of the sixteenth parallel, British occupation was swift and communists did not have the opportunity to consolidate their organization as they did in North Vietnam. There was considerable terrorism but little open insurgency'.[10] By 1954 the French acknowledged their defeat and the Geneva Agreement was concluded, which ended French rule in Indochina and recognised Ho Chi Minh's government in North Vietnam.

The French having departed, the United States, acting on the basis of the policy of containment, decided to assume responsibility for the defence of South Vietnam, where about 1 million North Vietnamese (mostly Catholics) had fled .... It took five years for Vietnamese communists to regroup and reorganize. In

1959 communists killed about 100 anticommunists in South
Vietnam .... One thousand anticommunists were killed in 1960
and 2000 in 1961: this was guerrilla warfare and the United
States decided to intervene.[11]

Containment of communism had been the central element in
the foreign policy of the United States from March 1947, when
the Truman Doctrine had been enunciated, to March 1968,
when President Johnson announced a reversal in the conduct of
the war in Vietnam. For many years the policy of containment
had reflected the position of the majority of the American
public. .... American leaders of the early 1960s, who had
experienced World War II and the postwar period, found it
natural to do in Vietnam what had been done in 1950 in Korea
and in 1947 in Greece. Until 1968 they had the lukewarm
support of about three-fifths of the public. .... The visual
evidence of the war in every American living room, the mounting
American casualties, and the long duration of the conflict
stimulated a protest movement which contributed to the rapid
weakening of national cohesion in the later 1960's and led to the
demoralization of part of the American armed forces. The
Nixon administration would have liked a Korean-type solution
to the conflict; all it could achieve was an orderly withdrawal
which left communist forces in control of much of South
Vietnam and Laos, and of Cambodia .... Whatever the balance
sheet of American involvement in Vietnam, the policy of
containment had come to an end.[12]

This treatment of the Indo-Chinese conflict in a very brief book,
claiming to explain the rise of communism, has been quoted here
at length with a purpose. A very superficial analysis will demonstrate
that even if the French military and colonial interests thought they
could step back into Indo-China after five years of disruption, war
and Japanese occupation, the Americans and the British should
have had enough realism to attempt to stop them. If that proved
impossible, the size of the French defeat should have been sufficient
to deter the Americans from attempting to substitute for them.
Further, it is clear that the lessons of de-Stalinisation had not sunk
in in the early 1960s, when the theory of containment was practised
with the same or more vigour as in the 1950s. Further, the
development of the 'domino theory' in the 1960s virtually precluded

any modification of American foreign policy, even though this theory was, like dominos, knocked down the first time it was tested. Moreover, the American withdrawal was neither orderly nor honourable, and it occurred because of a conviction among the Americans that the war could not be won, not because American public opinion became 'soft' or pro-communist.

When Nixon was elected in 1968 he already had a commitment to end the war. For various reasons this was not possible till he was elected for a second term of office, and one authority suggests that it was only made possible then because 'the Soviet leaders, desiring economic assistance from the West and therefore preparing the detente policy, put pressure on Hanoi....'[13] In January 1973 the ceasefire was declared. In the spring of 1975 North Vietnamese and Vietcong forces occupied Saigon. Ho Chi Minh died in 1969 and did not see what was in effect a personal triumph. To compensate for this, Saigon was renamed Ho Chi Minh City. 'Our Great Spring Victory', as the Vietnamese chief of staff called it,[14] was the combined result of a very long history of nationalist struggle, the generous help which North Vietnam received both from the USSR and China, and a series of appalling mistakes by the Americans. However, it is perhaps too strong to call it a complete victory for communism, particularly in view of what has happened in South Vietnam since unification.

One look at the situation will illustrate this point. When confined to North Vietnam, the Vietnamese practised an austere kind of egalitarianism which fitted in well with a war of liberation, wearing one type of clothing, eating limited rations of food and sleeping in deep shelters to avoid American bombing. They were sustained not by terror but by the idea of liberation and victory. They gave the impression of a deeply committed, simple, peasant folk, intent on one thing only: the victory over the corrupt South Vietnamese. Their leaders, particularly till Ho Chi Minh's death, gave the impression of having sprung from the people themselves, of doing the same things and of not enjoying any privileges above those which the people had (and these were very few). Occasional travellers to North Vietnam gave a glowing account of the bravery, self-sacrifice and simplicity of the regime and contrasted it with the corrupt South Vietnamese government, people and the American forces in South Vietnam. The sins of the South Vietnamese were legion, from an addiction to coca-cola to drug-pushing, and the American troops in South Vietnam came in for far more criticism. Indeed, it was this 'corruption' which hastened the end of the war, as it had undesirable effects in America when the veterans were sent home. When the North Vietnamese entered Saigon, there were accounts to settle with the South Vietnamese who had served the Americans, but whom their allies had abandoned literally at a moment's notice. Nevertheless, the new regime has, even its critics admit, been relatively mild in its treatment of most South Vietnamese.

But only a few years later, a Western reporter visiting Saigon could hardly hide his amazement. In place of the austere virtues, he found that 'Saigon is very much the same kind of city that it was before 1975 — irrepressibly commercial, wise in the ways of corruption, and determined to maintain its self-respect ... by finding new ways to beat the system .... Along the main street of Tu Do you can still see street-corner clusters of young men with no visible means of support ... and you can still have your pocket picked by innocent-looking children. The black market in money — offering four times the official rate for the dollar — is almost open in Saigon, rather than the hole in the corner affair it is in Hanoi.'[15] This correspondent concluded that while Saigon has not changed, Hanoi was beginning to be penetrated by the same type of corruption. The main reason for the economic and social problems is the fact that Vietnam has to maintain huge armed forces, which produces inflation and reduces resources available for the civilian population. And the main reason for keeping a large army is the fact that Vietnam is at war — not with the capitalist powers, but with two communist powers: China and Kampuchea. It is here that the ultimate paradox lies.

The situation in Kampuchea was the direct result of the American decision to bomb Kampuchean territory to eradicate refuges granted to the Vietcong by the then ruler, Prince Sihanouk. The first air raid was authorised by President Nixon on 18 March 1969.[16] On 18 March 1970 Prince Sihanouk, who was considered anti-American, was deposed by a military junta headed by General Lon Nol. Sihanouk immediately joined the Khmer Rouge, communist guerrillas, who had been his enemies till then. The American bombing of Kampuchea continued, despite sporadic protests by Lon Nol, up to 1973. The devastation caused by the bombing was such that the Khmer Rouge, not particularly popular till then, began to gain ground rapidly.

On 17 April 1975 the Khmer Rouge entered the capital, Phnom

Penh, now empty of American troops and evacuated by Lon Nol, and began a rapid evacuation of the city. The Khmer Rouge terror[17] was of massive proportions, though it was merely the result of the application of the pseudo-Marxist doctrine that re-education could only come through work on land and that cities are corrupt, combined with a particularly ignorant and brutal leadership. It has been admitted that at least a million people, out of a population of seven million, died. Finally, the Democratic Republic of Kampuchea was overthrown in January 1979 by the forces of the Democratic Republic of Vietnam.

Despite the traditional hostility of the Kampucheans towards the powerful Vietnamese, the brutality of the Pol Pot regime has been such that the invaders were greeted as liberators. The new People's Republic of Kampuchea, headed by Heng Samrin, was recognised by the Soviet bloc and has recently gained official recognition from other Asian countries. India recognised it in the summer of 1980, apparently under pressure from the USSR. The new government has 'Vietnamised' Kampuchea, which meant that there was a complete reversal of deportation to the countryside, a return of some urban activity and a considerable easing of terror. However, the years of American bombing and defoliation, of guerrilla activities and of Pol Pot's policies have produced a famine in Kampuchea which the Vietnamese were unable to check on their own. The spread of Kampuchean refugees into other South-east Asian countries further contributed to chaos.

There was a sequel to the story. The Pol Pot regime had been supported by China. Its overthrow by the Vietnamese was considered provocative. The Chinese decided to punish the Vietnamese by making a quick expedition across the border — the same territory in which some forty years earlier the nationalist guerrillas of Ho Chi Minh operated with Chinese blessing. Significantly, the war started a few weeks after Den Xiaoping's visit to Washington, where he was treated to fulsome hospitality by President Carter. 'All smiles at the White House', said a heading under a photograph of the two leaders, but there was a warning: 'China's throw of the dice across the Vietnam border has gambled much of what the new, non-Maoist administration in Peking has struggled to achieve ... since 1976.'[18] Further, the correspondent stated that: 'Foreign analysts calculating the enormous risks involved see only uncertain benefits for China in its attempt to "punish the Vietnamese as they deserve"'. The conduct of the Sino–Vietnamese war - though it was not a war because diplomatic relations were never severed — was one aspect of the picture. The other was the possible retaliation by the Russians, which the Chinese anticipated, because they were already evacuating population from Xinjiang, bordering onto the USSR and Mongolia.

The Chinese invasion was not very successful. The Vietnamese army, highly mechanised (thanks to the American equipment left behind) and skilled in battle, gave a good account of itself and the Chinese were forced to withdraw their struggling troops within a few weeks.

Early in March 1979 a Western correspondent announced that 'China and Vietnam struggle to save face', and added that both sides claimed a victory. Naturally, both sides could not have won — China had experienced real difficulties with its antiquated equipment and poorly trained army: on the other hand 'Vietnam may not have been overawed, but midweek reports from Hanoi indicated that the leadership was chastened enough to be split between the unrepentant who wanted to counter-attack, and others who wanted a conference'.[19] At any rate, both sides began negotiations to settle the dispute.

However, a year later the Chinese foreign minister announced that his country was ready to go to war with Vietnam again if necessary. The key to the problem was that the Vietnamese troops were still in Kampuchea and intended to stay there till the threat of return of Pol Pot was removed. The Vietnamese felt aggrieved. They have attempted to re-establish relations with the USA, they opened up the country to Western oil companies and they liberalised their regime considerably. In return the West continued to play the 'China hand', and Vietnam finally fell back on the USSR, joining the Comecon in 1977 and depending heavily on Soviet economic and military aid.[20] The Western states even refused to recognize the Heng Samrin government in Kampuchea.

Moreover, the difficulties in Indo-China did not end there. Partly to upset the Chinese and partly because of an economic crisis in the country, the Vietnamese encouraged a huge exodus of the Chinese population from Vietnam in the summer of 1979. The numbers of these refugees were estimated at hundreds of thousands: no-one knows how many 'boat people' drowned on the high seas. Every South-east Asian country, already saturated with refugees, either refused to give them shelter or tried to evict them or even liquidate them. Captains of foreign ships were told not to 'rescue' any more refugees, and hundreds of women and children were drowned in their little boats as a result. Added to the Kampuchean tragedy, the tragedy of the 'boat people' makes it into one of the major man-made disasters even in the troubled history of Indo-China.

Political correspondents are disturbed by these events. One commented that Kampuchea was the Balkans of Asia, and that the consequences of Chinese impotence and Soviet successes would be bound to de-stabilise other countries in Africa and Asia.[21] It is certain that the Vietnamese have supported the invasion of Afghanistan in late 1979, and that the existence of a strong Soviet presence in the Indo-Chinese Peninsula is bound to influence events in Thailand and other areas.

But an analyst of Marxism must be puzzled. The developments in Indo-China are sufficiently interesting to consider what had happened to Marxism *en route* from the USSR to China and to Indo-China. As the Japanese Communists rightly say, the first outcome was that the communist countries started to fight among themselves rather than fight imperialism. Yet one of the basic tenets of Marxism was that only the capitalists fight for markets — socialists are fraternal. Does this development disprove Marx? There is the additional fact that foreign communist parties find it difficult to support one or the other side in the dispute, mostly limiting themselves to appeals to settle it. Where does this put the unity of the communist movement? Third, it is assumed (not without reason) that the Chinese Communists have the full support of the Americans, despite their ideological stance. Has this made the American government pro-Marxist?

These puzzling questions cannot be answered in full. However, some factors appear plain. The application of Marxism to an agrarian economy, first made by Mao, has not been very successful. This does not impinge on the theory itself, as it had been developed for a different kind of environment. It does show that Mao, while possibly right in his adaptation, was wrong to insist that it was Marxist. What had emerged from the Chinese experiment was an agrarian socialism of the kind once envisaged by the Russian Populists, supported by a large measure of military administration in place of the skilled communist proletarian cadres, who would tutor the ignorant peasants. To call the Chinese socialism 'neo-Marxism' would be bold because it lacks most of the basic Marxist conditions. Calling it 'Maoism' would be to adopt a name which many radical non-Chinese groups have taken for their own, and which has different connotations. It is not 'revisionism', as the Russians insist, because revisionism applies to the same category as Marxism. Perhaps the best description would be to call it 'pseudo-Marxism', and if this is too strong to apply to China, which at least has some industrial base, it would be right to apply it to Vietnam and to Kampuchea.

The reason why Vietnamese and Kampuchean brands of Marxism are 'pseudo-Marxist' is that they take a mechanistic view of the theory and apply it according to their own needs. Even a superficial glance at Marx and Engels will demonstrate that this was not the intention of the theory, the first 'scientific' theory of development. Neither was Lenin, who adapted the theory, as quick to drop the basics of Marxism as are the Asian leaders. Indeed, his hesitations and worries are clear in his writings between 1919 and 1922. Even Stalin's innovation of 'socialism in one country', while a divergence from Marxism in that it rejected the necessity of a global revolution, was not such a flagrant violation of theory as that which the Asian leaders are performing.

Further, the fact that two types of Marxist governments have been actively engaged in fighting undermines their claims to true Marxism. No true Marxist would fight another, if the theory were to be followed. This is a contradiction in terms. While it is useful to blame Soviet or American influence on such behaviour, the fact remains that the Indo-Chinese states have had a measure of choice since 1975, and that they preferred war to peace. This seems to prove the theory that the leaderships, under the cloak of Marxism, are simply indulging in the age-old power struggle in Indo-China — a struggle between the Chinese and Indian influence and the indigenous population. The label of 'pseudo-Marxism', is attached to these regimes because some of the measures they have introduced have their origin in Marxist theories. This is the nationalisation of land and the introduction of wide-scale welfare measures. However, for the rest, they appear to be purely nationalist, and, moreover, nationalist in the Indo-Chinese manner. They are intent on localised interests, on localised victories and pay little heed to global matters.

One may add, however, that it is hard to blame any of these regimes. They are confronted with unprecedented problems, many of them new and the result of twentieth-century developments. Apart from a tiny elite, the majority of the population is still in the same state as they were in the Middle Ages. If modernisation appeals, Marxism seems a quick and efficient way towards it. But what if it fails? And it is bound to fail because the necessary 'objective conditions' are missing. Then one is left with authoritarian, nationalist regimes, always dependent on economic and military aid from some great power. It is not always an attractive prospect.

Analysing Asian Pseudo-Marxism

If the Asian pseudo-Marxist regimes cannot claim to have been highly successful one has to look at the reasons why, despite all the problems, they have proliferated over the last twenty years or so. One of the reasons is that they are in essence nationalist, and appear to be anti-European, or anti-American. The second, and possibly more potent reason, is that even they compare favourably with other Asian regimes, which are based either on Islamic theocracy or on a badly digested version of parliamentary democracy or on frank and brutal military oppression.

The objectors to the 'sovietisation' of Afghanistan need only look beyond the border towards Pakistan. As the squalid end prepared for Bhutto was nearing, a Western journalist visited Pakistan. They told him, and that was before the Supreme Court's decision: 'There is going to be an important hanging here soon. They're going to hang Mr Bhutto.'[22] It is not without reason that an ex-revolutionary wrote some time later: 'One of the more grotesque aspects of the West's response to the Soviet military intervention in Afghanistan has been the propaganda barrage unleashed . . . in defence of "plucky little Pakistan". . . . The military regime has utilised Islam in order to put the overwhelming majority of the country into a repressive straitjacket. Those who attempt to break out are publicly flogged, imprisoned without trial or sentenced to death'. And further: 'An old pro-Moscow Pakistani Communist said to me last week: "You better treat me with some respect from now on". "Why?" I asked. "Who knows", he replied, only half-cynically, "I might be the next President of Pakistan".'[23]

Other states in South-east Asia are Singapore, the Philippines, Thailand and Malaysia. Gavin Young visited their leaders in late 1978, only to be met with assurances that their stability was quite complete.[24] But a year later a report in a British newspaper said that 'Three years after the United States abandoned its bases in

Thailand, it is quietly reassigning military personnel here under contingency plans to cope with a possible Vietnamese incursion into Thai territory. ... The return of a United States military presence ... is a highly sensitive matter. ... A renewed US military presence would undermine Bangkok's uneasy friendship with Hanoi, and could stir discontent among progressive Thais, who have come to regard American assistance as ... the kiss of death'.[25] After its abandonment of Vietnam and Kampuchea, the US has little standing even in the countries which are traditionally anti-communist or anti-Vietnamese. And few people will forget that Henry Kissinger in his memoirs claimed that his action had averted a catastrophe.[26] The Thais and other Asians may well ask: If Kampuchea was an averted catastrophe what would an accomplished catastrophe involve?

As Ascherson says:

Kissinger could not have anticipated what Pol Pot would do. But he made it possible for him to do it. ... Let the indictment rest here. ... But at least we can judge better now whether Kissinger passes his own 'statesman's test'. That 'exaltation of goals' came to mean that he exalted the national interests of the United States to a supreme moral imperative, something which justified the sacrifice of a small neutral country. He certainly didn't 'avert catastrophe' from Cambodia: instead he tried to throw an unexploded American catastrophe into that miserable land before it went off. He begged America always for a little more time to use a little more force, and then it would be peace with honour. In the end, Congress grew tired of this and took away his sword'.[27]

Leaving Kampuchea and Vietnam apart, and passing over the implications for Thailand and neighbouring territories, allowing for the fact that Bhutto was sacrificed because he tended to lean leftwards (thus paving the way for a repulsive but anti-communist regime), one has to look at other responses to the threat of communism in Asia. A good example was found in South Korea, a country which was saved from communism in the early 1950s. The South Korean president, Park Chung Hee, was killed by his own intelligence chief in October 1979. Park had for long been labelled as the West's 'difficult friend'. 'He could and did use the challenge from communist North Korea to extract support from the successive

American governments which disliked his political methods'.[28] Another correspondent commented later that 'Blunders of Seoul intelligence proved more dangerous than any communist plot', and further 'there can be little doubt in the minds of many South Koreans that some of the hamfisted tactics and blunders of the KCIA have ... done more than any communist plot to undermine South Korea's position in recent years'.[29]

In April 1980 student demonstrations broke out in South Korea, with the students calling for the abolition of the repressive constitution and general elections. The reason for the revolt was that Park's successor, Choi Kyu Hah, who promised to re-establish constitutional rule, was not doing so. The student revolts were brutally suppressed, the opposition New Democratic Party was prevented from entering parliament or holding press conferences and Park's assassin and his accomplices were hanged. To top this, Reuter reported that:

> North Korea yesterday called on the South Korean authorities to lift martial law and to release all students and opposition politicians arrested during recent anti-government demonstrations. The North Korean news agency ... quoted a joint statement by the ruling Workers's Party and other political organisations describing the resignation of the Government in Seoul as 'another coup d'état'. In New York, North Korea's chief delegate at the United Nations said his Government had no intention of invading the South. 'We want to realise reunification through a North-South confederation, leaving the different systems as they are now', he said.[30]

The irony of the situation in Asia as a whole is that the doctrine of 'containment' has been proven to be just as fallacious as the 'domino' theory. Many anti-communist regimes behave in a manner which would make Stalin green with envy. Faced with the sheer brutality of these regimes and their apparent dependence on the Americans, many Asians behave like Tariq Ali's friend, and opt for regimes which are frankly one-party and possibly just as oppresive, but which give the impression of being independent and which salve their national or 'local' pride.

In summing up, one can say from this survey of ruling Marxist parties that their doctrine matters little to the average Asian. The label of 'competitive communism' for the Indians, of 'pure Marxism' in the case of the Japanese Communist Party or of 'pseudo-Marxism' for the Indo-Chinese parties is immaterial. The issues may be ex-colonial, or economic, or even purely political as in South Korea. The real problem is that Asian conditions have distorted Marxist theory to a point where one must seriously doubt whether any of those parties could reasonably claim even to have a Marxist theoretical background.

The same applies to 'parliamentary' types of government. Asia has traditionally had authoritarian systems of government. For this reason, introducing parliamentary democracy is as unsuitable as introducing Marxism: neither the people nor the institutions can be bent so far. Western-type democracy is at least as distorted in Asia as is Marxism. This fact was fully realised by the USSR, when it turned its attention to Africa. It remains to be seen whether it will be understood by the USA.

Notes

1. R.A. Scalapino, 'Patterns of Asian Communism', in *Problems of Communism*, January-April (1971), p. 2.
2. Ibid., p. 3.
3. Ibid., p. 9, emphasis in text.
4. B.S. Gupta 'India's Rival Communist Models', in *Problems of Communism*, January-February (1973), p. 3 and n. 10.
5. Ibid., p. 3.
6. Ibid., p. 15.
7. B.S. Gupta, 'Indian Politics and the Communist Party (Marxist)', in *Problems of Communism*, September-October (1978), pp. 11-12.
8. P.F. Langer, 'The New Posture of the CPJ', in *Problems of Communism*, January-February (1971), p. 23.
9. M. Salvadori, *The Rise of Modern Communism*, p. 85.
10. Ibid., p. 91.
11. Ibid., pp. 121-2.
12. Ibid., pp. 150-1.
13. H. Seton-Watson, *The Imperialist Revolutionaries*, p. 133.
14. General Van Tien Dung. *Our Great Spring Victory*, published in English in 1976.
15. M. Woollacott, *Guardian*, 29 May 1980.
16. This is described in detail, based on original American documents, by W. Shawcross in *Side-Show: Kissinger, Nixon and the Destruction of Cambodia*; the reader can also consult Henry Kissinger's interpretation, *The White House Years*, (1979).
17. A fairly recent description will be found in J.J. Zasloff and McAlister Brown, 'The Passion of Kampuchea', in *Problems of Communism*, January-February (1979).
18. N. Wade, *Sunday Telegraph*, 25 Feb. 1979.
19. D. Bloodworth, *Observer*, 11 March 1979.

20. C. Mullin, *Guardian*, 15 March 1980.
21. M. Frankland, *Observer*, 15 Jan. 1979.
22. G. Young, *Observer*, 1 Oct. 1978.
23. T. Ali, *Guardian*, 14 Jan. 1980.
24. *Observer*, 3 Sept. 1978.
25. R. Whymant, *Guardian*, 27 Nov. 1979.
26. See Ascherson's article on the Kissinger Memoirs in the *Observer*, 18 Nov. 1979.
27. Ibid.
28. M. Frankland, *Observer*, 28 Oct. 1979.
29. P. Hazelhurst, *The Times*, 7 Jan. 1980
30. R. Richardson, *Financial Times*, 21 May 1980.

20

Eurocommunism and Its Consequences

The Origins

The resolution ... emphatically declares that it is *permissible* in principle for Social-Democrats to participate in a provisional revolutionary government. ... By this declaration we once and for all dissociate ourselves both from the anarchists, who answer this question in the negative in principle, and from the tail-enders in Social-Democracy ... who have *tried to frighten* us with the prospects of a situation in which it might prove necessary for us to participate in such a government. ... It stands to reason, however, that the question of permissibility in principle does not solve the question of practical expediency. ... What we can and must do is to determine the nature and aim of our participation. That is what is done in the resolution, which points to the two purposes for which we participate: 1) a relentless struggle against counter-revolutionary attempts, and 2) the defence of the independent interests of the working class. ... We have now undoubtedly entered a new era — a period of political upheavals and revolutions has begun. In a period such as that ... it is impermissible to confine ourselves to old, stereotyped formulas. We must propagate the idea of action from above.[1]

[Eurocommunism] is not a matter of a *third road*, to use a term favoured by popular journalists. For if we were to set out to enumerate the different roads being followed in the world revolutionary process, there would be many more than three. Nor is it a question of a retreat to social-democratic positions, or of a denial of the historical reasons which justified the birth of communist parties. It must be recognised, however, that the approach to the problem of the State in the following pages involves a difference from Lenin's theses of 1917 and 1918. These were applicable to Russia and theoretically to the rest of the world at that time. They are not applicable today because they have been overtaken in the circumstances of the developed capitalist countries of western Europe. What has made them inapplicable is the change in economic structures, and the objective expansion of the progressive social forces, the development of the productive forces ... the advance of socialism and decolonisation, and the defeat of fascism in the Second World War. It may strike some people as blasphemous to read that some of Lenin's theses are out of date; there are those who are unaware that Lenin said the same thing about Marx, and that the Soviet successors of Lenin openly revised some of his theses.[2]

Lenin wrote the passage quoted above in 1905, Carrillo in 1976. Though more than seven decades divide these two quotations, the gist is not dissimilar: constant revision of practice is necessary to keep the dynamism of communism alive, even if the principle remains the same. When Lenin wrote his essay in 1905 the first Russian proletarian revolution was about to be put down by the Tsarist regime: when Carrillo wrote his book, the world had just witnessed a great surge of socialist victories. In the Far East, the Americans had just recognised the existence of Communist China, and left Indo-China to be occupied by a Marxist regime. In Spain, the last fascist dictator had just died, opening the way for a new, more liberal regime. In Italy, the Christian Democratic government had just accepted passive help from the Communist Party, which had come second in the national elections. In France, two years earlier, the joint candidate of the Left lost elections by a fraction of a per cent.

Even in Portugal, where one fascist dictator stayed in power for half a century, the dictatorship collapsed in 1974, and a new revolutionary junta, strongly dominated by left-wing officers, held power for a few months. True, there were some setbacks. The Portuguese officers were deprived of power and a series of governments of centre-left and later centre-right took over. but Portugal would never be the same after Salazar, just as the USSR would not return to Stalinist ways. On the other side of the globe, the world's only freely elected Marxist government was overthrown, and here the trend was reversed: the military dictatorship which followed it seemed to be one of the most oppressive ones in Latin America.

But there were lessons to be drawn from the Portuguese and Chilean experience, just as there were lessons to be learnt from the successful developments. What did all these events forecast for the future, and where did the impetus for change come from? In the first instance, as can be seen from Lenin's quotation, Marxism had never been intended as a static statement of faith. This aberration had come into force during the Stalinist period, but this was for a good reason. While Stalin was building up the USSR's potential and later pursuing an imperialist line of expansion, ideology had to take second place. After Stalin's death, the new Soviet leadership realised the harm Stalinism had done to the movement on a global scale, and agreed to scale down the imperialist policy and to promote the extension of socialism by ideological means, admittedly, only insofar as the USSR's geopolitical interests would allow.

These changes were also dictated by historical necessities. The communist parties everywhere had changed their character. The generation trained during the years prior to 1935, during the war and in the Cold War period had been phased out, giving way to new leaders, whose main experience was of preparing for elections, dealing with economic problems, and attempting to reconcile the differences within the Socialist bloc (or intra-party quarrels) rather than that of international communist solidarity. In most Western European countries, the communist parties were either safely established as major parties (as in Italy, and France) or at least legitimised within the state (as in Spain and Portugal). The age of heroism, at least in Europe, was over, particularly as the myth of Soviet encirclement could no longer be sustained.

There were also outstanding examples of an independent 'road to socialism', as in the case of Yugoslavia, and of Mao's China, whose emissaries were exercising a strong influence on various left-wing movements but with particular emphasis on the Third World countries. If 1956 the lowest point of communist self-esteem, the reformist tendencies were soon to the fore. The Yugoslav road to socialism influenced Poland and Hungary, who were soon followed by Romania. All four countries changed their economic systems considerably and experienced some degree of political liberalisation. The Italians were the first to espouse the cause of reformism, with Togliatti giving a blessing almost from his deathbed in his famous Yalta Memorandum. In the mid-1960s the

PCI was joined by the PCE, still illegal and in exile, but led by the pragmatic Santiago Carrillo, and after the death of Maurice Thorez, the PCF, under Waldeck Rochet, joined forces. These three parties were openly critical of the anti-liberal policies within the socialist bloc, such as those of the Ulbricht regime in East Germany, the anti-semitism in Poland in 1968 and the 1966 trials in the USSR of the dissidents Sinyavskiy and Dan'yel.

The events of the 'Prague Spring' produced a genuine enthusiasm among the Western European communists. Dubcek's 'socialism with a human face' was broader in scope and went further than other Eastern European countries had dared to progress, especially with regard to pluralism and human rights. After his visit to Czechoslovakia in May 1968, Luigi Longo, Togliatti's successor, declared that the Czech experiment helped communist parties in capitalist countries to create a new socialist society. In April, Waldeck Rochet pledged support for Dubcek, who, he held, had contributed to the 'expansion of Socialism'. Carrillo stated later: 'If the term "Eurocommunism" had been invented in 1968, Dubcek would have been a Eurocommunist.'[3] The Czech movement was seen in the West as an example of democratic socialism of the kind which could be introduced in a developed and democratic European country.

When the pressure on Czechoslovakia began to mount, the PCI, PCE and PCF mobilised seventeen Western European communist parties to support it, they even threatened to convene a separate conference to condemn the USSR, and Waldeck Rochet served as a mediator between the Czech and Soviet leadership. The ensuing invasion of Czechoslovakia by the forces of the Warsaw Pact marked a crucial turning point for the Western European communist parties: their opposition was not merely based on ideological grounds, it was based on the reasonable fear that the unpopularity of the invasion would lose them votes and a chance to come to power through the ballot box.

It was in this climate of uncertainty and hesitation that the PCF startled the world by signing the Common Programme of the Left in 1972, and co-operating with the Socialists in the 1973 legislative and 1974 presidential elections. The surprise was even greater when the presidential candidate of the Left, the Socialist, François Mitterand, polled 49.5 per cent of the total vote, against 50.5 per cent polled by Giscard d'Estaing. The success of the coalition, however temporary (for a serious rift broke it up in the late 1970s) gave the other Western European communist parties some food for thought.

But other events were also of importance. If the cause of socialism was to succeed in Western European conditions, what were the conditions for its success? First of all, it had to be demonstrated either that the USSR had changed its imperialist policy — which, if 1968 was anything to go by, it did not — or that Western European communist parties were independent of it. Second, strong anti-communist activity and propaganda carried out by various interests had to be counteracted in a subtle way. This is where the Chile lesson was particularly important. In Chile a Marxist government, freely elected, was de-stabilised: this made the PCI, in particular, decide on a course of allying itself with elements which are strong in Latin countries, especially the parties associated with the Catholic Church. In the Italian case this was a tacit alliance with the ruling Christian Democratic Party and an open wooing of the Church. As Berlinguer put it in 1975: 'It is necessary to bring face to face and to stimulate positive collaboration between Catholic ecumenism, and the cosmopolitan universalism of the great rationalist tradition of Europe. This is the most fundamental and most general significance of the Historic Compromise.'4

There was a dual type of reasoning behind the Historic Compromise: on the one hand, the anti-Communist forces were too strong for Communists to retain power without the use of force; and second, the use of force was an antiquated and at best a crude tool. On the other hand, the use of brutal techniques by the anti-communists had turned many traditionally anti-communist bodies into willing or unwilling allies of the Left. This applied particularly to some elements in the Catholic Church: but both the liberal laity and the progressive clerics were appalled by the methods used by the extreme right and by the continuation of social injustice by those regimes. In Latin America, the Jesuits, spurred by the American Jesuits' participation in the Civil Rights struggle, were particularly keen to join the struggle for liberation. In Chile, after 1973, the traditionally anti-Marxist Christian Democrats allied with the Marxists to defend the population against the junta. Even the highest hierarchy of the Catholic Church, while preaching that Marxism was spiritually pernicious, allowed that some social and economic aspects of right-wing dictatorships were so repulsive as to allow the Church to ally itself with the 'progressive' forces. So the PCI's conversion was not all onesided; the Church had made it possible to open a dialogue, and the Communists responded.

The second argument concerned the past, not the present or future. It concerned the Portuguese Communists' attempt to institute a dictatorial regime in that country, and its swift failure. On 30 April 1974 the Secretary-General of the CPP, Alvaro Cunhal, returned to Lisbon from exile abroad. It was announced that he came from Paris, but the informed ones knew that he had merely changed planes there, and had actually begun his journey in Prague. The Portuguese revolution of 1974 was not only directed by left-wing officers, joined in the Movement of Armed Forces (MFA), but it took an extremely left-wing line. As one commentator notes: 'The Portuguese "revolution" of 1974 startled the world not only by its suddenness, but also by the left-wing orientation of its presidium of middle-ranking officers. "We knew something was going to happen", said one American diplomat. "What surprised us was the direction it took".'[5] The officers were led by three middle-ranking officers, the best known among whom was Major Otelo de Carvalho, soon to be promoted to brigadier, and commander of the COPCON, the Operational Command for the Continent, a force created in July 1974 to combat right-wing forces.

If Cunhal was little known, Carvalho had charismatic qualities and was popular both among the armed forces and some sections of the population. Yet, within a year, and despite many social changes, such as the land reform, which were popular among the poorer peasants, the MFA was downgraded. Communist influence was all but eliminated and a centre-right government firmly installed. Carvalho himself was under house-arrest awaiting trial for violations of legality. What went wrong with the apparently invincible coalition of the armed services and the left wing, strongly supported by the Communist Party? Part of the blame must be attached to destabilisation by the right. Part must lie with the lack of political literacy of the masses and their willingness to be led by extremely reactionary forces. But a very large part of the blame lay with Carvalho himself, who indulged in dictatorial tactics and was distrusted by other political parties, and most of all with the leadership of the Communist Party. As one historian says:

The communists, by far the largest group to the left of the

socialists, assiduously courted soldiers 'incapable of resisting the temptations of power.' Early autumn opinion polls commissioned by several parties indicated that they would be the big losers in the promised national elections, gaining no more than 15 per cent of the vote. Cunhal's obvious task was to adapt party tactics to the exigencies of Western democracy like his French and Italian counterparts, setting his well-oiled machine to the business of vote winning. . . . However, Cunhal was a man whose ideas were frozen in the past. His long, bitter struggles with Salazar had moulded him in the crude image of his persecutor. . . . His long years in Prague had insulated him against the forces of change and left him untutored in the political conditions of the West. He was a Stalinist of the 1930's who dreamed of becoming the Lenin of his country, . . . a conspirator more at home in 1917 than 1974. 'Cunhal does not understand the Portuguese people' Soares complained. 'He wants to impose on them schemes that run against their psychology and their way of life . . . . He is outmoded. Cunhal is Prague'.[6]

How far the Portuguese and Chilean experience moulded the birth of Eurocommunism may never be known. What we do know is that repeated failure of communist parties to retain or gain power, coupled with the dissatisfaction with Soviet policy of repression within its own sphere, gave it an added impetus. This was complemented by the development of a much more open attitude towards the Left on the part of many social forces, the strongest of them being the Catholic Church. Just as the Church took a large part in the American Civil Rights Campaign, and supported the equal rights campaign in Rhodesia, so it felt it had to join the campaign for social and economic advancement, which was, in essence, the programme of the Left. The fact that it could do so without compromising its spiritual standing says a lot both for the stand initiated by Pope John XXIII of allying the Church with the oppressed of the world and for the new generation of clerics, who were spurred in their efforts to speak up for the deprived by a sense of social justice, precisely because theirs was now a vocational and not a professional calling. This synthesis of social and spiritual is very well demonstrated in the person of Pope John Paul II, who is able to show a strong anti-communist stance while exhibiting the greatest degree of concern for social and economic advancement.

Eurocommunism in Practice

Writing in 1976, Carrillo defined Eurocommunism in these terms:

> The parties included in the 'Eurocommunist' trend are agreed
> on the need to advance to socialism with democracy, a multi-
> party system, parliaments and representative institutions, sover-
> eignty of the people regularly exercised through universal suffrage,
> trade unions independent of the State and of the parties,
> freedom for the opposition, human rights, religious freedom,
> freedom for cultural, scientific and artistic creation, and the
> development of the broadest forms of popular participation at
> all levels and in all branches of social activity. Side by side with
> this, in one form or another, the parties claim their total
> independence in relation to any possible international leading
> centre and to the socialist states, without ceasing on that
> account to be internationalist. . . . These parties are striving for
> cooperation and peaceful coexistence, for overcoming the policy
> of military blocs, for the dismantling of foreign bases . . . for the
> prohibition of nuclear weapons and for disarmament; non-
> interference in the affairs of other countries; and the exercise of
> the right to self-determination for all peoples.[7]

The programme was as sweeping as the term itself. While the
term 'Eurocommunism' was said to have been coined by a Yugoslav
journalist in 1976 (though there are different opinions on this) the
Japanese and Mexican parties have adopted it, while on the other
hand the Portuguese party rejected it emphatically. Nevertheless,
the acknowledged leaders and participants in the movement were
the three Western European parties: the Italian, the French and
the Spanish. In 1977 the PCI participated (if passively) in
government: the PCF was assumed to have a good chance of
coming to power as part of the Left Alliance in the parliamentary
elections of March 1978, and the PCE was thought to be sufficiently
strong for the prime minister, Suarez, to invite it to take part in
negotiations on stabilising the economy in October 1977.

The Eurocommunist summit meeting in Madrid in March 1977
gave rise to alarm on the part of the European right that the three
major parties would form a dynamic bloc which would be difficult
to stop, and to hopes on the left that a unification of the forces of
the left could not be far off. In the event, this unification failed to

materialise, and even more surprisingly, the communist parties did not manage to come either to direct power or to retain their share of it after 1978. The PCF failed to come to power in the 1978 elections partly, though not completely, because of the rift in the Union of the Left.[8] The PCE trailed far behind in the national elections of 1977, getting 9.2 per cent of the total votes.[9] Perhaps the most disappointing of all was the drop in the standing of the PCI, which had gained 34.4 per cent of all votes in the elections of 1976 as against 38.7 per cent gained by the Christian Democrats. Local elections held in May 1978 showed that it had dropped its vote by almost 10 per cent, a poor record for a party which had gone all out to convince the voters that it was democratic and which, moreover, had a solid and praiseworthy record of local government.

It is not easy to analyse all the reasons for this poor showing, after such a promising start. Some authors point to the fact that: 'by relinquishing their comfortable positions in permanent opposition and engaging themselves more and more in the existing societal and institutional frameworks of their countries — i.e., by exposing themselves to what former West German Chancellor Willi Brandt has called the "venture of democracy" — the Eurocommunists opened the way to factional tensions within party ranks. Such tensions developed independently of whether the Eurocommunists followed a consistent course of constructive cooperation with other "progressive" political forces, as in Italy and Spain, or eventually shrank from responsibility and deliberately sabotaged a possible . . . victory of the Left, as in France.'[10] Another reason given is that in the wake of electoral alliances the electoral gains went not to the Communists but to the Socialist parties, making the Communists fearful of long-term consequences of such policies.

Other reasons quoted are personal incompatibilities between Communist and Socialist leaders (this was certainly the case in relations between Georges Marchais and François Mitterand) and differences of opinion between the leaders of the three main parties on issues concerned with national interest. It is true that each communist party had a different view on such issues as the Common Market, NATO, free trade and other matters, but these views had in no way previously stopped them from coming together.

Two reasons which emerge at this juncture appear to have more credibility. The first one is that in co-operating with the Socialists (as in France) or with the Christian Democrats (as in Italy) the Communists have lost their appeal to the radical left without compensating for it by gaining the support of the left wing of the Socialist parties. Italy is a particularly good example, as the growth of extreme left-wing groups after 1976 has been a marked phenomenon. There is good reason to suspect communist co-operation with socialist parties which attract, throughout Western Europe, voters who are, to use the famous meaningless phrase, 'moderates'. In other words, voters who are dissatisfied with centre-right policies vote socialist to register their dissent. Being allied with these parties could only lose the Communists support among such radical elements as still gave them their votes. But the fact is that since 1968 the Communists have also lost their traditional support among the young: Czechoslovakia, the student revolutions and the growth of much more appealing extreme left-wing groups have made the Communists seem stodgy and old-fashioned. If there is sense in changing the slogan of 'dictatorship of the proletariat' to the slogan of 'parliamentary democracy' as far as the moderate voter is concerned such a slogan will have no appeal to the young extremist intent on 'direct action' and seeing it coming only 'through the barrel of a gun'.

It was not the 'venture of democracy' which lost the Communists support; it was the radical, extremist left, often allying itself with the most unlikely causes which was to blame. The Communists were thus caught between two fires: that of wanting to belong to the legitimate parties, parties which uphold constitutional government and law and order, and that of seeing their traditional support wane in favour of extremism. Since they have already had to jettison some of their most important ideological baggage on the way, they have lost the best of both worlds and have acquired little in return.

But this is only part of the story. Other factors have undermined Eurocommunism to a point of disappearance only three or so years after it emerged.

The Superpowers and Eurocommunism

It has been assumed that Eurocommunism was a spontaneous phenomenon, brought about by 'objective' conditions in Europe. Yet one has some doubts. In view of the worsening economic situation since the oil boycott of 1973 one would expect proletarian politics to become more radical, not less so. In fact, all parties which claim to speak for the working classes have become ever more ready to come to terms with the West European mixed economy. In Marxist terms, this is nonsense. While the workers are not starving in the nineteenth-century sense, there has been a real erosion of their living standards since 1973. Yet instead of radical policies the communist parties talk of a compromise with the capitalists. Have they lost their teeth, or is there some other factor at work?

Soon after the Madrid Conference, an interviewer asked the US National Security Adviser, Zbigniew Brzezinski: 'What would you do if Eurocommunists came to power? Do you feel you would *have* to do something, some kind of response is necessary?' to which the reply was:

> Well, first of all, we do not wish the communist parties to come to power in Western Europe. Secondly, we have confidence that the West European electorates will use their best judgement to preserve democratic systems and will therefore opt for democratic parties. Thirdly, we have to deal with the world as it is. Fourthly, the existence of Eurocommunist parties ... does encourage change in the nature of Communism, and it is unwise for the United States to engage in direct interference in domestic affairs of other countries, of the sort that could make the Eurocommunist parties symbols of national independence. Lastly, Eurocommunism is a highly differentiated phenomenon. All it is really is a catchword for West European Communist parties.[11]

While the Carter administration was prepared to compromise in 1977, Kissinger was 'still sternly opposed to Eurocommunism. He reproves the "many people on both sides of the Atlantic who have permitted themselves to be convinced that Eurocommunism is only social democracy with a Leninist face". He also believes that "a Communist breakthrough to power or a share in power in one country will have a major psychological effect on the others, by making Communist parties seem respectable, or suggesting that the tide of history in Europe is moving in that direction".[12]

One of the reasons why Kissinger opposed Eurocommunism was his concern for NATO. The fact that the PCI stated that it preferred to be in NATO because it felt protected against the

USSR, that the PCF in government would have had no more part in NATO than any other French government and that Spain was not in NATO at all, did not seem to matter.[13] A similar view obtained on the Eurocommunists' attitude to the EEC, even though they endorsed it for many years. One study, which concedes that the Eurocommunists have changed their attitude to the EEC, still maintains that some parties are unremitting opponents: 'The British party played a significant role in the campaign for British withdrawal from the Common Market during the referendum in 1975.'[14]

The key to this attitude may perhaps be found in one quotation from Berlinguer: outlining the PCI's attitude to NATO he said:

> This decisive question of getting free of the bonds of subordination that tie our country to NATO cannot be reduced to a single declaration for or against the military pact. The struggle against the Atlantic Pact will rather, become more effective the more it is identified with a general movement of liberation of Europe from American hegemony and the gradual surpassing of opposed blocs, up to the point of their liquidation.[15]

If the US finds Eurocommunism fulfills one purpose while undermining another, the USSR's dilemma is even greater. On the basis of a simplistic philosophy it should like Eurocommunism because the US dislikes it. But the Eurocommunists have declared an independence of Moscow. Worse still, some of them, like Carrillo, are anti-Soviet. Soviet attacks on Carrillo started as soon as his book was published in 1977: they continued well into 1978, though by this time the movement was in some disarray.[16] And even if the Eurocommunists' claim to want a dissolution of both power blocs is doubted by some[17] it has enough force to make the denunciations of Eurocommunism sound genuine. Some authorities maintain that, however uncomfortable the Eurocommunists are to Moscow, they are important enough to keep within the fold, and their claims to independence doubtful enough to be ignored.[18]

But if this were so, why would the CPSU devote so much energy to denouncing the phenomenon? And why did it, in fact, condemn specifically a party which has little support in the country, like the PCE, whereas it treated a party with large support, like the PCF, with kid gloves? It has been obvious for many years that Soviet praise is equal to a kiss of death for Western European communists and the CPSU cannot be unaware of it. Hence, the conclusion must be that there is a genuine desire to break up the Euro-communist movement but an unwillingness to be seen to be interfering in the internal affairs of foreign communist parties.

Yet it would be easy to interfere. It is acknowledged that the finances of European communist parties owe much to the help of the CPSU. Even if there are no direct subsidies, the trading organisations which are jointly set up, the long and luxurious holidays which the Western leaders enjoy in the Eastern bloc and similar factors would be sufficient to put pressure on them. The result would be to resume the hegemony over European communism which produces total cooperation, even if some of the leaders resigned in the process.

One must look for other reasons. One of the reasons is that the USSR had for long felt embarrassed on its eastern and south-eastern flank. The Chinese situation and the experience of Afghanistan and Iran in 1979–80 proved that its outlying territories are in a very vulnerable position. It has long been the favourite occupation of political analysts to show the Soviet encirclement of the US on global maps: the Russians dare not show the encirclement of the USSR, but they feel it none the less acutely. Hence a period of disengagement in Europe may be very much in Soviet interests. Its interests are threatened not only in the Far East and South-east Asia but in Africa.

Second, the Carter Administration had effected a disengagement towards Europe similar to that which the USSR had shown towards Eurocommunism. In place of Kissinger's intense personal involvement in European organisations the Americans have assumed that Western Europe will always stay pro-American. While it is perhaps too strong a term to say that Europe had become 'Finlandised', it certainly came a long way between 1976 and 1980. The decision of European athletes to go to the Olympic Games in Moscow, despite American pleas, was an example of the new independence from America. The pilgrimages which President Giscard made to Warsaw and Chancellor Schmidt to Moscow in the summer of 1980, despite strong American objections, were a symbolic expression of this independence.

This development has long been envisaged by events. The EEC became an organisation sufficiently similar to the Comecon for the two to be able to engage in numerous trade deals which are mutually profitable. The West Germans have become engrossed in attempts to unify with East Germany. Their economic strength has allowed them to develop an independent Eastern Policy, while protesting their ultimate loyalty to NATO. The French, not to be outdone, wooed the USSR out of fear of a united Germany. And the Kissinger era had fuelled the trade between East and West, having built up a tremendous Eastern debt to the West. And, finally, the Eurocommunists have shown the way. The USSR has treated them with some hostility but has left them alone. Hence, the same treatment may be given to Western European governments.

On 24 June 1980 *Le Monde* carried the ironic title: *Mr Schmidt also hopes to gain 'something in Moscow'*, but was this irony, or was there more than a grain of truth in it? Is it possible that the Eurocommunists have ceased to be Soviet clients but that their governments have taken up this position? Time alone will tell.

Notes

1. V.I. Lenin, *Two Tactics of Social-Democracy in the Democratic Revoluton*, in *Selected Works*, pp. 61-2: emphasis in text.

2. S. Carrillo, *Eurocommunism and the State*, pp. 9-10: emphasis in text.

3. *L'Unità*, 14 July 1977: see also J. Valenta, 'Eurocommunism and Eastern Europe', in *Problems of Communism*, March-April (1978), p. 44.

4. Interview in *Rinascita*, 10 July 1975.

5. Quoted by D. Porch, *The Portuguese Armed Forces and the Revolution*, p. 25.

6. Ibid., p. 131.

7. Carrillo, *Eurocommunism*, p. 110.

8. For a detailed analysis of the reasons, see F.L. Wilson, 'The French CP's Dilemma', in *Problems of Communism*, July-August (1978).

9. See E. Mujal-Leon, 'The PCI in Spanish Politics', in *Problems of Communism*, July-August (1978).

10. H. Timmermann, 'The Eurocommunists and the West', in *Problems of Communism*, May-June (1979), pp. 31-2.

11. J. Power, *The Times*, 10 Oct. 1977: emphasis in text.

12. C. Page, *Guardian*, 21 June 1977.

13. Kissinger stated that 'It is difficult to see how we could have NATO discussions if these various communist parties of Western Europe did achieve control of governments . . . the alliance, as it is now, could not survive': quoted by K. Manzo, *Eurocommunism* (unpublished dissertation, 1979), n. 16, p. 24 (from *New York Times*, 7 April 1977).

14. R. Godson and S. Haseler (eds.), *Eurocommunism*, p. 98.

15. Ibid., p. 108.

16. See Reuter's despatch in the *Guardian*, 24 June 1977, and M. Binyon in *The Times*, 25 April 1978.

17. See L. Schapiro, 'The Soviet reaction to "Eurocommunism"', in *West European Politics*, May (1979), pp. 172-3.

18. See R. Lowenthal, 'Moscow and the "Eurocommunists"', in *Problems of Communism*, July-August (1978).

21
Revolutionary Marxism - an Assessment

The Proletarian Elite

The starting point of Marxist theory was that the proletarians were a small, exploited class which would unite across national borders to fight the bourgeoisie because its common interests were sufficiently strong to override national interests. This was very understandable in the period when Marx wrote the Communist Manifesto. However, the developments in the second half of the nineteenth century and in the twentieth century made the theory implausible, because in place of a small united class of proletarians the industrial age produced a large mass of differentiated working classes whose only point of reference was the national entity. Thus, alienation, in Marxist terms, did not arise from being an exploited, international class, but from being deprived of national status. This attitude of the proletariat was fully reflected in the decision of most Social-Democratic parties in 1914 to pursue a national war, instead of refusing to fight an 'imperialist' war. The length and bitterness of the war brought the idea of internationalism nearer.

> International socialism, which had disintegrated at the outbreak of war, seemed to be reviving. Previously only a few socialists of the extreme Left had met in Switzerland (at Zimmerwald and Kienthal). Now the moderate Russian socialists, themselves in the provisional government, proposed a wider meeting at Stockholm; and they were supported by 'Pro-war' socialists in Great Britain and France. ... In July 1917, Ramsay MacDonald, not usually a revolutionary, looked forward to the rule of workers' and soldiers' councils in Great Britain.[1]

However, the decision to pursue the war to a total victory frustrated the attempts of the Social-Democrats to bring about a negotiated peace and a socialist commonwealth in Europe.

In the post-war era the difficulties which the Bolsheviks were experiencing in introducing socialism in Russia, combined with the collapse of other European revolutions, brought about a new climate of nationalist revival among the Social-Democrats, but the new communist parties were internationally-minded. This situation obtained till the introduction of Stalin's theory of 'socialism in one country' and the elimination of the internatonalist leaders from all communist parties. Moreover, whether as a result of the Bolshevik Revolution and the apparent granting of all power to the proletariat or as a result of developing technology (and most likely because of the interaction of these two), the capitalist system changed almost imperceptibly to a system of a mixed economy, and the proletariat changed from an oppressed class to a consumer society. Such a consumer society would have been impossible to foresee in the mid-nineteenth century when Marx wrote, because the means of mass production were not yet invented.

But a consumer society demands several things: first, large markets (which Marx did foresee); second, a well-paid proletariat (which he did not); and third, a degree of planning, both on a national and international level, in order to distribute the goods rationally. This last had been one of the socialist aims from the start, but was very difficult to introduce because the degree of international consensus was lacking. Hence the problems Marxist theory encountered in the twentieth century were bigger than could have been expected and had much more to do with new developments than with a faulty prognostication — after all, Marx did not set out to become a prophet, he was merely building on the existing body of knowledge.

Therefore, however faulty Stalin's Marxism may have been, his practice was realistic. But it was owing to his support for 'national communism', as Trotsky called it, that the world-wide communist movement gradually broke up into national parties, each intent on its own national problems. The weakness of communism in the period of the 1920s and 1930s did not come from the strength of the capitalist system, or even from the strength of fascism: it came about as a result of Stalin's attempts to deform the theory of socialism in order to safeguard the USSR. It has been discussed in the first and second parts of this book how this policy undermined the revolutionary wing of the CPSU and of foreign communist parties, and how it led to a wholesale purge of leaderships in order to ensure Stalin's supremacy. While one must condemn Stalin's methods, one cannot but see that in terms of 'realpolitik' his policy was successful, even though the brief period of Popular Fronts undermined some of the national aims of each communist party. However, the Popular Front policy failed, and the impossible happened: the Nazi–Soviet Pact of August 1939 seemed to prove to all (communists and non-communists alike) that the CPSU had abdicated its responsibility for the furtherance of world communism and was embarked on a national road.

The brief period of internationalism in the 1930s was revived suddenly and unexpectedly as the German invasion of the USSR started in June 1941. This time Stalin did not hesitate to call on the world communist movement to come to the help of the first socialist country in the world, and it did, though it was the aid of the capitalist USA which proved conclusive in the end. But the left throughout the world forgot about August 1939, and came to the aid of the USSR, though without being certain whether it was helping Stalin or socialism. Thus the theory of the proletarian elite and the continuing revolution gave way first to national communism, then to an alliance with fascism and finally to an alliance against fascism, with all the possible opponents of fascism. The proletarian revolution was put in cold storage, while the first socialist state was fighting its recent fascist friend. The international solidarity of the working classes was being used externally, but at home, in the USSR as much as in the occupied European countries, the process was rather different.

How Nationalism became a Priority in the USSR and desirable Elsewhere

In the USSR itself, the nationalist myth was strengthened and enhanced as the population was exhorted to defend the fatherland with the help of religious flags, Orthodox priests and a new 'Soviet' brand of patriotism. In the occupied countries the communist partisan leaders were nationalists first and communists second. This applied equally to old communist parties like the French and Italian ones, and to new parties, like the Yugoslav or Albanian ones.

The new-found popularity of 'national' communist parties during the resistance period was very useful. There is no doubt that the communists were brave, well-organised and anti-fascist and that their following consisted of many non-communists who found their resistance effort much more effective than that of other political parties. In many European countries (as in Italy) the communists worked well with all the resistance parties throughout the Second World War: in others (as in France) they eventually found accommodation with other parties; in some (as in Yugoslavia, Greece and Albania) they became the leaders of the resistance effort. Only in a few countries which had good reason to fear the USSR — if not communism — were the communist partisans left to their own devices. This was the case in countries like Poland, Romania and Hungary. But even there, some communist partisans fought on their own, deprived of help and co-operation and, more in faith than in hope, prepared for the final defeat of fascism to be followed by the defeat of capitalism.

In some countries the communists were included in the governments of newly liberated territories, and served loyally. In others, they were helped to power through the progress of the Red Army. Between 1944 and 1948 there was communist participation in almost all European governments recently liberated from the occupier, though in some countries they were the dominant partner, in others they were retained because they were too popular to be dismissed. By 1948, though, the situation changed. In Western European countries the communist ministers were dismissed from office, while in Eastern and South-eastern Europe, the process was reversed: the non-communists were eliminated, leaving the communists and their closest allies in government.[2]

Thus the national dimension was reinforced by the regional dimension: the East was communist, the West was anti-communist. This simple paradigm was enhanced by the nationalist policy which Stalin pursued after 1945. The USSR after the war became not just a world power; it also became a national world power. The fate of communist parties within the Soviet bloc was to ape Soviet chauvinism while simultaneously to buckle under it. The non-ruling communist parties were in an even worse situation: they were forced to praise Soviet nationalism while bound by the strict anti-communism of the West. It was probably fortunate for the communist parties that the USA began an anti-communist crusade soon after the war, and that the result of the Soviet–US confrontation developed into the 'Cold War'.[3]

The nationalism exhibited by the USSR could be compared to the anti-communism exhibited by the USA, and each side collected support from the uncommitted as a result.

Communism after Stalin's Death

Stalin's death in the spring of 1953 brought about a relaxation of
tensions in the USSR and should have brought about a relaxation
in the Eastern European bloc. However, as has been discussed in
Part Three of this book, this relaxation was difficult to achieve,
and most Eastern European governments were simply interested
in retaining their power. As a result of Soviet pressure, changes
were eventually made, and in place of the Stalinist leaders,
'national' leaders were installed in several countries. Unfortunately,
this did little to further the cause of socialism: it did a lot to
increase the already strong nationalism, particularly among the
nations which felt they had been sacrificed to Soviet interests.

Such change was, basically, a mistake. National communism on
Yugoslav lines could not be introduced in Poland, East Germany
or Czechoslovakia without the massive injection of capital which
enabled Yugoslavia to prosper. On the other hand, all these
countries had already changed their economic and political systems
so drastically that it was impossible (even if it was allowed) to
return to a system of mixed economy.[4] Hence what was left of the
ideology and economic change was a watered-down version of
state socialism, a nationalistic government trying to compensate
for its shortcomings by stressing its patriotism and a disoriented —
hence a discontented — population. The Western European
communist parties were in an even worse state. They were now
being blamed for having supported Stalinism against all odds, for
intellectual dishonesty and for departing from ideological purity.

The situation would have become unmanageable had it not
been for a new development: this was the Chinese bid for the
leadership of the socialist world. Parts Four and Five of this book
discuss the changes which occurred in the communist movement
as a result of de-Stalinisation in the USSR and Europe and the
upholding of Stalinism by the Chinese Communists. The Sino–Soviet
split not only produced two different kinds of Marxism in socialist
countries, one hardline, the other revisionist; it also brought about a
polycentric development. Instead of one capital of socialism, Moscow,
there were now two, Moscow and Beijing, competing with each
other for the leadership of the world communist movement.

This allowed both the ruling and non-ruling communist parties to make their own choices of doctrine and, while it damaged the unity of the bloc, it also made possible various compromises which in the long run produced a more vital movement, but one which became even more regionally or nationally orientated.

Competitive Communism in Retrospect

The most significant changes did not occur till the next decade. In the 1960s the emergence of Cuba as the first 'national communist' state in Latin America, the lack of American successes in the Vietnam War and European disillusionment with American economic policies in Europe[5] brought about a wave of anti-American feelings on a world-wide basis. This, however, did not prove to be to the advantage of the orthodox Moscow-led communism. While a great many of the New Left appeared to follow a Maoist line of doctrine, a new policy, which owed little either to orthodox or to revisionist Marxism, was being developed.

It is not intended here to discuss how far such a policy was shaped by the original Marxist theory, and how far by the new thinkers, like Marcuse, whose condemnation of state capitalism was based on the disillusionment with Soviet policies: the result, however, was plain to see. The New Left called for a reappraisal of the theory, and for a change of practice. The appearance of the New Left in the United States and Europe coincided with several important events: the Warsaw Pact intervention in Czechoslovakia in 1968; the establishment of a Marxist government in Chile and its de-stabilisation with active US support; the development of Marxist regimes in Africa; and finally the American withdrawal from Vietnam, allowing the Indo-Chinese Peninsula to be almost totally taken over by socialist governments.

These developments are discussed in the final parts of this book. It is pointed out that the regional or national orientation of ruling and non-ruling communist parties was encouraged in this period at the expense of global communism. While this added to the viability and vitality of separate parties, it made a world communist movement less probable than in the first half of the century.

Moreover, the development of Eurocommunism in Western Europe ensured that the communist parties in those countries accepted the existing order and, implicitly, acknowledged that both in socialist and non-socialist countries, the *status quo* would be maintained to the detriment of the development of pure Marxism. This gave added impetus to the New Left to find the so-called 'third way'; neither Marxism nor capitalism, neither pro-Sovietism nor pro-Americanism, but an orderly way in which capital could be transferred for the benefit of the working classes, and the setting up of a system of collective ownership.[6] In other words, a return to Saint-Simonian visions of an orderly, collective society appears to be the only remedy to rescue the industrial age from ruin and the world from destruction.

Who are the Revolutionaries?

In the course of several decades it was inevitable that the Marxist theory of a revolutionary proletariat should be both questioned and revised. The first revisionist theory, that of Bernstein, noted that the proletariat had changed from an oppressed class to that of a highly skilled, respected and well-paid class. The second revision was carried out by Lenin, when he opined that revolutionary peasantry could co-operate with revolutionary proletariat in an underdeveloped country like Russia. The third revision was brought about in Yugoslavia, when a 'national road' to socialism was introduced, an extension of the Stalinist theory of 'socialism in one country'. The next revision occurred in China, when Mao placed his wager on revolutionary peasants without the help of the proletariat. Finally, the contribution the Latin Americans made, by developing the 'hispanic' brand of Marxism in which revolutionary peasantry, liberal intellectuals and progressive clergy participate in a national socialist revolution, is only equal to the revisionist theories propounded by the New Left in the importance it had on shaping future events.

But throughout this period one factor remained constant: the proletariat played a very small part in the development of Marxism. The new and often powerful trade unions were not interested in socialist theory but in improving their members' standard of living. The 'embourgeoisement' of the proletariat — already noticed by Lenin, when he spoke of the proletarian aristocracy in Britain — was only matched by the growing revolutionary tendencies among peasants of all nations and continents. However, this was not exactly a new phenomenon. Peasant revolutions were the only revolutions Europe had known for centuries. In the eighteenth and nineteenth centuries the ideological basis was developed by the intellectuals not by the proletarians. This, it was thought, was because the proletariat was either small or politically illiterate. However, in the twentieth century, this is not the case. But the revolutionary activity came, in every instance, first from the intellectuals and was then supported by the peasantry. The one exception which proves this rule is Poland, where the 1970, 1976 and 1980–81 revolutions were carried out by the proletariat, led by the intellectuals. It must be noted, however, that the majority of Polish industrial workers are either recent recruits from the countryside or worker-peasants.

The pattern of revolutions in the twentieth century had become fairly constant: the ideology is developed by the intellectuals and is then taken up by the oppressed; in most instances these are the peasants. But peasant disturbances are not confined to poor peasants alone: the highly subsidised and officially-favoured French farmers have been the most vocal — to the point of violent revolutionary activity — in the defence of their interests.

One is left with the impression that the 'revisionists' of the 1950s and 1960s were quite correct when they envisaged the leading revolutionary role of the intellectuals, and disputed the theory of the dictatorship of the proletariat. The revolution, at the end of the twentieth century, is still in the hands of the intellectuals, as it was in 1789, 1848, 1870 and in 1917. If the intellectuals can find allies in their activity, they are more likely to come from the peasants than from the proletariat.

Notes

1. A.J.P. Taylor, *The Struggle for Mastery in Europe, 1848–1918*, p. 559.
2. Some authors maintain that this was done purely as a result of American pressure. See, e.g., A. Grosser, *The Western Alliance*, Ch. 3. 1948 is taken as a median date when most of the changes occurred.
3. The development of the USA as a 'national security state' during this period is described by D. Yergin, *Shattered Peace*, who maintains that it was not inevitable but was the result of the 'Riga Axiom', the American school of diplomacy which was tutored by White Russian emigres after the Bolshevik Revolution.
4. It has been tried in one instance: the collectivised agriculture in Poland was returned to private owners. Poland has suffered from massive agricultural shortages as the small farmer is unable to cope with the socialist economy of the rest of the country.
5. On the opposition to American policies in Europe in the 1960s see Grosser, *The Western Alliance*.
6. See, in particular, Ota Sik, *The Third Way*.

Select Bibliography

Aguilar, L.E. 'Fragmentation of the Marxist Left' *Problems of Communism*, July-August (1970)

Alexander, R.J. 'The Communist Parties of Latin America', *Problems of Communism*, July-August (1970)

Amendola, G. *Gli Anni Della Republica* (Ed. Riuniti, Rome, 1976)

Auty, P. *Tito* (Longman, London, 1970)

Baevskii, D.A. *et al.* (eds) *Ot Oktyabryia K Stroitelstvu Kommunisma* (Nauka, Moscow, 1967)

Barker, E. *British Policy in South East Europe* (Macmillan, London, 1976)

Barnard, J.P. *et al. Guide to the Political Parties of South America* (Penguin, Harmondsworth, 1973)

Barnet, R.J. *Intervention and Revolution* (Paladin, London, 1972)

Baum, R. (ed), *China in Torment* (Prentice-Hall, Englewood Cliffs, New Jersey, 1971)

Bauman, Z. *Socialism, the Active Utopia* (Allen and Unwin, London, 1976)

Blackmer, D. 'Italian Communism: Strategy for the 1970's', *Problems of Communism*, May-June (1972)

Unity in Diversity: Italian Communism and the Communist World (MIT Press; Mass., 1968)

Blackton, C.S. 'Sri Lanka's Marxists', *Problems of Communism*, January-February (1973)

Boggs, C. and Plotke, D. (eds.) *The Politics of Eurocommunism* (Macmillan, London, 1980)

Bonachea, R.E. and Valdes N.P. (eds.) *Cuba in Revolution* (Anchor Books, New York, 1972)

Borkenau, F. *World Communism. A History of the Communist International*, 2nd edn. (Ann Arbor, Michigan, 1962)

Bridgham, P. *Mao's Cultural Revolution: Origin and Development* in Baum (ed.) *China in Ferment*

Carrillo, S. *Dialogue on Spain* (Penguin, Harmondsworth, 1975)

Eurocommunism and the State (Lawrence and Wishart,

London, 1977)

Childs, D. *East Germany* (Ernest Benn, London, 1969)

Ciechanowski, J. *The Warwaw Rising of 1944* (Cambridge University Press, Cambridge, 1974)

Claudin, F. *The Communist Movement* (Penguin, Harmondsworth, 1975)

Cliff, T. 'Russia: A Marxist Analysis', *International Socialism* (London)

    State Capitalism in Russia (Pluto Press, London, 1974)

Collier, J. and Collier, E. *China's Socialist Revolution* (Stage 1, London, 1973)

Communist Party of Great Britain, *The British Road to Socialism — Programme of the Communist Party* (London, 1978)

Conquest, R. *The Great Terror*, Revised edn. (Penguin, Harmondsworth, 1971)

Cotter, S. 'Charter 77 and the Czech Dissidents', unpublished dissertation, Dept of European Studies, UMIST, Manchester, 1980

Crankshaw, E. *Khrushchev* (Collins, London, 1966)

Cranston, M. 'The Thought of Roger Garaudy', *Problems of Communism* September-October (1970)

Davidson, B. *Which Way Africa?* 3rd edn. (Penguin, Harmondsworth, 1971)

    In The Eye Of The Storm, Revised edn. (Penguin, Harmondsworth, 1975)

Deakin, F.W. and Storry, G.R. *The Case Of Richard Sorge* (Chatto and Windus, London, 1966)

Debray, R. *Prison Writings* (Penguin, Harmondsworth, 1975)

Degras, J. (ed.) *The Communist International (1919 - 1943)*, 2 vols. (Oxford University Press, Oxford, 1956-65)

Derfler, L. *Socialism Since Marx* (Macmillan, London, 1973)

Deutscher, I. *Stalin: A Political Biography* (Oxford University Press, Oxford, 1961)

    Russia, China and the West 1953–1966 (Penguin, Harmondsworth, 1970)

Dung, Van Tien *Our Great Spring Victory* (Monthly Review Press, 1977)

Dziewanowski, M.K. *The Communist Party of Poland* (Harvard University Press, Harvard, 1959)

Fejto, F. *A History of the People's Democracies* 2nd edn. (Penguin, Harmondsworth, 1974)

Fiori, G. *Antonio Gramsci: Life of a Revolutionary* (Schoken

Books, New York, 1973)

Fischer, L. *The Soviets of World Affairs* (Vintage Books, New York, 1960)

Fischer, R. *Stalin and German Communism* (Harvard University Press, Harvard, 1948)

Fitzgerald, C.P. *The Birth of Communist China* (Penguin, Harmondsworth, 1973)

Florinsky, M.T. *Russia: A History and an Interpretation* 2 vols (Macmillan, New York, 1960–1)

Foley A. 'An Analysis of Church and State Relations in Poland 1945–1979', unpublished dissertation, Dept of European Studies, UMIST, Manchester, 1979

Foot, P. 'Why You Should be A Socialist', *Socialist Worker*, 1977

Foster, W.Z. *A History of the Three Internationals* (International Publishers, New York, 1955)

Franklin, B. (ed.) *The Essential Stalin* (Croom Helm, London, 1973)

Freymond, J. (ed.) *Contribution à l'Histoire du Comintern* (Geneva, 1965)

Garaudy, R. *Marxisme au XX Siècle* (La Palatine, Paris, 1966 and 1970)

Gelman, H. 'Outlook for Sino–Soviet Relations', *Problems of Communism*, September – December (1979)

Ginneken, J.Van *The Rise And Fall of Lin Piao* (Penguin, Harmondsworth, 1976)

Gittings, J. *Survey of the Sino–Soviet Dispute* (Oxford University Press, Oxford, 1968)

Godson, R. and Haseler, S. (eds.) *Eurocommunism* (St Martin's Press, New York, 1978)

Golan, G. 'The Road To Reform', *Problems of Communism*, May – June (1971)

Gonzalez, E. 'Complexities of Cuban Foreign Policy', *Problems of Communism*, November – December (1977)

Goure, L. and Suchlicki, J. 'Whither Chile', *Problems of Communism*, May–June (1971)

Guevara, Che *Guerrilla Warfare* (Penguin, Harmondsworth, 1969)

Gupta, R.S. 'India's Rival Communist Models', *Problems of Communism*, January–February (1973)

　　'Indian Politics and The Communist Party (Marxist)', *Problems of Communism*, September–October (1978)

Hoffman, G.W. and Neal, F.W. *Yugoslavia And The New Com-*

munism (Twentieth-century Fund, New York, 1962)

Hottinger, A. 'The Rise of Portugal's Communists', *Problems of Communism*, July–August (1975)

Hsieh, A.L. *Communist China's Strategy in the Nuclear Era* (Prentice Hall, Englewood Cliffs, New Jersey, 1962)

Humbert-Droz, J. *Mémoires de Jules Humbert-Droz*, 4 vols (Neuchatel, Paris, 1969)

Joll, J. *Gramsci* (Fontana, London, 1977)

Khesin, S.S. 'Revolyutsionnye Svyazi Petrogradskogo Proletariata s Baltiiskimi Moryakami v 1917g', in Baevskii *et al., Ot Oktyabryia*

Kousoulas, D.G. *Revolution and Defeat; The Story of the Greek Communist Party* (Oxford University Press, Oxford, 1965)

Kriegel, A. *Aux Origines du Communisme Français 1914–1920* (Paris, 1964)

   Les Internationales Ouvriers (PUF, Paris, 1970)

Lamberg, R.E. 'Che in Bolivia: The Revolution that Failed', *Problems of Communism*, July–August (1970)

Lane, D. *The Socialist Industrial State* (Allen and Unwin, London, 1976)

Langer, P.F. 'The New Posture of the CPJ', *Problems of Communism*, January–February (1971)

Lazitch, B. and Drachkovitch, M. *Lenin and the Comintern* (Stanford University Press, Stanford, 1972)

Leibzon, B.M. and Shirinya, K.K. *Povorot v Politike Kominterna* (MYSL, Moscow, 1965)

   (eds.) *Iz Istorii Kominterna* (Moscow, 1970)

Lenin, V.I. *Selected Works* (Lawrence and Wishart, London, 1969)

Lowenthal, R. 'Moscow and the Eurocommunists', *Problems of Communism*, July–August (1978)

Loebl, E. *Sentenced and Tried: The Stalinist Purges in Czechoslovakia* (Elek Books, London, 1969)

Malinowski, M. *Geneza PPR* (Ksiazka i Wiedza, Warsaw, 1972)

Mammarella, G. *L'Italia dopo il Fascismo* 2nd ed. (Il Mulino, Bologna, 1971)

Mandel, E. *Marxist Economic Theory*, 2 vols (Merlin Press, London, 1968)

   The Inconsistencies of State Capitalism (International Marxist Group, 1969)

   From Stalinism to Eurocommunism (NLB, London, 1978)

Manzo, K. 'Eurocommunism', unpublished dissertation, Dept of European Studies, UMIST, Manchester, 1979

Marcuse, H. *Soviet Marxism: A Critical Analysis* (Columbia University Press, New York, 1958)

Matthews, H.L. *Castro — A Political Biography* (Allen Lane, London, 1961)

McCauley, M. *Marxism—Leninism in the German Democratic Republic* (Macmillan, London, 1979)

Meijer, J.M. *The Trotsky Papers* 2 vols (Mouton, The Hague, 1964)

Minter, D. *Portuguese Africa and the West* (Penguin, Harmondsworth, 1972)

Morawski, A. 'The P.C.I. And The Italian Road To Socialism', unpublished dissertation, Dept of European Studies, UMIST, Manchester, 1978

Morgan, D.W. *The Socialist Left and the German Revolution. A History of the German Independent Social Democratic Party 1917—1922* (Cornell University Press, Cornell, 1975)

Moss, R. 'Urban Guerrillas in Uruguay', *Problems of Communism*, September—October (1971)

Mujal-Leon, E. 'The P.C.I. in Spanish Politics', *Problems of Communism*, July—August (1978)

Nahas, D. *The Israeli Communist Party* (Croom Helm, London, 1976)

Narkiewicz, O.A. *The Making Of The Soviet State Apparatus* (Manchester University Press, Manchester, 1970)

   The Green Flag (Croom Helm, London, 1976)

Nettl, P. *Rosa Luxemburg* (abridged edn) (Oxford University Press, Oxford, 1969)

Neubert, W. 'Maoist and Imperialist Ideological Alliance on an Anti-Communist Platform', *Far Eastern Affairs,* No. 1 (1976)

Payne, S.G. *The Spanish Revolution* (Weidenfeld and Nicolson, London, 1970)

Polonsky, A. and Drukier, B. (eds.) *The Beginnings of Communist Rule in Poland* (Routledge and Kegan Paul, London, 1980)

Ponomaryov, B.N. (ed.) *History of CPSU* (Moscow, 1960)

Porch, D. *The Portuguese Armed Forces and the Revolution* (Croom Helm, London, 1977)

Pelikan, J. *The Czechoslovak Political Trials 1950—1954: The Suppressed Report of the Dubcek Government's Commission of Inquiry, 1968* (Macdonald, London, 1971)

Raptis, M. *Revolution and Counter Revolution in Chile* (Allison and Busby, London, 1974)

Reale E. (ed.) *Avec Jacques Duclos au Banc des Accusés à La Réunion Constitutive du Kominform à Szklarska Poreba 22–27 Septembre 1947* (Plon, Paris, 1958)

Rieber, A.J. *Stalin and the French Communist Party 1941–1947* (Columbia University Press, New York, 1962)

Robinson, J. *The Cultural Revolution in China* (Penguin, Harmondsworth, 1969)

Salvadori, M. *The Rise of Modern Communism* (Dryden Press, Hinsdale, 1975)

Scalapino, R.A. 'Patterns of Asian Communism', *Problems of Communism*, January–April (1971)

Schapiro, L. *The Communist Party of the Soviet Union* (University Paperbacks, London, 1960)

   'The Soviet Reaction to Eurocommunism', *West European Politics*, May (1979)

Schram, S. *Mao Tse Tung* (Penguin, Harmondsworth, 1975)

Searle, J. *The Campus War* (Penguin, Harmondsworth, 1972)

Seniga, G. *Togliatti e Stalin. Contributo alla biografia de Segretario del PCI* (Ed. Sugar, Milan, 1961)

Seton-Watson, H. *The Imperialist Revolutionaries* (Hutchinson, London, 1980)

Shawcross, W. *Side Show; Kissinger, Nixon, and the Destruction of Cambodia* (Fontana, London, 1980)

Sigmund, P.E. 'Chile: Two Years of "Popular Unity"', *Problems of Communism*, November–December (1972)

   'Allende in Retrospect', *Problems of Communism*, May–June (1974)

Sik, O. 'The Economic Impact of Stalinism', *Problems of Communism*, May–June (1971)

Sobolev, A.N. *et al.* (eds.) *Kommunisticheskiy Internatsional — Kratkiy Istoricheskiy Ocherk* (Moscow, 1969)

Spriano, P. *Storia del Partito Communista Italiano* (Turin, 1969)

Stalin, J.V. *Sochineniya*, 13 vols (Moscow, 1946 - 1953)

Starr, R.F. *Communist Regimes in Eastern Europe*, 3rd edn (Hoover Institution Press, 1977)

Strong, J.W. (ed.) *The Soviet Union under Brezhnev and Kosygin* (Van Nostrand Reinhold, New York, 1971)

Szulc, T. *The Winds of the Revolution* (Thames and Hudson, London, 1964)

Taber, R. *The War of the Flea* (Paladin, London, 1974)

Taborsky, E. *Communism in Czechoslovakia 1948–1960* (Princeton

University Press, Princeton, New Jersey, 1961)

'Czechoslovakia: The Return to Normalcy', *Problems of Communism*, November–December (1970)

Tiersky, R. *French Communism 1920–1972* (Columbia University Press, New York, 1974)

Thomas, H. *The Spanish Civil War*, 2nd edn (Penguin, Harmondsworth, 1965)

Thompson, E.P. (ed.) *Warwick University Ltd* (Penguin, Harmondsworth, 1970)

Thomson, G. *From Marx To Mao Tse Tung: A Study In Revolutionary Dialectics* (China Policy Study Group, London, 1971)

Thorez, M. *Fils du Peuple* (Editions Sociales, Paris, 1960)

Timmermann, H. 'The Eurocommunists and the West', *Problems of Communism*, May–June (1979)

Trotsky, L. *The Struggle against Fascism In Germany* (Penguin, Harmondsworth, 1975)

The Permanent Revolution and Results and Prospects (Pathfinder, New York, 1970)

The Spanish Revolution (1931–1939) (Pathfinder, New York, 1973)

Valenta, J. 'Eurocommunism and Eastern Europe', *Problems of Communism*, March–April (1978)

Vorontsov, V. and Kapustin, D. 'Collective Security in Asia', *Far Eastern Affairs*, No. 1 (1976)

Vyunova, N.M. *et al.* (eds) *Partiyno-Politicheskaya Rabota v Krasnoy Armii* VIMOSSSR, Moscow, 1964)

Weber, H. *Die Wandlung des Deutschen Kommunismus*, 2 vols (Frankfurt am Main, 1969)

Weissman, St.R. 'CIA Overt Action in Zaire and Angola', *Political Science Quarterly* (N.Y.), Summer (1979)

Wilgus, A.C. and d'Eca, R. *Latin American History*, 5th edn (Barnes and Noble, New York, 1967)

Wilson, F. 'The French CP's Dilemma', *Problems of Communism*, July–August (1978)

Zasloff, J.J. and Brown, M. 'The Passion of Kampuchea', *Problems of Communism*, January–February (1979)

Zetkin, C. *Reminiscences of Lenin* (Moscow 1925; New York 1934)

Index